OTTOMAN TULIPS, (

To my parents, Amal and Wael, whose names mean exactly what they have given me: Hope and Refuge

# OTTOMAN TULIPS, OTTOMAN COFFEE
## *Leisure and Lifestyle in the Eighteenth Century*

Edited by Dana Sajdi

Tauris Academic Studies
LONDON • NEW YORK

Published in 2007 by Tauris Academic Studies, an imprint of
I.B.Tauris & Co Ltd
6 Salem Road, London W2 4BU
175 Fifth Avenue, New York NY 10010
www.ibtauris.com

Copyright © 2007, Dana Sajdi

The right of Dana Sajdi to be identified as editor of this work has been asserted by the editor in accordance with the Copyright, Design and Patents Act 1988.

All rights reserved. Except for brief quotations in a review, this book, or any part thereof, may not be reproduced, stored in or introduced into a retrieval system, or transmitted, in any form or by any means, electronic, mechanical, photocopying, recording or otherwise, without the prior written permission of the publisher.

ISBN 978 1 84511 570 8

A full CIP record for this book is available from the British Library
A full CIP record is available from the Library of Congress

Library of Congress Catalog card: available


Copy-edited and typeset by Oxford Publishing Services, Oxford

# Contents

List of Tables and Figures      vi
Notes on Contributors      vii
Preface, Note on Transliteration and Acknowledgements      ix

1. Decline, its Discontents and Ottoman Cultural History: By Way of Introduction
   *Dana Sajdi*      1

2. The Perception of Saadabad: The 'Tulip Age' and Ottoman–Safavid Rivalry
   *Can Erimtan*      41

3. The First Ottoman Turkish Printing Enterprise: Success or Failure?
   *Orlin Sabev (Orhan Salih)*      63

4. Nahils, Circumcision Rituals and the Theatre State
   *Babak Rahimi*      90

5. Janissary Coffee Houses in Late Eighteenth-Century Istanbul
   *Ali Çaksu*      117

6. The Heart's Desire: Gender, Urban Space and the Ottoman Coffee House
   *Alan Mikhail*      133

Notes      171
References      224
Index      257

# List of Tables and Figures

## Tables

| | | |
|---|---|---|
| 3.1 | Book sales and sale percentages of the Müteferrika Press | 89 |
| 5.1 | Some Zorba proprietors and their coffee houses | 132 |

## Figures

| | | |
|---|---|---|
| 3.1 | Sale percentages of *Tercümetü's-Sihāh-i Cevheri [Lugat-i Vānkūlu]*, 1141/1729 | 84 |
| 3.2 | Sale percentages of *Tuhfetü'l-Kibār*, *Tārīh-i Seyyāh*, *Hindi'l-Garbī*, *Tārīh-i Tīmūr*, *Tārīhü'l-Mısır*, 1141–42/1729–30 | 84 |
| 3.3 | Sale percentages of *Gülşen-i Hulefā*, 1143/1730 | 85 |
| 3.4 | Sale percentages of *Grammaire turque*, 1730 | 85 |
| 3.5 | Sale percentages of *Usūlü'l-Hikem*, *Mıknātısiyye*, 1144/1732; *Ahvāl-i Gazavāt der Diyār-i Bosna*, 1154/1741 | 86 |
| 3.6 | Sale percentages of *Kitāb-ı Cihānnümā*, 1145/1732 | 86 |
| 3.7 | Sale percentages of *Takvīmü't-Tevārīh*, 1146/1733 | 87 |
| 3.8 | Sale percentages of *Tārīh-i Naʿīmā*, 1147/1734 | 87 |
| 3.9 | Sale percentages of *Tārīh-i Rāşid Efendi*, *Tārīh-i Çelebizāde Efendi*, 1153/1741 | 88 |
| 3.10 | Sale percentages of *Ferheng-i Şuʿūrī*, 1155/1742 | 88 |

# Notes on Contributors

CAN ERIMTAN is an independent scholar. He received a D.Phil. in 2003 in modern history from Oxford University, where he wrote a thesis on the historiography of the 'tulip age'. In 2004–5, he was research fellow at the British Institute of Archeology at Ankara, where he worked on the perception of the Hittites in early republican Turkey. He was senior fellow at the Institute of Anatolian Civilizations, Istanbul.

ALI ÇAKSU is assistant professor and chair of the Department of Philosophy, Fatih University, Istanbul. From 2000 to 2006, he was a research fellow at the Research Centre for Islamic History, Art and Culture (IRCICA), a subsidiary organ of the Organization of the Islamic Conference (OIC). He earned his BA in 1991 from the Department of Political Science and International Relations at Boğaziçi University in Istanbul. He received his MA in Islamic thought in 1993, and a Ph.D. in philosophy in 1999, from the International Institute of Islamic Thought and Civilization (ISTAC), Kuala Lumpur, Malaysia.

ALAN MIKHAIL is a Ph.D. candidate in the Department of History at the University of California, Berkeley. His interests include the history of science, agricultural history and the cultural history of Ottoman cities. He has published numerous articles in Arabic on various topics in Egyptian history, and is currently writing a dissertation on the cultural history of water, irrigation and health in Ottoman Egypt.

BABAK RAHIMI is assistant professor of Islamic Studies at the

NOTES ON CONTRIBUTORS

Department of Literature, Program for the Study of Religion, University of California, San Diego. Rahimi received his BA from the University of California, San Diego, his MA from the University of Nottingham, and his Ph.D. in 2004 from the European University Institute's Department of Social and Political Science. He was a visiting fellow in the Department of Anthropology at the London School of Economics and Political Science, 2000–2001. He has published articles in Iranian studies and critical theory and historical sociology; his main research interest evolves around state–society relations in Islamic societies.

ORLIN SABEV (ORHAN SALIH) is a research fellow at the Institute of Balkan Studies, Bulgarian Academy of Sciences, Sofia. He received his Ph.D. from the same institution in 2000. His dissertation on Ottoman educational institutions in Bulgarian lands between the fifteenth and eighteenth centuries was published in Bulgarian under the title *Ottoman Schools in Bulgarian Lands 15th–18th Centuries* (Sofia: Ljubomadrie-Chronia, 2001). His second book, also in Bulgarian, *The First Ottoman Journey in the World of Printed Books (1726–1746): a Reassessment* (Sofia: Avangard Prima, 2004) is now forthcoming in Turkish. He received the Professor Marin Drinov Prize for Young Scholars of the Bulgarian Academy of Sciences in 2002.

DANA SAJDI is a post-doctoral fellow at the Wissenschaftskolleg zu Berlin. She received her Ph.D. from Columbia University in 2002. She was assistant professor of Middle East history at Concordia University, Montreal, 2002–4; and a Mellon fellow at Princeton University 2004–5. She is currently working on a monograph entitled *The barber of Damascus: nouveau literacy in the early modern Middle East*. On the subject of her book, she has published an award winning article 'A room of his own: the "history" of the barber of Damascus (fl. 1762)' (The MIT Electronic Journal of Middle East Studies, 4 (2004), pp. 19–35).

# Preface, Note on Transliteration and Acknowledgements

The present volume is a result of a conference, 'Rethinking culture in the Ottoman eighteenth century', which took place in Princeton on 15–16 January 2005. Although a very large number of excellent proposals were submitted in response to the call for papers, all things being equal, priority of participation was given to junior/graduate students and international scholars. After the conclusion of the conference, a committee of five senior and junior scholars was formed for the purpose of selecting the conference papers to be published. Once chosen, the papers were sent out for anonymous peer review and subsequently revised by the authors. Thus, this volume is the end result of a long process that could not have been completed without the work and dedication of a number of colleagues.

Given the multilinguistic legacy of the Ottoman Empire, however, no attempt has been made to privilege any one of the relevant Middle Eastern languages in terms of transliteration, especially with regard to shared terms between Arabic, Persian and Ottoman. Similarly, the choice of rendering titles and names into English or Turkish has been left to the individual authors.

I offer my first consignment of gratitude to Michael Cook, who invited me 'to organize a conference on the eighteenth century'. To that end, he entrusted me with some of his Mellon Foundation grant funds with no strings attached. He interfered in neither conceptualization nor logistics; however, he always came through

## PREFACE, NOTE ON TRANSLITERATION AND ACKNOWLEDGEMENTS

whenever his support was needed. In short, he proved to be the ideal patron.

At Princeton, Şukru Hanioğlu generously offered funds from the M. Munir Ertegün Foundation to cover some outstanding expenses. Kathy O'Neil gave her indispensible administrative help and Kim Hegelbach enthusiastically shared her knowledge of the nooks and crannies of the university campus and bureaucracy. Relief from constant organizing and busy deliberation was provided by the tradition of Tuesday dinners with the happy company of Shahab Ahmed, Yossi Rappoport and Gilat Levy.

Through the duration of the conference and beyond, I benefited from the advice and support of various scholars. I thank Norman Itzkowitz and Rifaʿat Abou-El-Haj for sharing their wisdom, and Elizabeth Frierson for a stellar performance at the conference and after. Immense gratitude is due to Madeline Zilfi for so kindly investing in this project time and work well beyond the call of duty. For their work behind the scenes, I am grateful to Heghnar Watenpaugh, Baki Tezcan, Selim Kuru and Shahab Ahmed.

I also thank the individual contributors to this volume for being patient with a particularly demanding editor, and for taking the risk of participating in a project composed entirely of young scholars.

Dana Sajdi
2007
Berlin

# Chapter 1
# Decline, its Discontents and Ottoman Cultural History: By Way of Introduction
*Dana Sajdi*

Those who have not been keeping careful track of recent monographs in Ottoman history, the time has come to stop and take notice. ... Dina Rizk Khouri's study ... joins the monographs of Çızakça, Darling, Fahmy, Hathaway, Hickok, Hoexter, Salzmann, Todorova and Zeʾevi ... adds to the earlier studies (but all since 1980) of scholars such as Abou-El-Haj, Aksan, Barkey, Cohen, Cuno, Doumani, Faroqhi, Kunt, Marcus, and Toledano ... *these works in aggregate have made obsolete all discussion of Ottoman stasis in the period from the death of Suleiman I in 1566 to the reform era initiated by Selim III in the late eighteenth century. Those who persist in portraying those interim centuries as a time of decline, Ottoman ineptitude, and weakness ... do so out of sheer laziness.* Read together, the works mentioned portray an empire whose leadership continually adjusted methods of taxation, assessment, landholding, revenue-holding, and military formations in an attempt to respond to the changing circumstances and demands of the empire for money or military might.[1]

This excerpt from a book review by Amy Singer published in 1999 warrants several observations. Mirroring the general state of the field of Ottoman studies on the period between the late sixteenth and early nineteenth centuries, the monographs cited above are characterized by an overwhelming collective concern to topple a single problematic, namely the 'decline thesis'. The listed works also reflect the manner in which the decline thesis was tackled, that is by focusing on the Ottoman state in order to demonstrate the ability of the state to adapt to changing circumstances, and by writing Ottoman provincial histories within the sub-disciplines of social history, economic history and political economy to show transformations in the polity, economy and society symptomatic of indigenous moves towards modernity. Culture, however, is decidedly absent both as an object of study, and as a method of analysis.

The present volume contains studies in Ottoman culture of which the temporal scope converges on the eighteenth century with necessary glances backwards and forwards into the period between the sixteenth and nineteenth centuries. While the focus on culture in each chapter is a response to a deliberate call by the editor, the topics and methods are not. The relative uniformity of the topics covered in this volume, which deal with either a deconstruction of the history and historiography of the so-called 'Tulip Period' (roughly, the first three decades of the Ottoman eighteenth century), or the rethinking and characterization of the institution of the coffee house, is itself indicative of the direction that the field is taking. Conceptually and methodologically, there is an implicit leitmotif that informs the chapters as a collective – namely, the social and political uses of cultural products and institutions ranging from architecture to ritual, to coffee houses, to the printing press and to historiography itself. Later on in this essay, we will have the opportunity to locate these studies within the new field of Ottoman cultural history; for now, it suffices to mention that this volume is one of the first collective treatments to focus on culture and thus seeks *to add culture* to the study of Ottoman early modernity.

The historiography of Ottoman early modernity has been almost intractably entangled in the overarching dialectic of 'decline/anti-decline'. Within the folds of the dialectic of decline and its anti is a long history of epistemological (and political) complications. By now one can comfortably state that, at least in the academy and specifically within Ottoman studies, the decline thesis has been overwhelmingly and successfully discredited. Thus, if one were to provide a quick characterization of the location of the present volume in the field, it would be between the tail end of anti-decline scholarship and the emerging field of cultural history. The obvious question is, therefore, is there a relationship between the rise of cultural history and the near closure of anti-decline scholarship?

This question is one of the issues that will be raised here. However, to address it I take this opportunity to devote much of this introduction to anti-decline scholarship, with the aim of exposing and thematizing its contributions. This will not only shed light on the circumstances surrounding the subsequent rise of Ottoman cultural history, but will serve to provide the widest possible context in which to locate, and appreciate, the contributions of the current volume. While the reader will find here the accustomed brief introduction to the various chapters (in the section entitled 'Tulips and coffee houses' below), the general thrust of this chapter is to acknowledge the contributions of the scholarship in the past 25 years, while simultaneously sketching rough contours of the state of the field.[2] Since the geographical coverage of the contributions to this volume overlap on the imperial centre, Istanbul, and the provinces of Damascus and Egypt, the majority of the scholarship reviewed here will be about these areas.

In the first section I delineate the decline thesis along with its theoretical and paradigmatic bases. The section following is devoted to the effort to dismantle the category of decline starting from the earliest calls in the late 1950s, but focusing on scholarship in the 1980s and 1990s. In this part I shall review the different frameworks and theories that were advanced in place of the decline thesis by exposing one or more salient studies in each of the fields of political economy, economic history, state formation studies, gender studies, urban social history and intellectual history. I then approach the emergence of Ottoman cultural history by exploring the attitudes of modern scholars towards the text and using the example of recent studies on textural production and book history. I will do so by asking two questions. The first, asked above, has to do with whether there is a relationship between the rise of cultural history and the end of anti-decline scholarship, and the second attempts to explore the enabling effect anti-decline scholarship has had on cultural history. In the fourth section I introduce the studies in this volume, while in the epilogue I temper the general optimistic tone by asking whether in the current political atmosphere it is really possible to dismantle the decline thesis and to transcend Eurocentricism.

## The category of decline

Since the eighteenth century, first European observers and then academics have employed the notion of 'decline' to describe the post-sixteenth-century Ottoman condition. This notion, popping up in different guises, the most familiar of which is the 'sick man of Europe', while initially used to explain the military setbacks, territorial contraction and/or economic deterioration of the Ottoman empire, came to represent an overarching category that subsumed every aspect of society, polity and culture.[3] This rather comprehensively damning view of the Ottoman sixteenth to nineteenth centuries, resembling the attitude to the premodern histories of many regions that came under colonial rule, served the purposes of, or perhaps was propelled by, a Western hegemonic agenda. This view fitted neatly into Enlightenment progress discourse, coalesced in Orientalist scholarship, and acquired further academic rigour in formulations such as the Marxian 'Asiatic mode of production' and 'Oriental despotism', and Weberian-inspired modernizationist and developmentist theories. The process of the epistemological consolidation and academic legitimation of such Eurocentric and imperialist views has been sufficiently delineated, and need not delay us here.[4] However, a brief outline of the meanings and manifestations of 'Ottoman decline' is necessary.

The category of decline assumes an isolated and unique Islamic society/civilization, which, because of its essential difference, is not susceptible to meaningful comparison. This society/ civilization functioned according to its own particular institutions and ideals. Though successful during the 'Golden Age' of Süleyman the Magnificent, Ottoman society/civilization soon witnessed a decay of its institutions and a woeful departure from its ideals. Incapable of adapting to changing circumstances or technological innovations, both the Ottoman state and society remained unchanged, insisting on rigid traditionalism and retaining decayed institutions, thus receding on the civilizational scale into a backward stage. Deliverance – read modernity – came in the form of the 'impact of the West', injecting or inspiring reform and paving the way for modern nationalisms. Consequently, the dates fixed to demarcate Middle Eastern modernity are the Napoleonic invasion with regard to Egypt (1798), the first wave of Zionist migrations in Palestine (1882) or the Egyptian invasion of the Levant (1831), and the Western-inspired Tanzimat (1839–76) for the rest of the empire.

A host of indications are cited in support of the foregoing conceptual framework, the starting point of which is the weakening authority of the Sultan over both polity and economy in the seventeenth and eighteenth centuries. The sultanic loss of control is seen in phenomena ranging from the passage of power from the person of the Sultan to the harem and the eunuchs of the imperial household, to frequent urban rebellions in the centre and some provinces, to rampant banditry in the countryside, to treasury deficits, to price inflation and currency deflation, to the overexploitation and flight of the peasantry, to the loss of the military identity of the once exemplary Janissary corps, to the empire's shrinking borders. Mirroring these phenomena was moral decay in the bureaucracy and other state institutions, where rules of fair play were suspended in favour of bribery, venality, corruption and favouritism. And, despite the reforming efforts by the Köprülü viziers in the seventeenth century, and by Sultan Ahmed III in the early eighteenth century, the Sultan's increasing loss of control is evinced in the eighteenth century by the rise of provincial notables *aʿyān/ayan* who asserted their regional power, challenging the grip of the imperial centre, Istanbul. The system needed an overhaul, which came with the reforming, institutionalizing and centralizing effort of the Tanzimat, which, in turn, gave the Ottoman empire its last breath before its collapse in the First World War.

For our purposes, it is important to stress that the concept of the rise and decline of empires is frequently associated with the civilizational paradigm. The latter assumes that societal complexity is gauged by the aesthetic and originality value of cultural products. Often, when decline or stasis is assumed, cultural production is also neglected on the basis of absence of value. This treatment of cultural production thus reserves historicity only to cultural products that are deemed beautiful or original. I shall return to this point later in this chapter.

## Dismantling decline

In their collective effort to tackle the assumptions of the decline thesis, modern scholars had to demonstrate the following (whether individually or severally):

1. the changing nature and adaptability of Ottoman state and society;
2. indigenous or internal social, economic, and/or intellectual processes displaying signs of modernity *prior* to the advent of the West;
3. the comparability of Ottoman state and society with their counterparts in the world in the same period; and
4. a logic, or a framework, alternative to decline and the Eurocentrism implied therein, that takes into account the phenomena of the seventeenth to eighteenth centuries.

*Early calls*
While the anti-decline scholarship of the 1980s and 1990s was

explicitly or implicitly given theoretical fuel by the publication of Edward Said's *Orientalism*,[5] scepticism of the decline thesis had begun a quarter of a century earlier. These early ventures deserve more than a brief treatment, not only as antecedents to anti-decline scholarship, but also because they were departure points for much of the research to come.

The first hints of displeasure with the decline thesis were raised on empirical grounds. In a masterful and elegantly written essay published in 1957, 'The changing face of the Fertile Crescent in the XVIII century', Albert Hourani proposed to look at the eighteenth century anew 'to ask whether in fact it was decaying and lifeless; whether indeed we can speak of a self-contained Ottoman Moslem society 'before the full impact of the West was felt'.[6] This was probably one of the earliest (if not *the* earliest) exposition of the dynamics of change in the eighteenth century, and contained in its pages the seeds not only of Hourani's later works, but of a whole generation of Ottomanists. The critical apertures opened in that seminal essay eventually became, without exaggeration, entire trajectories that allowed for the establishment of the great masters in the field. Hourani's observations about the change in imperial centre–provincial relations in the eighteenth century would later be officially dubbed 'decentralization' by the master of Ottoman studies, Halil İnalcık.[7] The phenomenon of the assertion of provincial local authority and the emergence of semi-dynastic rule in the eighteenth century was similarly highlighted by Hourani, and would soon after be studied by Abdul-Karim Rafeq, the eventual doyen of Ottoman–Syrian studies.[8] Hourani took up the idea of the assertion of provincial authority to develop the model of the 'notables' (aʿyān), which still serves as a productive analytical category.[9] As late as 1999 Rafeq developed Hourani's observations on the proto-nationalist tendencies of eighteenth-century Damascene ʿulamāʾ.[10] Hourani's essay also drew attention to renewed Mediterranean trade in the eighteenth century and the consequent rise of certain trading minority communities, a subject that Thomas Philipp would develop into a fully fledged study.[11] However, the significance of what was perhaps one of Hourani's subtlest observations in the article has only relatively recently been manifested in the scholarship of the field.

We tend to think of the Empire of Suleiman the Magnificent as the 'true' Empire, and judge all that came before and after in terms of it. Seen in this light, what came after was sheer decline; and in saying this, *we are indeed only reflecting what the Ottomans themselves believed, or at least what they were in the habit of saying.* From Khoja Bey [Koçu Bey] onwards, it was the custom of Ottoman writers to put their proposals for reform in the shape of exhortation to return to the great days of Sultan Suleiman.[12]

Here, Hourani precociously and intuitively unveils the constructed nature of historical discourse, in this case, the myth of the golden age of Süleyman the Magnificent. Although stated in a reflective mode rather than as a methodological assertion, Hourani's statement about the modern historian 'reflecting what Ottoman [writers] themselves believed' would encourage the next generation of scholars to exercise a healthy and productive scepticism towards their sources, and a vigilance not to take at face value what Ottomans tell us about their society for fear of falling into the trap of their myths. The search for the politics of, in and behind the text is something that Ottomanists would take seriously, especially when treating the genre of *nasihatname* (advice literature or 'mirrors for princes') to which Hourani refers in the passage quoted above ('From Khoja Bey onwards, it was the custom of Ottoman writers to put their proposals for reform in the shape of exhortation to return to the great days of Sultan Suleiman'). The consideration of this reform-driven literature informed at least parts of the individual works of three important Ottomanists: Cornell Fleischer, Rifaʿat ʿAli Abou-El-Haj and Cemal Kafadar.[13] Hourani's 'The changing face of the Fertile Crescent' was, and in many ways still is, to use the words of Karl Barbir, 'the gateway to the field' of Ottoman studies.[14]

But to whom was Hourani speaking in 1957? And why, in his proposition to re-evaluate the eighteenth century, is the sentence 'before the full impact of the West' in quotation marks? And why is it without a reference? The probable target was just too famous for citation – H. A. R. Gibb and H. Bowen, *Islamic Society and the West: A Study of the Impact of Western Civilization on Muslim Culture in the Near East*.[15] This was the canonical work that enshrined the decline thesis with all its implications: it assumed an autonomous, isolated, rigid, lethargic and decidedly premodern eighteenth century Muslim society as it existed 'before the full impact of the West'. The process of decanonizing this work was taken up, after Hourani's discreet attempt, by two more direct ventures.

Norman Itzkowitz did his own genealogical homework on Gibb and Bowen's project, and in 1962 published his famous 'Eighteenth century Ottoman realities'.[16] Itzkowitz's concern was not 'decline' *per se* – despite a footnote calling for the reconsideration thereof[17] – but the pedigree of empirical inaccuracy and prejudice of Gibb and Bowen's *Islamic Society and the West*. Itzkowitz identifies the pedigree of Gibb and Bowen as descending from Albert Howe Lybyer's *The Government of the Ottoman Empire in the Time of Suleiman the Magnificent*, published in 1913.[18] Lybyer, Itzkowitz demonstrates, offered his European readers a familiar, easily comprehensible formula based on state and church: 'the ruling institution' comprising the Sultan's household and the executive and military branches of government, staffed by slaves of Christian origin; and 'the Moslem institution', which oversaw religious education and the promulgation and upholding of Islamic law, and was staffed by free-born Muslims. Itzkowitz shows that Gibb and Bowen's adoption of Lybyer's schema included their own special twist: they attribute the purported eighteenth-century decline to the entry of free-born Muslims into the ruling institution to replace slaves of Christian origin. Thus, the view of the authors is religion-determined: the Ottoman empire could only be successful if 'state' is run by Christian slaves and 'church' is run by Muslim clerics. Very astutely, Itzkowitz remarks that the thesis 'has the ... merit of being comforting to the Christian West's deep-seated sense of superiority',[19] and quotes Kipling's racist verses describing the 'Oriental mind' as an explanation of the world-view that informs such a line of historical enquiry.[20] To refute the Lybyer–Gibb–Bowen thesis, Itzkowitz provides abundant examples of Muslim-born men holding offices in the so-called 'ruling institution' and Christian-born officials in the 'Moslem institution' at different periods of the history of the empire, thus invalidating the religious determinism that guides the vision of Gibb and Bowen. Itzkowitz further proposes tracing individual career trajectories of state officials as a guiding principle, rather than focusing on their religious origins. 'Career trajectories' could perhaps be considered a sub-school in Ottoman studies that falls at the juncture of intellectual history, historiography and state history, with Norman Itzkowitz at its centre. Itzkowitz's study of the career of the grand vizier and litterateur, Raghip Pasha (d. 1763), is bracketed between two classic studies of the lives, works and careers of Ottoman historian-bureaucrats Naima (d. 1714) and Mustafa Âli (d. 1600), by Itzkowitz's teacher Thomas V. Lewis, and Itzkowitz's student Cornell Fleischer, respectively.[21]

If Itzkowitz decried the attitude towards the 'Oriental mind' in 1962, Roger Owen, not an Ottomanist but an economic historian of the modern Middle East, announced the 'end of Orientalism' in 1976, two years before the publication of Said's *Orientalism*, in an article that delivered the blow that knocked Gibb and Bowen's *Islamic Society and the West* out of the canon (although their assumptions and conclusion would be restated by Bernard Lewis, as we shall see presently).[22] Owen links the approach of Gibb and Bowen to government and society with, among others, Marx and Engels's model of 'Oriental despotism', and demonstrates the over-simplifying and ideologically-determined categories of 'Islamic' (as a specific and distinct category different from other societies) and 'decline' as well as the unsupportable assumption of the 'isolation' of that society. Over and above Hourani and Itzkowitz's empirical correctives and lines of enquiry, and Itzkowitz's ethico-political considerations, Owen suggests a new methodological approach – political economy or the analysis of economic processes and their role in shaping society.²³ Political economy had already been in the offing, and became one of the leading frameworks of analysis and sub-disciplines in Ottoman studies.

But before turning to political economy, it is worth doing a playback to note the study that continued to promote the decline thesis. When Hourani and Itzkowitz were questioning it, Bernard Lewis was doing exactly the opposite: he had made Ottoman decline the object of his study. Lewis bemoaned the fact that Ottoman decline had not received serious study – with the notable exception of Gibb and Bowen's *Islamic Society and the West*.²⁴ He then proceeded to offer a 'broad classification and enumeration of some [of] the principal factors and process which led to, or were part of, or were expressions of the decline of Ottoman government, society, and civilization'.²⁵ The findings of this article would be published in a book – *The Emergence of Modern Turkey* – that would replace Gibb and Bowen, soon to be decanonized, as the *locus classicus* of the decline thesis.²⁶ (Interestingly, one of Lewis's informants is none other than Koçu Bey, whose complaints Hourani had warned us not to take at face value in the above-mentioned 1958 article, and whom Rifaᶜat Abou-El-Haj would later recontextualize.)

Remarkably, though many (most?) contemporary anti-declinists have cited Lewis's book to express their discontent, few scholars have embarked on studies that solely and primarily deal with the question of decline *per se*. A singular exception in this regard is Cemal Kafadar's 'The question of Ottoman decline'.²⁷ While not expressly presented as such, Kafadar's essay can be posited as an *anti-text* to Bernard Lewis's above-mentioned article and book. I shall return later to Kafadar's essay, but in the meanwhile let us visit one of the early correctives to the decline thesis.

*Political economy and the transformation to capitalism*
A full programme for the application of the political economy

model to the study of the Middle East was proposed by Peter Gran in 1980.[28] Gran had executed the model a year earlier in his path-breaking work *Islamic Roots of Capitalism: Egypt, 1760–1840*.[29] Rejecting the Napoleonic invasion as the moment of Egypt's modernity, Gran posits the emergence of capitalist accumulation in Egypt in the second half of the eighteenth century – that is, prior to the arrival of Europe. But the title of the book is deceptive, for Gran moves beyond political economy to tackle the domain of culture. While the career and work of the scholar Ḥasan al-ᶜAṭṭār (d. 1835) lie at the heart of the study, the author consults a remarkably large body of literary products in equally remarkable variety of fields and genres – from Ḥadīth, to jurisprudence, to history, to literature, to philology, to science. The author recontextualizes towering intellectual figures, who had previously been seen either as atypical luminaries in a dark age, as in the cases of al-Jabartī (d. 1825) and al-ᶜAṭṭār, or as mere Westernizers, as in the case of al-Ṭahṭāwī (d. 1873). Gran inserts these intellectual figures into a local cultural landscape, itself shifting and being shaped by socio-economic factors. Despite the excessive number of errors and inaccuracies that the book contains – something the many reviewers, albeit sympathetic to the enterprise, did not hesitate to point out[30] – the book remains singular in its attempt to offer a comprehensive treatment that regards literary production as culture.[31] For a long time after the book's publication, the study of seventeenth to nineteenth century Middle East remained bifurcated into two separate realms – intellectual history belonging to Islamic studies on the one hand, and social and economic history belonging to Ottoman studies on the other. Culture fell through the fault line between these disciplines.

At about the same time as Peter Gran was advocating political economy, others were offering a particular theory as a corrective within political economy: the Wallerstinian world-systems theory.

*World-systems theory and the logic of peripheralization*
To replace the notion of Oriental despotism and other essentialist

explanations of the Ottoman empire, Huri İslamoğlu-İnan and Çağlar Keyder offered the model of integration/incorporation into the capitalist world economy (or world system).[32] They suggest that prior to the penetration of European capital, the Ottoman social formation was defined by the Asiatic mode of production, where the state had control over land, surplus, production, and regulated both internal and external trade. The reproduction of this social formation was enabled through the state's close management of commercial capital and of the feudalized areas of the economy, two elements potentially destabilizing to the social formation. However, starting in the late sixteenth century, the change in trade routes due to the rise of the Atlantic economy, the rise in demand for raw materials for the European market, the Europe-wide phenomenon of price inflation, and population growth in the Ottoman empire, precipitated various trends that undermined the Ottoman state's political and economic control. Contraband trade increased in volume and contributed to the integration of Ottoman merchant capital into the capitalist world economy, while the state could no longer control prices that were now determined by the world market outside its borders. The Ottoman state's resort to tax farming allowed for the emergence in the eighteenth century of commercial estates (*çiftlik*) for the production of cash crops for the European market.[33] Thus, the social formation of world empire collapsed as the Ottoman empire was integrated into the periphery of the capitalist world system in the role of supplier of raw materials in exchange for finished products. Thus, to explain the phenomena of the seventeenth and eighteenth centuries, İslamoğlu and Keyder offer the logic of peripheralization instead of the thesis of decline.[34]

While accepted in its broad contours, the logic of peripheralization became yet another master narrative, the heavy handed application of which came to eclipse at least as much as it clarified. In the 1990s, several studies altered and nuanced the incorporation paradigm by offering local provincial perspectives.

One of these, Beshara Doumani's *Rediscovering Palestine*,

achieved several objectives.³⁵ By writing the history of merchants and peasants of Nablus and its hinterland, Doumani not only gave agency to these hitherto silent social groups in a peripheral region of both the Ottoman empire and the world economy, but also contested competing Arab and Israeli nationalist historiographies of Palestine. In looking at the processes of production and circulation of four commodities (textiles, raw cotton, olive oil and soap) in the context of merchant-dominated commercial, social and cultural networks, Doumani exposes a number of institutions and practices that evince an indigenous capitalist transformation emerging prior to the penetration of European capital.

He outlines a strong local commercialized and monetized economy that was initially unperturbed by European demand. He also demonstrates the rise of both a new capitalist urban elite and an integrated middle peasantry. The significance of the emergence of these groups is not only on the socio-economic level, but also on the socio-political level: the middle peasantry facilitated the forging of new (namely modern) discourses of citizenship in their appeals to the state to break the hegemony of the urban political elite. Thus, in Doumani's rendition, modernity is not brought in wholesale by any of the events that had been traditionally viewed as its markers (the 1831 Egyptian invasion of Syria; the Tanzimat reforms of 1839–56, or the first European Jewish migration to Palestine in 1882). Rather, the already transformed social and economic situation in Palestine facilitated integration into the world capitalist market and justified the centralizing effort of the Tanzimat. Doumani departs from a reductively economistic approach and further complicates the integration into the world economy narrative by taking into account culture, specifically the manner in which family, religion and ritual facilitated the production and perpetuation of socio-economic relations. Thus, Doumani introduces culture not merely as a super-structure, but as an important constitutive element in its own right.

## DECLINE, ITS DISCONTENTS AND OTTOMAN CULTURAL HISTORY

*Economic history and the logic of the 'general crisis of the seventeenth century'*
Prior to the Wallerstinian turn, economic history as propounded by the *Annales School* was championed most prominently by Ömer Lütfi Barkan.[36] Seminal studies of the demographic, economic and political crises of the seventeenth century were published by Barkan and Halil İnalcık, among others.[37] Barkan showed the penetration into the Ottoman empire of the price revolution that was taking place all over Europe as a result of the influx of new world silver. İnalcık further linked economic crises and currency devaluation to demographic changes and the diffusion of firearms. Due to changes in war technology, the Ottoman empire could no longer retain the twin institutions of *sipahi* (cavalry) supported by *timar* (land grants given to cavalry officers). As part of its reorganization strategy, the empire came to depend on armed mercenaries made up of vagrant peasants who, for one reason or another, had fled their villages. Once demobilized, they became discontented and wreaked havoc on the countryside. These disruptions, along with a number of rebellions led by provincial administrators (like Canbuladoğlu Ali Pasha in Syria) came to be known as the Celali rebellions. The works of Barkan and İnalcık laid the path for the next generation of scholars exemplified in the prolific career of Suraiya Faroqhi, who has worked tirelessly on the minutiae of the economic history of Anatolia.[38] Her cogent construction of the seventeenth century (which *inter alia* summarizes the state of the field) places the Ottoman empire within the wider European context of the 'general crisis of the seventeenth century' where the demands of a centralizing and bureaucratizing state that was in the business of war-making coincided with economic difficulties due to expansion of the Atlantic trade. This resulted in overwhelming economic distress, which, in turn, effected political upheavals.[39] In the logic of the 'general crisis of the seventeenth century', the Ottoman empire is seen as neither displaying signs of decline nor as being peripheralized by the *external* factor of European capital. Rather, these crises are viewed as manifestations of both internal and external

transformations similar to those taking place in Europe, thereby reinstating the Ottoman empire in its European context.

*State formation: the logic behind banditry, venality and corruption*
In her revised 1987 version of the applicability of world systems theory to the Ottoman world, İslamoğlu-İnan called for new conceptions of the Ottoman state.[40] This seems to have been a 'general feeling' in the field over the next decade, which saw the publication of several studies showing that the fiscal measures adopted in the seventeenth century and the administrative decentralization of the eighteenth century did not represent loss of either the authority or legitimacy of Ottoman rule. Rather, they signified the transformation and adaptability of the Ottoman state in rapidly changing circumstances.[41]

In 1991 Rifaʿat ʿAli Abou-El-Haj published his prescient study *Formation of the Modern State: The Ottoman Empire, Sixteenth to Eighteenth Centuries*.[42] Abou-El-Haj looked at the state's experimentation with revenue collection practices over time, and noted a tendency towards privatization of landholding, which, in turn, resulted in a change in social formation. The early modern state formation in the sixteenth century was a centralized system that was at once 'feudal, military and hereditary' and in which the ruling elite espoused merit in matters of public service just as long as that service remained the exclusive domain of that selfsame elite.[43] The transformation brought about by the privatization of land, the monetization of the economy and various external factors precipitated the breakdown of the old order, as manifested in the crises of the seventeenth century, and resulted in the rise of new classes and a concomitant change in the constitution of the ruling elite. At the same time, the changes brought a decentralization of state power that found form in the emergence of ruling households headed by a 'grandee' (or *aʿyān/ayan*) whose politics was characterized by a utilitarian attitude to public office that entailed the purchase and sale of office, as well as nepotism. Thus, rather than taking such 'corruption' as symptomatic of decline – as previous historians had done – Abou-El-Haj regarded it as a sign of a changed order and value system. In this regard, Abou-El-Haj draws instructive comparisons with similar practices in eighteenth and nineteenth century England. Particularly original in Abou-El-Haj's book is his use of literary sources as a reflection – or more accurately a deflection – of the social and political transformations between the sixteenth and eighteenth centuries. In his reading of the historical literature of *nasihatname*, he seems to take Hourani's above-mentioned warning about the treacherous nature of the sources to its logical conclusion. Abou-El-Haj sees the reform proposals in these 'mirrors for princes' as reflecting the social position and ideology of each of their authors: the historian Koçu Bey bewailed the collapse of the social order and the value system it contained because he was a representative of that collapsing order. The new order, on the other hand, found an apologist and legitimizer in the work of one of its beneficiaries: the historian Na'ima.

Abou-El-Haj thus achieves two goals in his book. Like Doumani in the next decade, he is able to debunk the notion that the Tanzimat, the Western-style state-driven reform movement was the *beginning* of modernization in the Middle East, and demonstrates that it was, rather, the logical *culmination* of processes that had been going on in previous centuries. Second, in demonstrating the changing nature of the Ottoman state and society between the sixteenth and eighteenth centuries, Abou-El-Haj was able to establish the comparability between the Ottoman empire and its European counterparts.

Following up on some of the themes raised by Abou-El-Haj, Ariel Salzmann examines *malikane*s (lifelong tax farms) and venality, not as obstacles to the evolution of the modern state but as a deliberate fiscal policy of *privatization* that allowed the transition of the Ottoman state from its 'precocious' early modern state formation in the fifteenth and sixteenth centuries to its centralized manifestation in the nineteenth century.[44] To maintain its rule and territorial integrity, the Ottoman empire, like its counterparts in Asia and Europe, had to resort to privatization to access cash in times of crisis. Conceding to the demands of a new political elite over both fiscal and political rights, the state extended tax farms into lifelong contracts and auctioned them on the market to a select elite. The *malikane* contract had a distinctly entrepreneurial aspect and functioned like a firm with shares to which agents and financiers were attached. It thus came to be viewed as an important source of revenue for the aspiring investor. On the provincial level, these tax-farm contracts, though much smaller in scale, were important for establishing a set of obligations between the state and provincial contractors, which, in turn, allowed for a mutually confirming relationship that functioned to entrench rather than challenge Ottoman rule. For various reasons the *malikane* system faced a crisis towards the end of the eighteenth century, but despite several hesitant attempts at its abolition the system continued into the next century to be eventually abolished by the Tanzimat. And, it was none other than the beneficiaries of the *malikane* system who constituted the main supporters for the Tanzimat effort. Thus, tax farming, venality and accompanying administrative decentralization did not threaten state authority 'so much as to rationalize it in a politically effective form' and to pave the way for the centralized modern state.[45]

Karen Barkey looked at the Ottoman state in the late sixteenth and early seventeenth centuries, not as a state in decline but as a 'wily state responding to challenges as they emerge'.[46] Barkey developed her argument by examining current theories of state formation – which are limited in application to European states – where state making in the seventeenth and eighteenth centuries was carried out through militarization, centralization and bureaucratization, despite opposition from, or at the expense of, sectors of society such as peasants or landed gentry. In other words, state making in the European context occurred as a contest between society and state in which the latter won. Barkey demonstrates that the Ottoman state similarly went through the process of state consolidation, but took the quite different route of negotiating with and co-opting discontented elements and incorporating them into its fold. According to Barkey, because of the specificities of the Ottoman system neither peasant nor elite class-based rebellions were possible. Rather, peasants who had become vagrants because of the crises of the seventeenth century were armed by the state to satisfy the latter's demand for mercenary armies. Once demobilized, however, these soldiers turned to armed banditry and became a destabilizing force that had to be contained through negotiation and bargaining. Thus, participants in the Celali revolts of the late sixteenth to early seventeenth century were not 'primitive rebels', and did not seriously undermine the legitimacy of the Ottoman order; rather, they were simply disaffected bandits who wanted to partake in the Ottoman order. In the end, the bandits were both created and absorbed by the state – and the processes of both creation and absorption were symptomatic of Ottoman state centralization.

*The logic of dynastic reproduction*
If political economy, economic history and the history of state formation tackled the decline thesis to offer correctives, alternative frameworks and periodization schema, gender studies too had a role to play. In declinist constructions, one of the major signs of weakening Ottoman sovereignty is the wielding of power by royal women in the last third of the sixteenth century and continuing through much of the seventeenth century. This was a period when the queen mother, or *valide sultan*, enjoyed unprecedented influence, at least until Turhan Sultan, as regent for her son, appointed Köprülü Mehmed Pasha as grand vizier and forfeited much of her power to him. This put an end to the 'Sultanate of Women'. Leslie Peirce, in *The Imperial Harem: Women and Sovereignty in the Ottoman Empire*, aimed to dispel both early modern and modern misogynist interpretations of the age of powerful imperial women, and to explain the phenomenon, in terms not of the weakness of the sultans but of an internal logic of dynastic reproduction.[47] Peirce notes that, despite the sultan's authority, from the beginning the Ottoman dynasty allowed all family members, irrespective of gender, to have a share in royal patrimony. The exercise of authority, or political maturity, was,

however, linked to sexuality. For men, it was effected by the capacity to father a child, but for women this authority came into being when they achieved a post-sexual status (that is they were either postmenopausal or had borne a son). Given the link between sexuality and the exercise of power, the sexual activity of royal members was highly controlled by the older generation. The logic behind the control of sexuality was to safeguard both the perpetuation of the dynasty and the integrity of the incumbent sultan's authority.

According to Peirce, the rise of the queen mother figure was an inevitable result of the Ottoman empire's change during the course of the sixteenth century from a military expansionist power to a sedentary, administrative bureaucracy. Initially, royal princes participated in state power through their appointment to princely governorates where they would get hands-on training, a chance to establish their reputation in conquest and, possibly, a 'constituency' of supporters. All this would be in preparation for accession to the throne whereby eligible princes would have to prove their fitness against each other, often in open combat. During the heyday of the princely governorate, the prince's mother would leave the imperial harem to accompany her son to the province (thereby achieving post-sexual status) to oversee his household and promote his interests. As the nature of the empire changed from expansionist to administrative, the prince as conqueror ceased to be a central figure. This transformation eventually led to the demise of the institution of the princely governorate and the reaggregation of the entire royal family into one imperial household in Istanbul. Once in the same household, with too many competing mothers of princes present, the sultan's mother naturally occupied the highest rung of the hierarchy.

At the same time, the principle of succession changed to one of seniority, with the throne reserved for the eldest surviving male member of the family, who rarely happened to be one of the sultan's sons. In such a system, the role of the mother as guardian and mentor was further strengthened. To ascertain the unchallenged authority of the incumbent sultan, royal princes were now divested of any political authority by means of confinement to the palace and postponement of their sexual maturity (they would only father children upon enthronement). Due to their confinement, princes ceased to be able to establish 'constituencies' of supporters prior to enthronement, with the result that several sultans would now be deposed and replaced by princes who were simply too young to rule. The *valide sultan* thus became not only the head of an entire centralized imperial household, but also the sultan's mentor and guide, and often his regent. The 'sultanate of women' was therefore, in contrast to the misogynist thesis, not an obvious cause and symptom of decline, but was rather the vehicle that ensured the perpetuation of rule by the House of Osman as empire and dynasty were undergoing major reorientation.

*Urban social history and new empiricism*
The discovery of Ottoman provincial judicial court records and central state archives as historical sources had the effect not only of facilitating more empirically grounded research but also of writing into history hitherto under- or unrepresented social groups like peasants and artisans.[48] In this regard, André Raymond's *Artisans et commerçants au Caire au XVIIIe siècle*, published in 1973–74, was a *tour de force*.[49] Raymond's nuanced study of a highly differentiated artisanate and merchant class, along with its institutions, such as guilds, and its relations with the ruling class, was a watershed in the field. The work's integrative approach brought out the role of minority communities in the economic and social life of the city, and situated the circumstances of manufacturing and trade within the urban physical layout. This, with Raymond's subsequent works, would propel the field of Ottoman urban social history.

Raymond's masterful work opened the way for discontented scholars to subject the decline thesis to empirical testing and verification through the study of urban social history. One such study is Abraham Marcus's *The Middle East on the Eve of*

*Modernity: Aleppo in the Eighteenth Century*.[50] Marcus asks several questions that challenge previous Orientalist assumptions about Middle Eastern cities. Had Aleppo been in a condition of stasis before the nineteenth century? Was Islam the sole and only referent in understanding the social and cultural history of the city? And had Aleppo conformed to the stereotype of the 'Islamic city' inhabited by a 'mosaic' of isolated confessional and/or neighbourhood communities.

Marcus takes an intimate and sweeping look at Aleppo; he examines its economics, politics and governance, as well as its social and cultural life (including popular and learned culture and the attitude to and treatment of health, disease and death). He also offers a characterization of the urban experience ranging from neighbourhood life to public services, personal privacy and the public spirit. Although the author detects both long-term and 'cyclical' changes in Aleppo in the eighteenth century, he does not see the radical change usually associated with modernity (though one must warn that the temporal span of Marcus's sources is limited to only three decades, hence generalizations about the eighteenth century as such may be inapplicable). While Marcus does see community-based social organization, whether according to neighbourhood or faith, he notes that class differentiation cuts across these groupings, allowing for city-wide action that transcends local community.

Perhaps one of Marcus's most important contributions is the demonstration of the extent to which there existed a variance between the ideal of Islamic law as found in legal texts and its daily application at the judicial court. The divergence between the legal text and the practice of the law shows that previous conceptualizations of the Middle East that focused mainly on the morphology of the city and explained it in terms of Islamic law are both inaccurate and insufficient for an understanding of the urban experience and the functioning of the city. In short, a determinedly philological understanding of Islamic society that assumes an essential uniqueness embodied in the text is demonstrably fallacious. To comprehend how the city operated and how its citizens experienced it, we need not only new conceptualizations of the city that go beyond morphology and the Islamic ideal but also new empirically-grounded research such as that of Raymond and Marcus.[51]

*Intellectual history: renewal, reform, enlightenment?*
In her survey of scholarship on the eighteenth century, Jane Hathaway described intellectual history as the 'big lacuna'.[52] Though there is still much work to be done on Ottoman intellectual history, the problem has less to do with the dearth of work than with the work being done under a different rubric: Islamic studies. There, too, the general thrust has been towards antidecline, but is concerned with *Islamic* decline at large and not specifically with Ottoman decline. Intellectual historians of the period have been following reformist trends, as well as the careers and ideas of individual intellectuals within the wider Islamic world.[53]

For two decades now attention has been paid to eighteenth-century intellectual reformulations and/or reformist thought. Fazlur Rahman noted a change in the attitude to and practice of Sufism, which he famously dubbed 'neo-Sufism ... Sufism reformed on orthodox lines' (that is *sharīʿah*-minded); it focused on the person of the Prophet (and was thus concerned with Ḥadīth studies) and was 'activist'.[54] Taking this phenomenon as a point of departure, John Voll led a trend in the field that sought to identify connections between the different reformist movements in chains of scholarly networks that overlapped in the holy cities of Mecca and Medina.[55] In Germany, Reinhard Schulze declared an *autochtone Islamische Aufklärung* (an autochthonous Islamic Enlightenment) and thereby sparked a controversy that lasted for more than a decade.[56] He located an indigenous subjective self-consciousness and rationalism in the mystical beliefs and activities of the eighteenth century, which, in turn, provided fertile ground for the emergence of an anthropocentric world-view and a concomitant liberation of the urban bourgeoisie from state control. Critics, most virulently Bernd Radtke, have objected to many of

Schulze's proposals, not least the use of concepts and terminology seen as the preserve of Western history.[57] While many disagree with Schulze's propositions, whether *in toto* or in detail, Stefan Reichmuth noted that, 'whenever Schulze's critics, after having done with "Islamic Enlightenment", set out to develop their own ideas about Islamic cultural and intellectual development in the eighteenth century, they can be seen as keeping remarkably close to Schulze's own concepts.'[58] Whatever its intrinsic merits, the Islamic Enlightenment debate has pushed the field towards a return to a reconstituted (post-Orientalist) intellectual history and an interest in the early modern period.[59] Moving away from Ḥadīth and Sufism, reformists and reform, Khaled El-Rouayheb has focused on the study of philosophy in the early modern Arab Middle East, which had been presumed to have abated in Sunni Islam since the medieval great masters. El-Rouayheb has patiently registered the resurgence in the study of logic, noting movements of texts and scholars between North Africa, Egypt, the Levant and Iran, while at the same time extending the temporal span back into the seventeenth century.[60]

But, what is Ottoman about the foregoing? The answer is everything and nothing. While many of the activities historians have charted have taken place within Ottoman domains, as I mentioned at the outset the thrust of contemporary scholarship in intellectual history has not sought to link these intellectual trends to those occurring at the imperial centre, probably because most modern scholars are proficient in either Arabic or Ottoman but rarely in both.[61] Furthermore, as is the habit of intellectual history in which state and power are treated as accidents rather than as part and parcel of the analysis, very few studies have linked intellectual currents to the politics and/or socio-economics of (in our case the Ottoman) empire.[62] Thus, things *Ottoman* seem to be at the margins of intellectual history. As such, discussions about reform, renewal and/or enlightenment in the eighteenth century have not seriously been linked to the different frameworks offered in lieu of Ottoman decline in the foregoing sections. Similarly, the work that has been undertaken on intellectual history at the imperial centre has not been linked to the wider context of the Islamic world.

While not concerned with Ottoman decline or intellectual history *per se*, Madeline Zilfi's study of the official learned/ religious institution (*ilmiye*) in Istanbul in the seventeenth and eighteenth centuries is of relevance.[63] Although the characterization of the evolution of the institution and its attendant social history is her main concern, a significant part of Zilfi's project is devoted to the rise and fall of the Kadızadeli movement in the seventeenth century. The movement had its roots in the writings of Birgivi Mehmed (d. 1573) and may have influenced later reform movements, both in terms of ideology and praxis. While Zilfi does not dwell on the intellectual and ideological import of the movement, she is able to locate Kadızadeli *activism* and popular support within a social context in which the *ilmiye* was simultaneously facing institutional instability. The connection between the Kadızadeli and eighteenth-century reform movements still awaits serious exploration.

Like Zilfi, Cornell Fleischer was unconcerned about decline as such when he wrote about the life and career of historian, bureaucrat and poet Mustafa Âli (d. 1600).[64] However, among other things like changes in the Ottoman bureaucracy and the place of non-religious law (*kanun*) in its workings, the study brings out a crucial aspect in Ottoman historiography – what became dubbed as 'decline consciousness'. Mustafa Âli's career frustrations led him to write a reformist critique of the Ottoman system that ushered onto the scene of historiography a whole genre of Ottoman 'mirrors for princes' (*nasihatname*) of which the central theme was Ottoman decline. In unveiling the personal motivation behind historiography, Fleischer's study opened the way for modern historians to treat the decline historiography produced by Ottomans with scepticism. Consequently, the 'decline consciousness' found in Ottoman *texts* was not immediately to be translated into *real* Ottoman decline. Differentiating between the textual and the real is something that Hourani advised in the late 1950s and that Abou-El-Haj executed in the early 1990s.

*Between the perceived and the real: decline and renewal?*
Earlier I mentioned Cemal Kafadar's 'The question of Ottoman decline' and posited it as an anti-text to Bernard Lewis's *Emergence of Modern Turkey*. But Kafadar's essay, published in 1998, was *also* a response to almost two decades of anti-decline scholarship.

On the one hand, Kafadar finds the category of decline woefully imprecise in that it inaccurately lumps together changes in 'all spheres of life – political, military, institutional, social, economic and cultural' – to cast them negatively in a linear and totalizing manner.[65] Taking declinists on their own terms without resorting to alternative frameworks, Kafadar offers a quick narrative of the Ottoman empire in which he looks at government apparatuses and institutions, the economy, the military and technological change. Although remarkably similar to Lewis in his choice of subjects, Kafadar arrives at a different conclusion in which he shows that decline as an overarching category lacks historicity and explanatory function.

On the other hand, Kafadar is dissatisfied with the political correctness that has come with the baggage of anti-decline scholarship ('one might even fear that "decline" is turning into "the d-word", shunned because it seems to be the incorrect thing to say').[66] One of his major concerns is precisely the above-outlined separation carried out by modern scholars between the textual and the real in decline-consciousness literature. Kafadar does not want to dismiss the complaints and diagnostics of the *nasihatname* literature as mere inaccurate perceptions. Simultaneously, he wants to show that the reform literature did not idealize Sultan Süleyman's rule as a 'golden age' and thus did not suffer from the 'traditionalism' purported in modern scholarship.[67] In attempting to save the *nasihatname* authors, Kafadar shows a certain congruence between Ottoman realities and textual claims by demonstrating (some would say conceding) a very relative and limited decline in terms of the empire's 'delivery of force and the ability to command obedience and awe' starting in the seventeenth century (a crude feminist interpretation would be that if one wants to look at history from a militaristic, testosterone-driven angle, then yes, there was decline).[68] Yet, Kafadar's conclusion is not one that confirms Ottoman decline, but rather sees that every 'warp of decline' was entangled in the 'weft of renewal'.

So, is the decline/anti-decline dialectic now resolved? I would suggest a hesitant positive answer (the anxiety surrounding the answer is explained in the Epilogue to this chapter). If, according to Amy Singer (in the opening quotation), it would have been intellectually lazy to espouse the decline thesis in 1999, then, given the state of the field today, it is equally lazy to espouse anti-decline in 2007. The invocation of decline is not only academically superfluous but it also undermines the achievements of scholarship in the past 25 years, which are many. Regardless of what one may think of an individual revisionist work, or a particular method or framework, the cumulative effect of the scholarship has demonstrated the empirical and theoretical invalidity of the decline thesis, and offered a portrayal of an internally dynamic Ottoman state and society. It has also established the comparability of the Ottoman empire to other – mainly European – societies and polities, and concomitantly revised the existing scheme of periodization. A Middle Eastern modernity marked by the Napoleonic moment or the Tanzimat effort is now a questionable equation, and 'Ottoman early modernity', not a 'post-classical age', has become tenable.[69] In addition to developing new and creative methods of writing Ottoman history, anti-decline scholarship has also demonstrated the importance of healthy scepticism towards the sources.

## Ottoman cultural history/studies: textual tribulations

Kafadar's above-mentioned essay reinforces our observation on the conspicuous absence of culture from the list of books mentioned by Amy Singer in the opening excerpt: 'Among the least studied aspects of Ottoman history, despite some recent stirrings, is cultural life.'[70]

But, ever since, the field has witnessed what one may term a 'cultural turn' both in terms of interest in cultural life and products, and in the utilization of cultural analysis. Some early 'stirrings' include the appearance in English in 2000 of Suraiya Faroqhi's *Subjects of the Sultan: Culture and Daily Life in the Ottoman Empire*.[71] In the same year, a volume on consumption history edited by Donald Quataert was published and, though it focused primarily on the social and economic aspects of consumption, it also evinced interest in material culture.[72] Over the past five to six years, the field has accumulated many studies on various aspects of culture, which include, just to name a few, body and disability, public gardens, homoeroticism, popular protest and coffee house culture.[73]

Given this particular history of contemporary Ottoman historiography, which witnessed the cultural turn only after a long wave of anti-decline scholarship in which cultural history was scant, two questions come to mind: First, is there a relationship between the fall of the decline thesis and the rise of cultural history/studies? Second, how has Ottoman cultural history dealt with the legacy of anti-decline scholarship?

Regarding what one may call the inverse relationship between cultural history and anti-decline scholarship one may conjecturally offer two possible reasons that might have precipitated this relationship, both of which involve (but of course are not limited to) *fear of the text*. The first has to do with the possibility of empirical research and the availability of sources for it on the one hand, and the decline thesis on the other. For a long time empirical research was obviated by the fact that the text, which delivered evidence that was anecdotal at best and unreliable at worst, provided the main source for history. The discovery of court records and other official documents was received with relief and excitement, for these sources delivered vast pools of data (which *inter alia* could be subjected to quantitative and statistical analysis) and allowed Ottoman history to move from narrative and institutional history to scientifically 'solid' studies and, in due course, to debunk the decline thesis. Interestingly, these records and documents lent themselves to social, economic and state history, while the text was mostly neglected (or given secondary status), to remain important only in the field of intellectual history. But if the first reason that I offered to explain the inverse relationship between anti-decline history and cultural history has to do with a fear of the text because of its inherent testimonial weakness, the second reason is linked to another fear, an epistemological one. This latter fear is related less to cultural history *per se* than to the method of cultural analysis, which is derived in large part from textual approaches. Both Orientalist scholarship and the related civilizationalist narrative had enshrined the text as the central piece of scholarship. Orientalist scholarship not only depended on the text for its primarily philological methods but also drew its generalizations from textual ideals and idealizations. The civilizationist narrative, as mentioned earlier, valorized the text (among other cultural products) in terms of quality and originality, and saw it as an indication of progress or backwardness. Thus, the associations between essentialist methods and the text may have resulted in a general distaste for the latter. But it was not only the text that was disposed of; the associated possibilities of discursive methods and cultural analyses were also ignored. It is highly instructive that in her excellent critique of essentialist methods, Huri İslamoğlu-İnan characterizes them as 'culturalist' in orientation and assumptions.[74] Culture, in other words, seems to have had a bad name.

Thus, in an attempt to establish new truths against the decline thesis, most anti-decline scholarship took a generally materialist approach based on archival research. In this approach society and economy take precedence over culture, which more often than not is seen as a superstructure. Similarly, the text is demoted because of its factual unreliability and association with essentialist methods. The urgency of the mission of anti-decline scholarship may have resulted in an impatience for the ambiguities of cultural analysis.

To return to the second question posed above, how has the emerging field of Ottoman cultural history dealt with the scholarship of the 1980s and 1990s? To answer this question I return to recent treatments of literary production, reading and book history (not taking into account print culture, which in the case of the Middle East only became entrenched in the nineteenth century).

*The cultural dimension of textual production: early modern order-preserving anxiety or modern subversive radicalism*
In his comment on the *nasihatname* literature, Kafadar characterizes this decline-conscious literature as 'part of a condition the Ottomans shared with their early modern European contemporaries: anxiety'.[75] He further advised extending this rubric (of early modern anxiety) to include other literary production of the period including popular literature, which he saw as equally decline conscious as its elite counterpart, the *nasihatname*. By placing cultural phenomena in the Ottoman empire in the context of general 'early modernity', Kafadar rejects limits that may hinder comparative analysis, either geographically (Europe versus the Middle East) or civilizationally (the West versus the Islamic/Ottoman world). As for broadening the analysis to include literary production beyond the 'mirrors for princes' literature, Kafadar had executed his own idea a decade earlier (in 1989) when he traced the emergence of 'first person narratives' in the social dislocation of the seventeenth and eighteenth centuries.[76] In this study, Kafadar also brought out the cultural specificity (namely the Ottoman variation) of early modernity by exploring Sufi (mystical) practices surrounding textual production. In the context of great social dislocation, individuals and groups found in mystical social and literary practices some anchorage in the sea of change. The literary result was the first-person narrative, which expressed anxieties about a changing order.

More than a decade later Kafadar's student, Derin Terzioğlu, took both the logic of 'early modern anxiety' and the Sufi connection to produce an excellent analysis of the diary of the mystic Niyazi Mısri (d. 1694).[77] While more concerned with the literary hybrid nature of popular texts, my own work on a barber historian in eighteenth-century Damascus also frames the analysis in terms of anxiety, disorder and dislocation.[78] Away from anxiety, but still within the frame of early modernity, Astrid Meier has identified a tendency to represent the characteristically early modern sentiments of melancholy and solitude in the historical writings of the *ulamā'* in Damascus.[79]

Nelly Hanna, who provided a much needed and overdue monographic treatment on book history, took a different approach from the one outlined above. In her *In Praise of Books* (2003) she explores the existence in Cairo in the seventeenth and eighteenth centuries of a sophisticated book culture outside the traditional domains of the courtly and religious, or learned, classes.[80] This book culture, according to Hanna, reflects concern for the secular and quotidian, and reveals a line of enquiry motivated by observation and empiricism. The certain tenor that Hanna attributes to the content of this culture is further assured by her explanations for its rise – the emergence of a literate, *modern middle class* that came about as a result of a prosperous Mediterranean trade. Thus, Hanna, like Kafadar, sees textual production as a reflection of larger transformations; she, however, portrays a more certain, even comfortable and convivial outcome. In her Cairo, the participants in the market of new texts are not anxiety-ridden subjective voices attempting to preserve the social order, but a confident group of progressive radical intellectuals.

This is no place to attempt to resolve whether new textual production in the Ottoman empire during the seventeenth and eighteenth centuries characterized early modern order-preserving anxiety *à la* Kafadar (and those who see early modern sentiments in the textual productions of the period), or modern subversive radicalism *à la* Hanna. Indeed, these two phenomena may not even be related and each may be specific to its particular geographical location (Egypt and the central Ottoman lands respectively). In short, these phenomena are not necessarily mutually exclusive. This is also not the place to quibble over methods of evaluating Hanna's materialist approach against Kafadar's inclination towards cultural analysis. What is important, however, is the identification of the phenomenon of textual production and the simultaneous recognition that literary culture in the seventeenth and eighteenth centuries is worth investigating. Would these studies have been possible without the anti-decline scholarship of the previous generation?

On the one hand, had it been pursued earlier, cultural history would have helped the anti-decline effort and reinforced work in other sub-fields. On the other hand, it is exactly the work done in these other fields that gave the next generation the licence to think of Ottoman history as being comparable, coeval in terms of periodization, and as fitting into categories beyond Islamic terms. Perhaps the most important leap that anti-decline scholarship achieved, and that constituted an enabling factor for cultural history, is the gradual departure from the civilizational paradigm, whose treatment of cultural products I have outlined above.

The belief in Ottoman civilizational decline seems to have hindered the investigation of cultural artefacts on the grounds that they were considered valueless. However, once new frameworks and logics (that were alternatives to decline and hence to the civilizational narrative) had been offered, it became possible to view cultural products differently. The point of cultural history is not the product *per se*, but rather that all of the product, its uses, and the value its users ascribe to it, become objects of study. From a cultural history viewpoint, every product – regardless of its aesthetic or novelty value – deserves a history. Once anti-decline scholarship had questioned the civilizational narrative it became possible to think culturally and to attribute historicity to all cultural products and not only a select few. The value of the text is no longer to do with aesthetics and originality; it is no longer merely a source from which to collect information, and its idealizations no longer guide our enquiry. Rather, the text is expressive of wider socio-economic transformations; it is indicative of specific cultural phenomena and is invested with meanings that need to be decoded. We now think it is possible and necessary to look at book culture, to trace the emergence of first-person narratives and to find melancholy and anxiety in Ottoman texts.

As it stands today, Ottoman cultural history can both contribute to old debates and shape new ones. Cultural history can add to processes begun by earlier scholarship, as well as independently chart completely new territories. Although cultural history has made a recent debut, its studies have already produced internal debates. This book includes all these possibilities of cultural history. Each study continues to undo, offers new beginnings, or engages with recent scholarship.

## Tulips and coffee houses

As a springboard from which to introduce the chapters in this volume, I will use Ariel Salzmann's 'The age of tulips', which appeared in 2000.[81] Significantly, that study was published in the same collection on consumption history that I located as a bridge between economic and social history on the one hand and cultural history on the other. Thus, this book comes as the logical next step: another edited collection, but one in which the main preoccupation is culture.

Taking the tulip as a transcultural sign and luxury commodity, Salzmann traces synchronically and diachronically both the symbolic and real value of this flower. She follows the course of the transposition of the form of the tulip across the various media from poetry to tiles, textiles, canvas and embroidery, *and* of the real flower (as a much demanded horticultural specimen) as it travelled throughout Eurasia.

She posits the tulip as a site of competition between early modern court societies, the characteristic theatricality of which compelled the elite to burst onto the public space displaying pomp and pageantry and taking as the *mise en scène* new forms of built environment (new gardens and new home and palace architecture).[82] Such an indulgence in and display of luxury is seen as a reflection of the 'expanded reach of exchange networks and the changing content of commercial interaction between regions and states' giving rise to a distinctly early modern preindustrial consumerist culture.[83] It is a 'transnational' elite culture that utilized shared vocabularies – in this case the tulip –

in the articulation of power and privilege within and outside their societies.

So what do tulips have to do with coffee houses and Ottoman history? The Ottoman elite was very much part of this early modern, transnational, consumerist culture and the fervent cultivation of and decoration with tulips. But Turkish nationalist historiography inscribed the Ottoman cult of tulips with multiple significations and packaged it in a neat civilizational narrative. The cult of tulips became emblematic of the first three decades of the Ottoman eighteenth century, dubbed *Lale Devri* (the Tulip Period), when Sultan Ahmed III (who ruled from 1703 to 1730) and his grand vizier Nevşehirli İbrahim Pasha (who held office from 1718 to 1730) undertook a series of reforms, including the establishment of the first Ottoman printing press set up by Ibrahim Müteferrika. This period is remembered not only for its reforms and tulip mania, but also 'theatrically' in its imperial circumcision festival and architecturally in the building of the Saadabad ('Abode of Happiness') palace. In 1730 a popular rebellion led by Patrona Halil, a coffee shop owner, ended with the abdication of the sultan and the destruction of the palace of Saadabad. Turkish nationalist historiography had posited this sequence of events as a story of 'precocious modernization' undertaken by an enlightened ruler that came to a tragic end with a rebellion initiated by the sultan's reactionary and benighted Muslim subjects.[84] In other words, historians had constructed the 'tulip period' as an attempt at a Western-inspired *rise* that met the fate of inevitable Muslim *decline*. Salzmann rewrites the narrative by exposing the underlying *social conflict* behind the rebellion. Rather than the preservation of religious and cultural identity or the fear of modernizing change, it was the harsh material realities and social conditions that instigated Patrona Halil and his artisan compatriots to launch their revolt. Significantly, the revolt was launched from a coffee house. Thus, if the target of the rebellion was the palace, both physically and symbolically, the coffee house had come to mean the *anti-palace*.

Tulips and coffee (as cultural products) and related institutions (like the palace, coffee house and so-called 'Tulip Period') have come to bear multiple meanings in both the history and historiography of the Ottoman empire. It is with aspects of these significations that the present volume is concerned.

In Chapter 2, Can Erimtan proposes a similar project to that of Salzmann's, but the cultural product here is the famed palace of Saadabad, the construction and eventual destruction of which in the aftermath of the Patrona Halil rebellion represents another of those emblems of the 'Tulip Period'. Supposedly as part of his Westernizing imperial project, Sultan Ahmed III commissioned the building of the palace as a replica of Versailles, or so the received wisdom has it. Erimtan takes a genealogical approach to the historiography of the narrative of the 'tulip period' and the building of Saadabad and reveals its 'manufacture' at the hands of the early twentieth-century Ottoman historian Ahmed Refik who, the author argues, was following his own political agenda of justifying the reform project underway in his own time. Having uncovered the politics and mechanics behind the narrative of the 'tulip period', Erimtan proceeds to offer an alternative narrative that sees Saadabad in the context of Ottoman–Safavid rivalry. He demonstrates that the Ottoman palace makes direct architectural references to Safavid architecture, especially the palace of Chihil Sutun. Thus, instead of a Westernization project, the commissioning of Saadabad and its architectonic features is placed in the context of a shared inter-Islamic competitive vocabulary and within a new Islamicate geography.

Yet another symbol of the 'Tulip Period' is the reputedly failed project of the first Ottoman printing press, that of Ibrahim Müteferrika. Like the destruction of Saadabad in the 'tulip period' narrative, the purported failure of the first Ottoman printing press has been posited as reflective of the general ill-preparedness of the Ottoman public for enlightened reform. In Chapter 3, Orlin Sabev, like Erimtan, takes a genealogical approach to the historiography of the first Ottoman printing press to demonstrate that the sources of the alleged failure of Müteferrika's printing enterprise are rather unreliable. Having unearthed the probate inventory prepared after Ibrahim Müteferrika's death, Sabev is able to offer a statistical analysis showing the production and sale of the Müteferrika printed books. He concludes that Müteferrika had managed to sell 70 per cent of the books produced in his print shop, a figure that cannot be considered a failure by any measure. Indeed, in comparison with the earliest European printing ventures, the first Ottoman printing press was a resounding success. So, like Salzmann before them, Sabev and Erimtan make further inroads into shaking the foundations of the 'tulip period.'

In Chapter 4, Babak Rahimi treats the theatricality of the pageantry of imperial ritual. He traces changes in symbolism and participation in Ottoman imperial public circumcision celebrations between 1582 and 1720. He observes changes in the course of the ritual procession, the composition of its participants and the shape and make up of the procession marker – the fertility symbol of the *nahil* (wooden poles displayed in the public and court festivals associated with the circumcision of a prince). Grounding his study in the theories of Mary Douglas, works on the early modern 'theatre state', and Rifaʿat Abou-El-Haj's abovementioned monograph, Rahimi sees the change in significations of the eighteenth century imperial ritual as reflective of 'changes in state and collective identity formation processes ... where power was both *enacted* and *represented* to affirm state authority and social solidarity'. Rahimi ends his chapter by comparing Ottoman circumcision celebrations with contemporary Safavid Muharram rituals.

Moving away from the palace to the 'anti-palace', in Chapter 5 Ali Çaksu takes the reader to the Janissary coffee shops of eighteenth- and nineteenth-century Istanbul. Beyond serving as a rebel headquarters, the Janissary coffee shop, Çaksu shows us, performed a multiplicity of functions. Based on extensive original research in Ottoman chronicles and archives, the author paints an unprecedently vivid image of the Janissary coffee house, seeing it as a 'place to drink coffee and smoke tobacco, but ... also a cultural salon, rebel headquarters, police precinct, Sufi lodge, business office, and mafia club all rolled into one'. Given that the coffee shop served such a variety of functions over and above coffee sipping, the Ottoman coffee shop demands new theoretical consideration. This is exactly what Alan Mikhail will do in the next chapter.

Recent conceptualizations have posited the Ottoman coffee house as home to subversive political activity and as a public institution defined by male sociability. In Chapter 6, pushing theoretical limits, Mikhail eschews Jürgen Habermas's dichotomous category of 'public' and 'private' for Michel Foucault's 'heterotopia'. The author looks at the social, legal, architectural and literary dimensions of Ottoman coffee houses in the cities of Istanbul, Cairo and Aleppo and provides a counter-characterization for every recent depiction of the coffee shop. What emerges is a complex image of the neighbourhood coffee house as possessing overlapping (often seemingly contradictory) functions and multiple identities.

Thus, between the tulip and the coffee house, as a collective enterprise the contributors to this book visit elite and popular, state and society (and the spaces in-between) to examine aspects of Ottoman culture as they consider ritual, architecture, technology and sociability.

The authors continue to undo previous nationalist constructions that saw the early eighteenth century as a period of Western-inspired arrested change. Instead, they assume the commensurability of Ottoman culture by using categories applicable to other societies and cultures while underlining inter-Islamicate inspirations and interactions. At the same time, some of the studies offer new theoretical propositions and fresh data that may open up possibilities and problematics to induce further research. In the final analysis, the studies herein take change as a given, thanks to the enabling efforts of previous generations.

## Epilogue: decline dismantled?
## The political predicament and the defensive posture

In the foregoing I declare the end of decline and anti-decline scholarship, but a mitigating note is in order. Although there is undeniable consensus in the field that the decline thesis has been entirely debunked, a revised image of the Ottoman empire in the post-sixteenth century has not yet infiltrated other fields and has not yet been accepted in the world outside the academy. Thus, despite the effort of the past 25 years and the readiness of Ottomanists to participate in public history, the decline thesis persists.[85] What is the problem?

One can think of a host of reasons for the recalcitrance of the decline thesis, including intellectual and institutional ones, but here I shall briefly touch on the most obvious – the political predicament. It seems that we are caught in an epistemological hegemony that lies beyond our immediate academic field and that resides in global power relations, thus forcing us to remain in a defensive position.

While we have been and still are in the process of liberating the history of the Middle East from both imperialist and nationalist constructions, the Middle East has not yet been liberated from imperialism and, in turn, from defensive nationalisms. Nationalist sentiments in the Middle East aside (which have been current since the late nineteenth century but which may even go back to the eighteenth century), the very marking of the nation-state happened with the colonial pen in the aftermath of the First World War. Colonial and post-colonial imperial interests in the Middle East have not subsided since then and are bolstered and justified by a civilizing discourse. The most recent manifestation of both imperial interests and the concomitant discourse are the war on, and occupation of, Iraq, the continuing assault on Palestinian territories, and the brutal most recent invasion of Lebanon. All of this for the purpose of (yet another) drawing of a new Middle East.[86] Behind this is a rhetoric of democratization, creation of civil society and, in the case of Lebanon, a return to its old glory. This is not only remarkably reminiscent of declinist discourse, but it is also an actual extension of it: the Middle East, fraught with fanatic fundamentalism and tyranny, can only achieve secular democracy through pre-emptive wars and invasions by the 'civilized' world (namely the West). And as long as the powers that be demand the discourse of decline, supply is readily found, whether in the figure of the Middle East expert in the media or in popular histories and documentaries.

In the Middle East the decline thesis was upheld for a long time by Middle Eastern historians themselves, having partly internalized the Orientalist discourse and partly in service of the nationalist agendas of their fledgling nation-states. In an atmosphere of national liberation and decolonization, the nation-state seemed to be the inevitable and desirable end. In the name of ethnic-nationalist ideologies, a history of decline was written to justify these exclusivist states.[87] However, while historians have turned away (and continue to do so) from the nationalist historiographical project,[88] defensive regimes in the Middle East still require it as part of their legitimation routine. As such, school curricula continue to teach it and most national celebrations are annual reminders that imply former decline. This nationalist legitimation routine has been enhanced by and has become doubly necessary because of the continuing imperialist gaze and military menace.

A related issue that is not limited to the history of the Middle East but affects the rest of the non-Western world, and that I mentioned above when discussing the category of decline, is Eurocentrism. While the thrust of anti-decline scholarship has been to counter European hegemonic narratives, it sometimes inadvertently confirmed a position of European centrality. Anti-decline scholarship rightly understood that the yardstick of Ottoman decline was an assumption of European ascendancy. The negation of Ottoman decline and the emphasis on indigenous processes have, however, failed to disinvest us of the exemplary status attributed to Europe. What is implied in some anti-decline work is 'like Europe, the Middle East also', or 'this happened in the Middle East even before it did in Europe.' One's objection to this stems neither from jealousy of European specificity nor from a belief that it is impossible to draw comparisons between the Middle East and Europe (quite the contrary!), but is a criticism of our incapacity truly to transcend Eurocentricity. Thus, at an epistemological level, the defensive nature of the anti-decline stance has indirectly perpetuated centre–periphery relations instead of what it sought to achieve, namely decentering Europe.[89]

The foregoing problems are, of course, not new, and there exist no ready solutions. Aside from continuing to educate and to engage in public history, I can think of three immediate objectives for us to carry out. First, we need simply to continue to do new research in order to animate and 'add flesh' to Ottoman history and thus provide fresh images for both academic and public consumption. Second, we need to think of new comparative geographies in which Europe is not the sole referent. And third, while it is admittedly difficult to shift away from our defensive posture, it might perhaps be helpful if we were to cease invoking the decline thesis altogether. To change the terms of the debate, we may want to move beyond both decline and its discontents. As a collective venture by a group of young scholars, in this book we hope to achieve all three of these objectives.

## Chapter 2
# The Perception of Saadabad: The 'Tulip Age' and Ottoman–Safavid Rivalry
### Can Erimtan

The construction of Saadabad and its attendant structures on the Kağıthane river beyond Istanbul's city walls took place in the following sequence during Şevval 1134 (15 July–12 August 1722): the building project started with the clean-up (*tanzif ü tettahur*) of the river and subsequent transformation of a section into a regular canal of 1100 metres, the *Cedvel-i Sim*. Alongside the canal two rows of trees were planted, and next to the water an imperial summer palace (*bir kasr-ı hümâyûn*) (the actual Saadabad) was built on 30 'well-proportioned' pillars (*otuz aded sütûn-ı mevzûn üzerine*). Opposite this apparently opulent dwelling, a large reflecting pool (*pişgâhında bir havz-ı vâsi*) was laid out. In this artificial pond three fountains, of which one was in the shape of a three-headed serpent, threw jets of water into the air.[1] These were all features common to the practice of building gardens and garden palaces in the early modern Islamic world.[2] The contemporary visitor Charles Perry (1698–1780)[3] wrote down the following evocative description in his travelogue:

> [This] pleasure-house, called *Sadabat* ... is embellished in a very splendid elegant manner; its Roof is covered all over with Lead, resting upon little Arches, which are sustained by 30 small pillars: The Intercollumniations are filled with

Sheets of green Canvas, which, when stretched out, may serve as umbrella's [sic]. The Entrance is through a Pair of Brass Folding-doors ... between the Pillars in each Space rises a Balustrade about Two Feet from the Ground, upon which was a Sofa of very rich Brocade; in the Middle is a lovely Fountain, which plays its Water through a Cluster of little gilded Pipes, starting out of a Marble Cistern, against a large gilt Wall hung with Tassels: From thence the water is reflected upon a noble Tivan, or ceiling, of gilded Fretwork, which beats it down again in little sprinkling Showers.[4]

Fatma Müge Göçek's work is symptomatic of the conceptual confusion surrounding the appearance of Saadabad and the nature of the so-called 'Tulip Age'. In her aptly-titled book, *East Encounters West*, she deals with the Ottoman ambassador Yirmisekiz Çelebi Mehmed Efendi (who died in 1732), and his mission to Paris (from 7 October 1720 to 8 October 1721).[5] She unabashedly claims that Saadabad's 'construction tried to imitate Versailles and Fontainebleau, which Mehmed Efendi had visited. Mehmed Efendi [even] brought back plans of these palaces to apply them in Constantinople'.[6] By contrast, in his important work on Saadabad, the architect and architectural historian Sedad Hakki Eldem (1908–88) had in 1977 already stated that the building was completely congruent with the 'Turkish tradition', by which he obviously meant the Ottoman tradition.[7] Although this remark discloses Eldem's nationalist inclinations,[8] his standing as a serious architect and scholar should warrant a cautious approach to the issue of Saadabad and its supposed reliance on French models. Given Saadabad's character as a garden palace, which was apparently commonly encountered in the Islamic space and Ottoman world, it is difficult to believe that scholars persist in linking this Ottoman construction to French buildings.

In the first part of this chapter I analyse the concept of a 'Tulip Age' from a historiographical point of view. The idea that the Ottoman empire went through a short-lived but highly productive era of Westernization during Damad İbrahim Paşa's tenure as *sadr-i âzam* (grand vizier) will be exposed as a product of intertextual cross-fertilization and teleological agendas. In the second section I reinterpret the building of Saadabad in an attempt to appreciate the actions of Damad İbrahim and his patron Sultan Ahmed III in the context of the Ottomans' then current political and military concerns. In so doing I hope to illustrate that the Ottoman empire had at the time not necessarily been looking westward for inspiration. Rather than turning their attention to France, it is my belief that early eighteenth-century Ottomans were preoccupied with the lands of Iran and, to a lesser extent, with their Islamic contemporaries. As a corollary, I would like to offer a view of Saadabad that tries to hint at certain parallels with the architectural image of the Safavid empire, as constructed by Shah Abbas I (1588–1629) in Isfahan.[9]

Intellectual developments during the second constitutional period in Ottoman history (1908–18) have in many ways influenced the current practice of Ottoman historiography.[10] Today's emphasis on archivally-based research, for example, had a clear precursor in the activities of the *Tarih-i Osmanî Encümeni* (TOE), the state-sponsored academic institution for the study of the Ottoman past set up on 27 November 1909. The organization's policy statement (*İfâde-i Merâm*), published in 1326/1910, contains a section that states that research in the extensive Ottoman archive holdings (*Hazine-i Evrak*) opened in 1262/1846 was to be an important element of its members' activities.[11]

Quite aside from research practices popularized in the early years of the twentieth century, a number of historiographical *topoi* were also established in that period of frenzied intellectual and political activity. The idea that the Ottomans started to look to the West for inspiration in the early 1700s is one of the more persistent of these intellectual legacies from the late-Ottoman period. Nowadays, it seems like common sense to assume that the outcome of the treaties of Karlowitz (1699) and of Passarowitz (1718) led some Ottomans to imitate the ways of the 'infidel' Franks. The words of the historian Bruce McGowan epitomize this trend, for he argues that 'after a second round of punishment, ending with the Treaty of Passarowitz (1718), we see the first evidence, at the very top of society, of experimentation with Western models'.[12]

With respect to the survival of certain late-Ottoman historiographical *topoi*, the writings of one of the most prolific members of the TOE would in particular prove to be very influential: these were the popular publications of Ahmed Refik [Altınay] (1880–1937).[13] This historian, who had been a well-known figure on the intellectual scene of early twentieth-century Istanbul, not only contributed to the written output of the TOE, but also published numerous articles in the popular press of his day. He was in particular associated with the daily *İkdam*. In the period between 9 March and 4 April 1913/1328–9, he wrote and published his *Lâle Devri* or 'The Tulip Age' in serialized form in *İkdam*.[14] The serialized book popularized his then unconventional understanding of the life and actions of Ahmed III's grand vizier Damad İbrahim Paşa (1718–30). Ahmed Refik even gave Damad İbrahim's tenure as grand vizier the colourful name 'Tulip Age'.[15] In his daily instalments, he attempted to dislodge the then current negative perception of the Ottoman vizier as a sybarite – an image that had been firmly established by the eminent Ottoman statesman and historian Ahmed Cevdet (1822–95).

Cevdet's impressive *Vekayi-i Devlet-i Aliyye-i Osmaniyye* (or simply *Tarih-i Cevdet*), consisting of 12 volumes, appeared between 1270 and 1301 (1854 and 1884).[16] It was the first printed book in the Ottoman world to deal critically with the reign of Ahmed III. In the first volume published in 1270 (1854), Cevdet deals with the development of Ottoman history prior to the Treaty of Küçük Kaynarca (1774) in 12 separate entries called '*makâle*'. The seventh and eighth *makâle* partially deal with Damad İbrahim Paşa.[17] The relevant sentences in those sections display an image of the Ottoman vizier Damad İbrahim that shows him to have been a serious hedonist whose actions damaged the Ottoman state. Cevdet found this negative portrayal of İbrahim Paşa in the late eighteenth-century manuscript *Mür'i't-*

*Tevârih*, written by Şemdânizâde Süleyman Efendi, who died in 1193 (1779).[18] Ahmed Cevdet's agenda in writing his impressive work had been to explain the implementation of the *Tanzimat* in 1839, which was why he intimated that Damad İbrahim had been one of the men responsible for the decline of the Ottoman position. Ahmed Refik, however, was coming from a very different position. As an erstwhile member of the army and an active historian of the TOE, he was an Ottoman whose concern for the well-being of the empire was saddled in its past. In his writings he thus often tried to link the present to the past. In the 1930s the politician and intellectual Hasan Ali Yücel (1897–1961) coined the term *telmihî tarih* (allusive history) to describe Ahmed Refik's methodology of employing the past to comment on the present.[19] In other words, Ahmed Refik's methodology amounted to what one might today call 'presentism'.[20] And his book *Lâle Devri* was no exception.

The *Lâle Devri* text depicts early eighteenth-century Istanbul as an Ottoman place imbued with a desire to imitate the best of the West. As an intellectual primarily concerned with the survival of the Ottoman empire, Ahmed Refik depicts the Ottomans as beneficiaries of European military guidance. A parallel with the early twentieth-century situation was provided by the German general Otto Liman von Sanders (1855–1929) who was appointed adviser to the Ottoman army in November 1913.[21] Ahmed Refik's text intimates that Damad İbrahim, falling short of actually appointing a European specialist, nevertheless experimented with European forms and models. Ahmed Refik's depiction of Damad İbrahim shows an Ottoman statesman busy at work trying to update the army's structures and weaponry.

In what would appear to be a totally anachronistic fashion, the book *Lâle Devri* even mentions the *Nizâm-i Cedid*, 'the new order', in this context.[22] Ahmed Refik's source for this outrageous claim was a short piece on Damad İbrahim in Tayyarzâde Ahmed Atâ's (1801–c.1880) *Tarih*.[23] For biographical information on Damad İbrahim, Atâ had relied primarily on the eighteenth-century text

*Hadikat ül-Vüzerâ*, which was published in 1854–5/1271.[24] There, Dilaverzâde Ömer Efendi (who died in 1759/1172) had written the entry on Damad İbrahim and it contained no mention at all of army reforms or even the phrase *Nizâm-i Cedid*.[25] Thus, it would seem that Tayyarzâde had been taking liberties in devising a 'story' that combined elements of the reign of Ahmed III with themes from Selim III's day (1789–1807). The phrase *Nizâm-i Cedid* was nevertheless in currency prior to Selim III's failed attempts to reform the Ottoman armies. The phrase appears in a book written by İbrahim Müteferrika (1674–1745), namely *Usul ül-Hikem fi Nizâm ül-Ümem*, published in 1732 (1144) during Mahmud I's reign (1730–54).[26] This book, an eighteenth-century version of the traditional Islamic genre of the *Nasihatnâme*, or 'mirror for princes', effectively contrasts the worlds of Islam and Christianity.[27] The phrase *Nizâm-i Cedid* is employed in *Usul ül-Hikem* to explain the reasons behind the sudden successes of Austrian armies on Ottoman battlefields.[28] But Atâ's source, the *Hadikat ül-Vüzerâ*, mentions neither the phrase *Nizâm-i Cedid* nor Damad İbrahim's efforts to establish a new order in the Ottoman empire.

But aside from his spurious attempt to endow Damad İbrahim with a reformist vigour in the military field, Ahmed Refik also asserts that the vizier had been a cultural innovator, a modernizer who tried to acquaint the Oriental Ottomans with the fashions and styles of the Occident. The grand vizier's decision to commission the imperial palace of Saadabad outside Istanbul's city walls subsequently provided Ahmed Refik with an ideal opportunity to highlight the far-reaching vision of his protagonist Damad İbrahim.[29]

Ahmed Refik loosely links the small-scale Ottoman building on the banks of the Kağıthane river with France's royal palace of Versailles.[30] However, in a later publication, *Fatma Sultan* (1331/1916), a monograph on Ahmed III's daughter and Damad İbrahim's wife, Ahmed Refik strengthens the connection between the French and Ottoman buildings hinted at in *Lâle Devri* by calling Saadabad a copy or imitation (*taklid*) of Versailles that the enlightened İbrahim Paşa had commissioned.[31] Ahmed Refik is not forthcoming with a source for this connection, but close reading reveals that the Ottoman historian had unscrupulously copied a sentence written by the French historian Albert Vandal (1853–1912). In his book on the Marquis de Villeneuve, published in 1887, Vandal mentions in passing that the grand vizier had ordered an imitation of Versailles to be built on the Kağıthane river.[32] The Ottoman writer Ahmed Refik had clearly read Vandal's *Une Ambassade française en Orient sous Louis XV* (1887), referring to it, as he did on another occasion in his monograph on Fatma Sultan.

Ahmed Refik presents Ambassador Yirmisekiz Çelebi as the medium through which European ideas of 'progress', in this case the stylistic properties of Versailles, entered the Ottoman capital.[33] Yirmisekiz Çelebi had been sent to Paris in 1133/4 (1720/1). Adhering to a literary tradition established in the second half of the seventeenth century,[34] on his return to Istanbul he put his impressions on paper in a *takrir* (report).[35] This little book has subsequently received the lofty denomination *sefâretnâme* and has entered Ottoman historiography as an important text, which some even see as containing a manifesto on the desirability of European culture and civilization.[36]

The relevant literature on the Ottomans is littered with narratives that construct a link between the treaty of Passarowitz (1718), Yirmisekiz Çelebi's trip to Paris (1720–21) and the construction of Saadabad (1722). The chronological sequence appears persuasive and thus authors as varied as Göçek, Robert Olson and Münir Aktepe present Ahmed III and Damad İbrahim as enlightened patrons whose adherence to the principle of cultural modernization or rejuvenation necessarily led to a popular reaction managed by the backward religious classes, opposed to the West and its 'progressive' atmosphere.[37]

In general, scholarly as well as more popular narratives dealing with the 'Tulip Age' almost invariably end dramatically with the Patrona Halil uprising of 1730 when rebels destroyed the palace of Saadabad. The prolific and multi-disciplinary academic Andrew Wheatcroft, for example, says that the outbreak of the rebellion was 'followed [by] two days of rioting, arson and looting – a sudden show of cultural xenophobia towards anything thought to be "frankish" (western)'.[38] As a result, scholars regard the period that started with the conclusion of the Passarowitz Treaty (1718), and was followed by Yirmisekiz Çelebi's Paris mission (1720–1) and the construction of Saadabad (1722), as ending in the Patrona Halil rebellion (1730). The chronological sequence of 1718, 1720/1, 1722 and 1730 is thus moulded into a 'well-made story'. A 'well-made story', in the words of the professor of comparative literature Ann Rigney, is as a 'set of closely connected events forming a temporal whole with a well-marked beginning and [end] presented as if "telling itself" without the mediation of a retrospective narrator'.[39] The story of the construction of Saadabad in 1722, which ended in the destruction of the palace in 1730, is a good example of such a 'well-made story'.

The narrative of Ahmed III's and Damad İbrahim's supposed attempts to introduce Western forms into Istanbul's urban fabric led some specialists working in the early 1970s, such as architectural historian Godfrey Goodwin, to refer to the project on the Kağıthane river as 'pavilions [that] were Ottoman pomaded *à la française*', elaborating that 'the desire to copy Western ways and emerge from the restraints of a mediaeval past was genuine'.[40] Writing in the same period, historian Robert Olson sees the Ottoman empire and Christian Europe as undertaking a 'first serious attempt ... to try to understand one another' during the Tulip Age.[41] Sentiments like these have led scholars to view the 1718–30 sequence as containing 'a cautionary tale of the perils of precocious modernization', as quite recently critically recounted by Ariel Salzmann.[42]

As a consequence, this persuasive narrative of 'precocious modernization' has become the cornerstone of a teleological interpretation of Ottoman history that sees a move to the West as Turkey's destiny. Scholars leaning towards accepting *a priori* a so-called 'Tulip Age' paradigm understand Damad İbrahim's commission of the Versailles-inspired building of Saadabad as a provocative gesture that led religiously-inspired rebels to remove any trace of infidel forms from the city's architectural body. The destruction of Saadabad has become a 'hard historical fact', which proves that modernization understood as Westernization was taking place during the 'Tulip Age'. Sociologist and political scientist Şerif Mardin, who is renowned for his analytic insight into the relationships between religion, ideology and popular movements in Turkey, sees the Tulip Age as the beginning of 'the Westernization of Ottoman statesmen and the Palace through various attempts to copy the pomp of Versailles and the libertinism of eighteenth century France'.[43]

Current critical discourse on Ahmed III and Damad İbrahim sees the popular discontent with the introduction of architectural novelties as proving the existence of a centre–periphery dichotomy, with benevolent rulers trying to impose innovation on an unwilling populace steeped in religious bigotry and prejudice. Or, as Mardin put it, 'when called to arms to prevent the subversion of traditional ways, [the people] responded'.[44]

The academic community has accepted an assumed but unproven stylistic relationship between Versailles and Saadabad as a 'hard historical fact', which shows that the Ottomans had been moving West, away from the Ottoman tradition and certainties of Islam under the munificent leadership of Damad İbrahim. In 1994, for instance, the literary historian Kemal Silay postulated that 'the first ardent desire of the ruling Ottomans for a secular country was manifested in the Tulip Period.'[45]

So, *had* Ottoman culture been subject to direct Western influence during the early eighteenth century? *Had* early eighteenth-century Ottomans really been moving away from Islam in an attempt to revive their society and civilization?

Ahmed Refik, who coined the phrase 'Tulip Age' and introduced the Versailles narrative into Turkish literature, had simply copied the words of a French historian to describe the nature and makeup of Saadabad. From the second half of the twentieth century onwards, numerous historians and other writers have replicated Ahmed Refik's stance on the benevolent and pro-Western Damad İbrahim who commissioned Saadabad as a physical exteriorization of his policy decisions. It hardly seems possible any more to accept at face value the existence of a Paris–Istanbul axis suggested by the Versailles-inspired building of Saadabad.

Ahmed Refik produced texts that performed a teleological function in that they claim parallels between the past and present, parallels not necessarily reflected in historical reality. His book *Lâle Devri*, for instance, publicizes the existence of a beneficial 'Tulip Age' synonymous with a *rapprochement* between the Ottomans and the West. The appearance of Saadabad plays an important role in the rhetoric employed to give credence to the idea that prior to the *Tanzimat* (1839–76) there had already been a structured effort to introduce Europeanization into the Ottoman mainstream.

The Saadabad *topos* thus symbolizes vital issues in Ottoman-Turkish history and historiography, particularly the double concept of modernization and Westernization. As a result, conceptualizing Ahmed III and Damad İbrahim's architectural patronage involves more than just an episode in the socio-cultural and architectural history of Istanbul. The practice of historians and other intellectuals who have worked on Saadabad should be reassessed in the light of the theoretical and philosophical debates on the composition of historical narratives. The limited field of writing Ottoman history thus has to be related to the wider practice of writing historical texts and with the more extensive subject of historiography. Nowadays, it seems customary to question the role of the historian as an author of narratives purporting to be 'faithful' representations of past events, and thus to investigate the function of history texts as literary artefacts. The publication 30 years ago of Hayden White's article, 'The historical text as a literary artefact', stimulated a debate on the extent to which history as a discipline can accurately recover and represent the content of the past.[46] Hayden White's narratological model of historical understanding would have it that historians select and impose a story line, or an emplotment as he calls it, derived from the present to write about the past. The past is something that does not exist apart from a few traces and the historian's imagination, an imagination that is subject to his or her rhetorical, metaphorical and ideological strategies of explanation. History, or historical narratives and representations, on the other hand are primarily the product of historians' compositional skills, and thus firmly reside in texts and narratives produced to explain what happened in the past. The danger in accepting the validity of this narratological model is that historical texts in the end become totally 'self-referential' and detached from the 'real past'. For example, Frank Ankersmit's postmodernist approach holds that the meaning of historical representation 'is not found [in the traces from the past], but made in and by the text'.[47] This thus holds that resultant historical narratives become exercises in composition, or simply stories, and not attempts to describe the past in its own terms. It seems plausible to state that the *topos* of the Versailles-inspired Saadabad in historiographical reconstructions of early eighteenth-century Istanbul functions as a setting for the story of the Westernist Damad İbrahim to unfold. The narrative of a Paris–Istanbul axis as contained in the 'story' of Saadabad could be seen as a construction, an invention that was thought to be plausible in view of the available 'evidence', or rather the selected sets of supposedly known historical 'facts' like the conclusion of the Treaty of Passarowitz (1718), Yirmisekiz Çelebi's mission to Paris (1720–21) and the building of Saababad (1722).

I would like to offer a different interpretation of the Damad İbrahim and Saadabad episode in Ottoman history, using a different set of 'evidence'. This will necessarily also be an interpretation that cannot claim to be a truthful reflection of the past but that should be understood as an equally plausible rendering of the narrative of the building of Saadabad in 1722. This means that I accept that the validity of my narrative is equally delineated by its intertextuality. But, in contrast to Ankersmit's beliefs, I contend that my new interpretation of the Saadabad narrative has validity beyond a purely intertextual discourse. Rather than being a 'story' of Damad İbrahim and his 'new inclination to profit by European example', as Harold Bowen described the Ottoman leadership's changed world-view following the Treaty of Passarowitz (1718) in the *Encyclopedia of Islam*,[48] my proposed new take on Saababad will attempt to connect the building with the representation of the Ottomans' political, cultural and intellectual context. Although the original building of Saadabad was demolished under Mahmud II's rule (1809–39), thus leaving no recourse to physical evidence, the remaining information available on the *kasır* will be weighed against well-known samples of palatial and garden architecture following the types and models used in the building practices of the early modern Islamic world.

I would like to begin with the simple commonplace statement that the Ottoman state was built on Islamic foundations, a statement that bears repeating at this juncture. As Yaşar Ocak recently stated, in Ottoman studies scholars have traditionally focused on 'political-legal structures and institutions [of Islam], rather than on the ideology, beliefs and practical dimensions of Islam in the Ottoman context'.[49] This recognition implies that Ottoman culture was not just steeped in the cultural idiom of Islam, but was rather part and parcel of the wider culture of Islam.

Returning specifically to the building of Saadabad, one needs to bear in mind that the construction of canals, waterfalls, fountains and similar engineering projects was an important feature of building traditions in the premodern Islamic world. These enterprises were closely connected with the establishment of gardens and garden pavilions. In this respect Richard Ettinghausen's phrase about 'the ubiquitousness and popularity of horticulture in Islam' has literally now become nothing but a cliché.[50] The Ottomans' Muslim contemporaries could claim important achievements in the field of garden-related waterworks – the Paradise Canal (*Nahr-i Behisht*) in the Mughal capital of Shahjahanabad, and the main canal (*Shah Jub*) in the middle of Chahar Bagh Avenue (*Khiaban-i Chahar Bagh*) in the Safavid capital, Isfahan. Individual scholars such as Eba Koch[51] and Stephen Blake[52] have investigated artistic and cultural links between Mughal Shahjahanabad and Safavid Isfahan. But a possible Ottoman correlation has so far not received much serious study or consideration.[53]

In the context of Ahmed III and Saadabad, a possible linkup between Istanbul and Isfahan seems appropriate given the longstanding proximity and enmity between the Ottomans and Safavids.[54] The canal in the centre of Chahar Bagh Avenue leading into Isfahan was flanked by a double row of trees on either side, and the palace or reception pavilion of Chihil Sutun, a part of the same garden configuration as the Chahar Bagh complex,[55] originally built in 1647 by Shah Abbas II (1642–66), was erected on approximately twenty columns, which become forty when reflected in the pool opposite.[56]

Recently, Shirine Hamadeh has also highlighted the 'conceptual, if not formal, link between, on the one hand, Isfahan's Chaharbagh ... and, on the other hand ... Sa'dabad'.[57] In addition, it could be regarded as significant that in their layouts the Saadabad and Chihil Sutun buildings were given a specific number of columns.[58] Their reflections in the Isfahan pool showed (approximately) forty columns; whereas, in Istanbul the reflections counted sixty. In 1942, the Byzantinist and architectural historian Richard Krautheimer (1897–1994) published a piece on the iconography of mediaeval architecture in which he argued that patrons of architecture in premodern societies often regarded 'figures and numbers' as important 'among the elements which determine the relation between copy and original'.[59] In the case of the relationship between Saadabad and Chihil Sutun, one could argue that the Ottomans' attempt to build a *kasır*, arguably somewhat reminiscent of the Safavid reception pavilion Chihil Sutun, with more columns than its ostensible model can be interpreted as an Ottoman attempt to surpass the Safavid accomplishment. One could argue that the Ottoman design was deliberately conceived to humble the Safavid palace symbolically, albeit in a very subtle and ostensibly inconsequential way.

Gülru Necipoğlu has convincingly demonstrated in one of her articles that symbolic interactions on an architectural plain were not unheard of in an Ottoman context. In doing so, she also demonstrates that the Ottomans and Safavids were aware of their respective cultural vocabularies and architectural idioms. Necipoğlu specifically talks about sixteenth-century Istanbul and Selim I (1512–20), the sultan at the root of the Ottoman–Safavid rivalry. She starts off by stating that 'the Ottoman garden tradition does not fit comfortably into the usual definitions of the so-called Islamic garden.'[60] In particular, she refers to the 'quadripartite formal gardens with straight water channels', the so-called 'chaharbagh' type, when making the aforementioned statement.[61] Mahvash Alemi describes this 'type' as a 'garden quartered by two intersecting water channels'.[62] Alemi declares that this particular scheme of garden layout was already considered a 'particular type' in the early sixteenth century, as Qasim Ibn Yusuf Abu Nasri Haravi unceremoniously mentions the chaharbagh as a model in his manuscript Irshad az-Zira'ah (921/1515).[63] In other words, in the early sixteenth-century Islamic world one seems to have regarded the construction of 'quadripartite formal gardens with straight water channels' as common. The exception was formed by the Ottomans, who favoured designs 'characterized by asymmetrical open compositions with an outward-looking orientation … in Istanbul … relatively informal landscapes with understated symmetry and axiality were … common'.[64]

Necipoğlu nevertheless goes on to say that there was 'at least one example of a Persianate chaharbagh among the suburban gardens of sixteenth-century Istanbul … the Karabali garden in Kabataş'.[65] In the context of sixteenth and seventeenth-century Istanbul, the Bagçe-i Karabâli,[66] as a quadripartite formal garden, stands out from the numerous other gardens and garden structures adhering to the classical Ottoman tradition. In view of its rather extraordinary nature in the context of Istanbul gardens and garden layouts, Necipoğlu argues that the Bagçe-i Karabâli with its deliberate Persianate character 'was created … to commemorate [Sultan Selim I's] victorious Persian campaign', which in 1514 crushed the Safavid forces of Shah Isma'il I (1501–24).[67] This sixteenth-century example of the cultural effects of the political and ideological Ottoman–Safavid rivalry[68] could be used as a template for a new interpretation of Saadabad, an interpretation that involves Ottoman interaction with the cultural modes of Safavid Iran rather than with those of eighteenth-century France.

The parallels between the *Cedvel-i Sim* and Saadabad in Kağıthane, on the one hand, and certain aspects of the architectural image of Safavid Isfahan,[69] notably the Chihil Sutun and the *Khiaban-i Chahar Bagh*, on the other, could be employed to furnish a different narrative of Ahmed III, Damad İbrahim Paşa and the Ottoman refurbishment of an area beyond Istanbul's city walls.

My narrative also takes an ambassadorial mission into account. In the year 1132 (1720) Damad İbrahim's government dispatched Dürrî Ahmed Efendi to Tehran, where the Safavid court then resided.[70] During the reign of Ahmed III's Iranian contemporary, Shah Sultan Husain (1694–1722), the territorial coherence of the Safavid dominions became more and more difficult to support. By the early 1720s internal incursions had become rife in Iran and the Ottoman ambassador was thus called upon to give details of the actual state of the Safavids' affairs.[71] On his return to Istanbul, Dürrî Efendi composed a report (*takrir*) that described the desperate situation of the Safavids in the face of internal instability and rising unrest among various of the Safavid dominions' population groups.[72] In Safer 1134 (December 1721) Shah Sultan Husain responded to the Ottoman delegate by sending an ambassador, Murteza Kuli Khan, to Istanbul. Damad İbrahim Paşa impressed the envoy with displays of cultural splendour, such as feasts at elegant kiosks interspersed with presentations of samples of Ottoman calligraphy set against a background of the finest Ottoman music, and displays of the Ottomans' military prowess through demonstrations of newly built three-decked galleons equipped with heavy artillery.

The Safavid ambassador Murteza Kuli Khan remained in Istanbul from 5 Rebiyülevvel to 16 Cemaziyelâhir 1134 (24 December 1721 to 3 April 1722). As soon as he left the capital İbrahim Paşa called a meeting of the great divan in which a decision was made to go to war.⁷³ And approximately three months after his departure, in the course of the month of Şevval 1134, which corresponded to the period from 15 July to 12 August 1722, Saadabad was constructed. The building was set up in an area that had been popular as an excursion spot since the reign of Murad IV (1623–39).

Meanwhile, Shah Sultan Husain was fighting a losing battle with Afghan rebels under Mir Mahmud's leadership and eventually, on 12 Muharrem 1135 (23 October 1722), Mir Mahmud forced the Safavid Shah to abdicate.⁷⁴ In Istanbul, this seems to have led the Şeyhülislâm Yenişehirli Abdullah Efendi (who died in 1743) to issue a *fetva* declaring the war against the heretics of Iran to be lawful and desirable in the months from Muharrem to Rebiyulevvel 1135 (October–December 1722)⁷⁵ – 'evidence' that presents us with an opportunity to provide a new interpretation of Saadabad. The sequence of the above events (namely 1720, 1721 and 1722) helps one to understand Saadabad in the context of the culture and value system of the Ottomans and of the wider early modern Islamic world. The traditional enmity between the Sunni Ottomans and the Shiᶜi Safavids provides an intra-Islamic dimension to a reassessment of the construction of Ahmed III's summer palace outside Istanbul's city walls and a re-evaluation of the so-called 'Tulip Age' in Ottoman history.

Rather than acknowledge that the Safavid state had been overthrown, the Ottoman government couched its territorial desires in language that implied that Ahmed III as defender of Sunni Islam was fighting Shah Sultan Husain, the Qizilbash champion of heresy. Shah Sultan Husain had been a ruler who pursued extremely oppressive religious policies against Sunni Muslims, mystics and other religious minorities, policies that included forcible conversion to Shiᶜi Islam. The shah also cultivated his personal piety by, for example, performing highly publicized pilgrimages to saints' shrines, and even creating a new post, the *mulla-bashi* (instituted 1124/1712), in the palace hierarchy that was meant to secure his personal moral and spiritual rectitude.⁷⁶ But aside from dealing with such lofty concerns about Islam as an ideological determinant, one could also look at the shah's architectural patronage as warranting a possible linkup between Saadabad and the Chihil Sutun. Shah Sultan Husain patronized the construction of new buildings as well as the restoration and refurbishment of already existing works. Especially relevant in this context seems to have been his refurbishment of the Chihil Sutun. At the beginning of the eighteenth century the palace had been destroyed by fire and, after this disaster, the shah had the palace rebuilt in the year 1115 (1703). According to Tadeusz Jan Krusinski (1675–1756), a priest who was present in Isfahan at the time, this was done 'with more Splendor than the former [version of the Chihil Sutun]'.[77]

It is important to remember that Saadabad was built at a time when the Ottomans seem to have thought that a final resolution of the Ottoman–Safavid rivalry could be attained. The actual building work was started and completed within the space of the month of Şevval 1134 (between 15 July and 12 August 1722), and was a relatively light, inexpensive and easy-to-build pavilion. In adhering to this form of architectural patronage, Damad İbrahim and Ahmed III seem to have continued a building tradition that had first been practised under Mehmed IV (1648–83), Sultan Ahmed's notorious father. Sedad Hakki Eldem remarks that Sultan Mehmed IV 'gave a new turn to kiosk building' in that he patronized methods of construction that were lighter and less expensive than had previously been the case when heavy constructions of ashlar and bricks were used for domestic architecture (roughly between the 1450s and 1640s).[78]

But Saadabad's 'light' character might also compare with the Safavid Chihil Sutun. After all, Robert Hillenbrand remarks that the Chihil Sutun has a 'deliberately unstable and impermanent air' that he links to the general nature of secular Safavid architecture, which he calls 'ostentatiously frail'.[79] Shah Sultan Husain had associated his name with the palace in Isfahan, and Damad İbrahim attached his patron Ahmed III's name to the construction on the Kağıthane river. Thus, in a retrospectively historiographic fashion, one could posit that the construction of Saadabad, which contained a number of allusions to Isfahan and its structures, was a cultural declaration of the Ottomans' political and military resolve to conquer the lands of Iran. Ahmed III spent a lot of his time in Saadabad, where he held numerous feasts and other pastimes. The chronicler Küçük Çelebizâde İsmail Asım Efendi, who died in 1173 (1760) noted in his *Tarih* numerous festive occasions organized at Saadabad.[80]

A contemporary illustration of the Ottoman appreciation and acclaim of Saadabad can also be found in one of the songs (*şarkı*) written by Ahmed III's court poet Nedim (1681–1730). The composition extols the attraction and beauty of Saadabad set within the framework of Ottoman–Safavid rivalry: 'Come a while and let [your] gaze wander, it is not forbidden to the eye Now Saadabad has become my favoured hill above garden. [Saadabad's] hill [and] garden have equalled Isfahan's Chahar Bagh Now Saadabad has become my favoured hill above garden.'[81]

At the outset of the song Nedim invites the listener to wander around the surroundings of Saadabad. In the following lines the beauty of the layout is underlined, while the gardens of the Chahar Bagh in Isfahan by comparison are said to have lost their attraction and charm. The quoted first strophe of Nedim's song portrays Damad İbrahim's commission for his patron Ahmed III to have clearly surpassed the earlier accomplishments of Shah Abbas I in Isfahan. Members of the Ottoman elite visiting the *mesire* excursion spot at Kağıthane may well have heard or even sung this tune, while enjoying themselves. The song is a eulogy to Damad İbrahim as a patron of the arts, and of his ability to commission architectural constructions able to challenge the Safavids' well-known accomplishments in Isfahan.

In an inter-dynastic context, however, it seems fair to say that in the minds of their contemporaries the figure of the *Sadr-ı Âzam* was easily replaced by that of his patron, Sultan Ahmed III. Hence, one could argue that the Ottoman Ahmed III competed in a symbolic rivalry with his Safavid counterpart Shah Sultan Husain. This symbolic rivalry was valid on a number of levels: in ideological terms, Ahmed III presented himself as the champion of the Sunni cause, who, in visual terms, challenged the Safavids through his ostentatious dislays of Ottoman wealth, culture and refinement at the attractive palace of Saadabad so reminiscent of the Chihil Sutun in Isfahan. That Ahmed III's *kasır* carried an ostentatiously Persianate name seems to underline a possible connection with Ottoman designs on the lands of Iran.

Another symbolic Ottoman gesture ostensibly directed at the Safavids was constituted by the Ottoman government's establishment of a tile workshop at Tekfur Sarayı in Istanbul during Damad İbrahim's tenure. Previously, the Ottomans had relied on the tile kilns at Iznik, established in the mid-sixteenth century, to supply them with high-quality glossy underglaze tiles in a colour spectrum of turquoise, blue and red against a white background. According to Gülru Necipoğlu, these tiles formed a 'decorative skin' that was strikingly different from the decorative appearance of the 'Timurid world', which was preserved 'with different emphases ... by the Safavids and Uzbeks'.[82] By Ahmed III's reign, the Iznik workshops were no longer producing any tiles, but Damad İbrahim's administration appeared to favour a revival of these specific tiles, which in Necipoğlu's words had become 'a stamp of Ottoman identity'. She continues by saying that Ahmed III's court historian Küçük Çelebizâde clearly stated in his *Tarih* that it was his patrons' 'wish to revive [the] textile-like ceramics of Iznik (*kumaş-i kaşi gibi münakkaş ve hoş kumaş kaşiler*) that led to the establishment of the workshop at Tekfur Sarayı'.[83] One could argue that Ahmed III and Damad İbrahim, in this instance, tried to secure the continued existence of a particular type of Ottoman visual language: a visual idiom that was meant to differentiate them from the Safavid image, still beholden to the norms established by Timur (1336–1402) who had defeated and humiliated the Ottomans in 1402.[84]

In other words, it would seem that, on a cultural plane, early eighteenth-century Ottomans appeared very preoccupied with their eastern neighbours.[85] In this connection, it seems equally significant that in Istanbul a committee was set up to translate the Persian historian Ghiyath ad-Din Muhammad Khwandamir's

(1475–c.1535) *Habib as-Siyar fi Akhbar Afrad al-Bashar* (929/ 1523) into Ottoman. Throughout the 1720s, Ottoman patrons encouraged the translation of literary works that had hitherto been inaccessible to Ottoman audiences.[86] Intellectuals working on the *Habib as-Siyar* comprised such figures as Mansurizâde, Fasihi Hasan, Nahifi Mustafa, Sadi Efendi and Sheikh Musa Dede.[87] Their project must have carried a special significance in the context of the then current Ottoman interest in the lands of Iran. The book describes the political events of Iran until the reign of Shah Isma'il (1501–24), the founder of the Safavid state. Also, for each historical period the author included an appendix with the biographies of notable writers and poets of the age. In all, no fewer than 211 individual figures are treated in this way.[88] By means of this book, the Ottoman court was able to familiarize itself with the cultural and political heritage of Iran, which was supposed to form part of the Ottoman sphere of influence because of Sultan Ahmed's occupation of the former Safavid dominions.

Quite apart from the above-mentioned cultural factors indicating an Ottoman preoccupation with Iran, one should also not underestimate the religious and ideological aspects of the Ottoman–Safavid rivalry. The *Şeyhülislâm* Abdullah Efendi issued a *fetva* supporting the Ottoman sultan's claims to the caliphate in 1138 (1726), demonstrating that Ahmed III took seriously his title as defender of Sunni Islam. In his *fetva* Abdullah Efendi argues that Ahmed III's appropriation of the title was legitimate because he had made conquests with the sword.[89] This line of argument resembles that of Ebussuud Efendi, in office from 952 to 982 (1545–74), who had earlier reasoned that the Ottoman sultan, as the most powerful potentate in the Islamic world, was in a position legally to call himself the 'Successor of the Prophet'.[90] The above 'story' of Ottomans, Safavids, summer palaces and Islamic rectitude seems to constitute a plausible way of reinterpreting the construction of Saadabad in 1722.

The new narrative I present of the role of Damad İbrahim in Ottoman history is, however, in sharp contrast with the received wisdom on Saadabad and the so-called 'Tulip Age'. The traditional understanding of Ahmed III's era is nicely encapsulated by the entry on the 'Lâle Devri' in the well-respected new edition of the *Encyclopedia of Islam*: Damad İbrahim's term of administration constituted 'a serious movement towards a secular society'. Along those lines, Saadabad is thought of as 'a new palace ... constructed on French plans'. The recognition of Saadabad's supposed French origins seems to indicate that the Ottomans had at the time been contemplating an ideological move to the West, a move away from the Islamic world. This Versailles narrative subsequently holds that a popular uprising, the so-called Patrona Halil rebellion, put an untimely stop to this premature form of Westernization. The composite *Tarih-i Sâmî ü Şâkir ü Subhî* (1198/1784) indicates, however, that the rebels had been unsuccessful in their attempts to destroy Saadabad and the attendant *kasırs*. The *vakanüvis* Mustafa Sâmî recorded the wording of an imperial writ issued by Mahmud I that indicated that the sultan did not want the rebels to burn down the site (*ihtirâk*) allowing (*ruhsat ve iznim*) them to enact some minor acts of destruction and damage (*hedim ve tahribi*).[91]

The proverbial coupling of 'continuity' and 'change' is a key feature in traditional appreciations of early eighteenth-century Ottoman culture. The academic community regards the 'Tulip Age' as a kind of harbinger of the idea that modernization is synonymous with Westernization in an Ottoman-Turkish context, and it depicts the small-scale palace of Saadabad as giving physical shape to this otherwise unverified notion. The received wisdom on the issue thus holds that early eighteenth-century Istanbul had seen a marked move towards 'change'. On the other hand, my alternative perception of Saadabad does not aim to burden the small palace with any ideological significance beyond Ahmed III and Damad İbrahim's Ottoman and Islamic contexts – their own cultural framework. In the end, the new 'story' that I presented here finds more credibility in an Ottoman past that persisted in its habits, unprovoked as it were, than in one that all of a sudden turned its face to the West. My 'story' of the construction of Saadabad holds that it was conceived as a building containing conscious allusions to the Safavid architectural image. Rather than claiming a Safavid inspiration for Saadabad, it is my belief that Damad İbrahim and Ahmed III were cultured Ottomans who were consciously reaffirming their allegiance to the cultural world of the early modern Islamic world by creating *kasır* that functioned as a visual reminder of the Ottomans' designs on the lands of Iran. Rather than implying that Yirmisekiz Çelebi Mehmed Efendi had made his patrons susceptible to the delights and pleasures of the Christian world of Europe, the sultan and his grand vizier proved to be fully cognizant inhabitants of the early modern Islamic world. I would thus like to claim that Ahmed III and Damad İbrahim had been conventional Ottomans in cultural and ideological terms, Ottomans who tried to stay connected with the traditions of their ancestry, and whose cultural patronage and political programmes disclosed a willingness to fashion a continuity and sense of cohesion with the wider culture and intellectual heritage of the early modern world of Islam.

## Chapter 3
## The First Ottoman Turkish Printing Enterprise: Success or Failure?

*Orlin Sabev (Orhan Salih)*

In the final scene of Jale Baysal's play, *Cennetlik İbrahim Efendi* (İbrahim Efendi in Paradise), the man who was a member of the Müteferrika corps at the Ottoman court,[1] but who became known for establishing the first Ottoman Turkish printing press in 1726, İbrahim Müteferrika is found on his deathbed complaining to the court poet Nevres, 'There will be in inheritance piles of unsold books. They did not read what I printed.'[2]

In 1986, the script of this play, which is an adaptation of the biography of the first Ottoman printer, İbrahim Müteferrika, won first prize in a theatre competition organized by the Foundation of the Turkish State Theatre and Ballet (*Devlet Tiyatrosu ve Bale Çalışanları Vakfı* – TOBAV). Unfortunately, we do not know whether the play was ever staged, but we do know that it was published in 1992. As a literary adaptation meant for performance, the play, perhaps expectedly, is a mixture of fact and fiction, with fiction utilized to 'fill in the gaps' of the factual details of the narrative, rendering it, as Christine Brook-Rose calls it, a 'history palimpsest'.[3] In 'history palimpsest' fiction tends to overwrite real historical events, thereby presenting an alternative version that is perhaps more entertaining and attractive to the reading public and/or audience, but less satisfying to the historian. In these instances, fiction obfuscates 'what really happened'.

Here I am not trying to discuss the historical accuracy or artistic merits of Jale Baysal's play, but rather to take its final episode as a starting point for the present discussion. Baysal's depiction of İbrahim Müteferrika's desperate final words about the failure of his book printing enterprise is one instance of a 'history palimpsest'.

Strikingly, the impression of the failure of Müteferrika's effort does not originate in semi-fictitious literary works such as Baysal's but in the first academic study of İbrahim Müteferrika's biography, namely Imre Karácson's article published in 1910.[4] Karácson cites a letter by the Catholic Hungarian nobleman Czezarnak (César) de Saussure who, as a companion of Ferenc Rákoczi during his exile to the Ottoman empire (1717–35), met İbrahim Müteferrika in Turkey in 1732. In this letter he stated that Müteferrika's profits were rather moderate.[5] So, Karácson took de Saussure's remark at face value and presented Müteferrika as a disappointed pioneer who had been unable to reap the fruits of his labour.[6]

César de Saussure's aforementioned letter was written in February 1732 and it provides one of the few sources of biographical data about Müteferrika. Although a subject of controversy in modern historiography,[7] until very recently this letter was the only source available that gave some idea of the commercial success of the first Ottoman printing enterprise. According to de Saussure, Müteferrika's press was unsuccessful because of insufficient sales, which he attributed to the limited number of literate Turks, a lack of interest in reading and the relatively high price of printed books. The author mentions that there was a fear that the enterprise would be suspended after İbrahim Müteferrika's death, for no Turk would take on an undertaking with such low profits.[8] Much later (in fact after 1759) de Saussure added to his 1732 letter a note that İbrahim Müteferrika had died in 1738 and left nothing but piles of books. He added that such a legacy only made his descendants feel an aversion to resuming the enterprise. (*'Ce qui a tellement dégoûté ses successeurs ou héritiers qu'ils ont entièrement abandonné son imprimerie.*')⁹ The exact date of the appended note is unknown, but the year of İbrahim Müteferrika's death given by de Saussure is incorrect. Rather than 1738, Müteferrika actually died a good eight or nine years later (in 1746 or 1747).[10] Given this error, the fact that we are unsure whether de Saussure was an eye witness to Müteferrika's death and the consequent situation of his printing house, we may legitimately ask if de Saussure's version is yet another 'history palimpsest' that overwrites the real events.

Given the paucity of sources on the subject, scholars and litterateurs alike had no option other than to refer to de Saussure's 'observations', while in the process giving his version credibility. The first was the above-mentioned Imre Karácson,[11] followed by people such as Lajos Hopp,[12] Jale Baysal and Hidayet Nuhoğlu, the latter two referring to Karácson's quotation after de Saussure.[13]

Since Karácson's article of 1910, scholars have accepted the claim that İbrahim Müteferrika's enterprise was rather unsuccessful and invested their efforts in searching for, and speculating about, the reasons for this alleged failure. Niyazi Berkes, a well-known specialist in Ottoman social history, points out three main conditions conducive to the successful progress of any printing undertaking, namely technological development, the production of the quantity of paper appropriate for the requirements of printing, and the existence of the necessary reading public. According to Berkes, these three conditions were absent in the Ottoman milieu. He also underlines the relatively high prices of the first Ottoman printed books and the nature of their subjects. He argues that the latter rendered the books insufficiently attractive to the majority of the reading public whose education was most likely attained through Islamic religious learning, such as the *medrese* students. Berkes concludes that the limited technical and restrictive economic conditions were responsible for the weak influence of the first Ottoman printing enterprise.[14]

A similar view is shared by A. D. Jeltyakov, who attributes the alleged failure of Müteferrika's venture to cultural and technological underdevelopment. Not only does he see the illiteracy prevalent in Ottoman society as an obstacle to the success of printing, but also conjectures that the literate elements of the population were uninterested in topics in the exact sciences of the kind Müteferrika printed.[15]

A combination of the above-mentioned views can also be found in J. S. Szyliowicz's 1988 article on the subject, in which the first Ottoman printing enterprise is considered in terms of the different social, economic and cultural conditions prevailing in western Europe and the Ottoman empire respectively. According to Szyliowicz, compared with western Europe, the Ottoman social climate was unsuitable for such an undertaking because of both mass illiteracy and the opposition of the numerous professional manuscript copyists who viewed the printing press as a threat to their profession.[16]

Hüseyin Gazi Topdemir, author of one of the most recent monographs on İbrahim Müteferrika, assuming the failure of Müteferrika's project, stresses the same reasons, namely the paucity or the prohibitively high cost of printing paper, the low output of Müteferrika's printing press, the availability of printed books only to select individuals, the books' topics not meeting the public's expectations and, finally, their relatively high cost in comparison with that of manuscripts.[17]

Topdemir's reference to the high prices of the first Ottoman printed books comes from an article by Osman Ersoy that is especially devoted to that issue. Ersoy, who is a prominent scholar of the history of Ottoman printing, concludes that the prices of the books printed in Müteferrika's typography were quite high given the average Ottoman standard of living in the first half of the eighteenth century. According to Ersoy, along with the constant paucity of printing paper and well-trained printers, high prices must have been a significant factor behind the alleged failure of the first Ottoman printing enterprise.[18]

Ersoy's article was published in a volume on the proceedings of a symposium dedicated to the 250th anniversary of Turkish book printing, which was held in Ankara in December 1979. The volume also includes the symposium participants' comments on the papers presented and Ersoy's paper seems to have sparked a lively discussion. One of the participants, Şerafettin Turan, pointed out a methodological flaw in Ersoy's paper in that the prices of the first Ottoman printed books should be compared with manuscript prices, as found in the probate inventories of deceased Muslims, rather than measured against the average standard of living. Turan's implication is that printed book prices should be seen in the context of the book market in general, whether manuscript or printed. Thus, the cost of printed books should be measured against the standard of living of those who owned manuscript books, namely the reading public. Turan added also that the first Ottoman printed books must have had a public with specific reading interests and a higher standard of living.[19]

Şerafettin Turan's remarks are insightful in their insistence on empirical research and the utilization of the rich and massive Ottoman sources of the probate inventories (*tereke defteri*). Oddly enough, although these documents have been widely used for exploring social and economic aspects of the history of Ottoman everyday life in different periods,[20] except for a few early studies, dealing only partially with the presence of books in probate inventories,[21] they have only recently attracted the attention of students of Ottoman book history.[22] This attention, however, has been overwhelmingly devoted to studying the circulation of manuscripts rather than of printed books. And if Turan did significantly point to the importance of probate inventories in Ottoman book history, it seems that he failed to consider the probate inventory of the most important personality of Ottoman printed book history, namely of İbrahim Müteferrika.

I have been fortunate enough to come across precisely that – the probate inventory relating to the possessions of İbrahim Müteferrika, preserved in the Mufti Archives of Istanbul,[23] in the collection *Kısmet-i Askeriye Mahkemesi* (register 98, folios 39a–40b). This source, dated 20 Rebiü'l-ahir 1160 (1 April 1747), is thus far the most illuminating with regard to many hitherto unknown aspects of Müteferrika's personality and printing activities.[24] Since the document provides an inventory of Müteferrika's possessions at the time of his death, it gives a relatively accurate idea of how many unsold copies of printed books were left in his possession. An interpretation of these figures of unsold copies, and their juxtaposition with the total number of initial prints made, not only allows us to gauge the degree of success or failure of Müteferrika's printing project, but also, subsequently, to see to what extent the discussions and speculations about the 'failure' of the first Ottoman printing press have been warranted. Thus, a statistical analysis of the Müteferrika printing venture is in order. Through the analysis, I propose to explore the following issues:

- a juxtaposition of print figures to sale figures in order to judge the commercial outcomes of the Müteferrika press;
- an assessment of the popularity of the titles;
- a contextualization of the findings by relating them to the book market and the reading public; and finally
- a reassessment of the significance of the first Ottoman printing press.

But before we get to the subject, there are several issues to be considered. The first has to do with what is meant by the term 'success' when used in reference to the first Ottoman printing press. If we are speaking of commercial success, then the term implies not only good sales figures but also a good turnover of the investments made. However, if we use the term in a broader sense, we need to consider the printing press as a cultural product and look at the extent to which the technological innovation is adopted or rejected by society at large. While I deal with the latter in the conclusion to this chapter, on the question of commercial success it is difficult to assess to what extent the net proceeds of the sales actually covered the investments Müteferrika had made. For now, it would be reasonable to turn our attention to sales figures because they reflect printing as a mutual process in which the printer/seller and the reading public/customers are involved.

## THE FIRST OTTOMAN TURKISH PRINTING ENTERPRISE

Another issue has to do with problems related to the sources used for this research. The above-mentioned inventory provides the number of printed books left on Müteferrika's death (2981 in total); however, it does so partly by listing individual titles and partly by listing groups of titles. Given this classificatory inconsistency, it is impossible to calculate the number of unsold copies of each publication; one can only do so for those that are listed individually, which is roughly half the titles. Thus, although I shall be unable to assess the popularity of each of the Müteferrika press titles, I am able to include these titles in the total figures, which is relevant for gauging the overall success of the Müteferrika printing enterprise.

Of course, book sale figures would be almost meaningless if not juxtaposed with figures for the total number of initial printed copies. Fortunately, we can find the relevant information in a source other than the above-mentioned probate inventory, namley a book printed at the Müteferrika press – *El-Cildü's-sāni min Tārīh-i Na'īmā* (second volume of History of Na'ima). This book happens to be the thirteenth of the Müteferrika press editions, and provides the number of copies for each previous title published by the press except for one book – *Grammaire turque ou Méthode courte & facile pour Apprendre la Langue turque* (Turkish Grammar or a Concise and Easy Method of Learning the Turkish language) by Holdermann (1730).[25] The author, however, provides figures for the initial print number of the latter. Unfortunately, we have no documentation for the total print of the last three of Müteferrika's 16 editions, namely Raşid Efendi's *Tārīh* (History) in three volumes, along with Çelebizade Efendi's appendix (*zeyl*) *Tārīh* (printed in 1741), Ömer Bosnavi's *Ahvāl-i Gazavāt der Diyār-i Bosna* (The State of Religious Wars in the Province of Bosnia) of 1741, and the two-volume Persian–Turkish dictionary, *Lisānü'l-'Acem* or *Ferheng-i Şu'ūrī*, of 1742. However, one may suggest that each had a run of *at least* 500 copies since it is the minimum number of copies of the initial prints found in the above-mentioned list (indeed, ten of the sixteen editions whose initial print number we know is at 500 copies).

Thus, figures for both the total initial print and final numbers of the unsold copies exist for six of the Müteferrika press titles, namely Vankulu's Arabic–Turkish dictionary of 1729, Nazmizade Efendi's *Gülşen-i Hulefā* (Rosary of Caliphs) of 1730, *Grammaire turque*, Kātip Çelebi's *Kitāb-ı Cihānnümā* (Mirror of the World, 1732) and *Takvīmü't-Tevārīh* (Calendar of Histories, 1733) and Naʿima's *Tārīh* (1734).

The category of books for which we know the initial total print but where the number of unsold copies is given in groups rather than individually falls into two groups. The first includes Kātip Çelebi's *Tuhfetü'l-kibār fī Esfāri'l-Bihār* (Select Gift in Voyages) of 1729, Juda Tedeusz Krusiński's *Tārīh-i Seyyāh der Beyān-i Zuhūr-i Ağvāniyān ve Sebeb-i İndihām-i Binā-i Devlet-i Şāhān-i Safeviyān* (History of Traveller about Afghans' Appearance and Reasons for the Decline of the State of the Safavi Shahs) of 1729, *Tārīhü'l-Hindi'l-Garbī el-Müsemmā bi-Hadīs-i Nev* (History of the West Indies Called the New World) and Nazmizade Efendi's *Tārīh-i Tīmūr-i Gurkān* (History of Tamerlane), and Süheyli Efendi's *Tārīhü'l-Mısri'l-Cedīd: Tārīhü'l-Mısri'l-Kadīm* (History of Contemporary Egypt: History of Ancient Egypt) of 1730. The second group includes Müteferrika's own writings such as *Usūlü'l-Hikem fī Nizāmi'l-Ümem* (The Fundaments of Wisdom with regard to the Order of Nations, 1732) and *Füyūzāt-ı Mıknātısiyye* (Features of the Magnets, 1732), as well as Ömer Bosnavi's *Ahvāl-i Gazavāt der Diyār-i Bosna* of 1741.

Before turning to the numbers of unsold copies, two observations are worth making. First, there were obviously fewer unsold copies of earlier than later editions because they had been on the market for a longer period of time. Second, at the time of the inventory, some books seem not yet to have been ready for sale, as in the cases of *Kitāb-ı Cihānnümā*, Naʿima's *Tārīh*, and Raşid Efendi's *Tārīh* and *Ferheng-i Şuʿūrī*. Most of these copies were unbound (*cildsiz*), unpolished (*mühresiz*) and without margins around the pages (*cedvālsiz*). The unsold copies of *Gülşen-i Hulefā*, *Tuhfetü'l-kibār*, *Tārīh-i Seyyāh*, *Tārīhü'l-Hindi'l-Garbī*, *Tārīh-i Tīmūr-i Gurkān*, *Tārīhü'l-Mısri'l-Cedīd;* *Tārīhü'l-*

Mısri'l-Kadīm and Takvīmü't-Tevārīh were sewn (dikilmiş), cut (kesilmiş) and partly bound. The books of which there were very few unsold copies, such as Grammaire turque, Usūlü'l-Hikem fī Nizāmi'l-Ümem, Füyūzāt-ı Mıknātısiyye, and Ahvāl-i Gazavāt der Diyār-i Bosna, were properly bound (tamām mücelled). It seems that there was some connection between the demand for certain books and the success of their sale, on the one hand, and the state of their preparedness for sale on the other.

By juxtaposing the numbers of unsold copies against the number of the initial print run of each of the Müteferrika editions, one is able to ascertain the degree of popularity that each title enjoyed. As shown in the table and figures presented in the appendix at the end of this chapter, where the number of copies left unsold is juxtaposed with the number of the initial print, among Müteferrika's bestsellers were the Vankulu Arabic–Turkish dictionary (see Figure 3.1) and Grammaire turque (Figure 3.4), followed by some titles such as Usūlü'l-Hikem fī Nizāmi'l-Ümem, Füyūzāt-ı Mıknātısiyye and Ahvāl-i Gazavāt der Diyār-i Bosna (Figure 3.5), as well as Naʿima's Tārīh (Figure 3.8). There are five other titles in history and geography like Tuhfetü'l-kibār, Tārīh-i Seyyāh, Tārīhü'l-Hindi'l-Garbī, Tārīh-i Tīmūr-i Gurkān, Tārīhü'l-Mısri'l-Cedīd: Tārīhü'l-Mısri'l-Kadīm (Figure 3.2), which seem also to have sold well but since they are inventoried in one group it is difficult to make a distinction between them.

Books such as Gülşen-i Hulefā (Figure 3.3), Takvīmü't-Tevārīh (Figure 3.7) and Kitāb-ı Cihānnümā (Figure 3.6) seem to have enjoyed moderate commercial success. Only Raşid Efendi's Tārīh (Figure 3.9) and Ferheng-i Şuʿūrī (Figure 3.10), which had been on the market for a good six years before İbrahim Müteferrika's death, sold fewer than half the print run.

Having examined the number of unsold copies and the degree of popularity of the individual titles, let us now turn to total figures to get an overall picture of the success or otherwise of the Müteferrika press. There are different estimates – 12,000,[26] 12,500,[27] 12,700[28] or 13,200 copies[29] in total. These figures, however, seem to be overestimations. In my opinion, the safest way to reach a more accurate estimate is to turn to the aforementioned list in Naᶜima's *Tārīh*, which, as I mentioned earlier, gives the total initial print of 12 Müteferrika press editions (*Grammaire turque* is missing). The figure for these 12 editions can be calculated at 7200.[30] We know from the author of *Grammaire turque*, Holdermann, that the total print run of the grammar was 1000 copies.[31] Thus, the cumulative figure of initial print runs, of which the number of copies is known (as opposed to estimated), is 8200. As for the books for which the initial print run is unknown, as I suggested earlier, an informed and conservative figure is 500 copies for each of the last three editions. If we add the estimated figure of 1500 to the figure calculated for those books for which the initial print number is known, the total number of copies of all the printed books would be 9700. However, if we take a less conservative estimate of 1000 instead of 500 for those in the unknown category, then the total print of all Müteferrika's printed books would equal 11,200 copies. While a definitive answer is impossible, one may opt to settle on a median number between the conservative figure of 9700 and the liberal figure of 11,200 to suggest that the total number of printed copies was in the range of 10,000 to 11,000 printed copies. If we juxtapose this figure against the number of unsold copies that Müteferrika left upon his death, which is 2981 unsold copies, as mentioned in the probate inventory, we could infer that 69.3 per cent of his editions were sold.

These figures clearly show that İbrahim Müteferrika's printing enterprise was far from the fiasco presented in scholarly and literary sources. Indeed, as we shall see later, as a first attempt at printing, Müteferrika's commercial enterprise was comparable with that of the early European printing presses. However, before we become euphoric about this newfound 'success', these figures need to be qualified and inserted in different contexts before we declare a final judgement. First, not all the printed books that were circulated in the market had actually been sold. Some of Müteferrika's copies were presented as gifts by him or by the Ottoman court to different royal libraries in Europe – in Austria (1730),[32] Russia (1731),[33] Sweden (1735)[34] and France (1741–

42).³⁵ Having said this, the number of such gifts could not have been high enough to warrant adjusting the sale figures we have suggested.

It is insufficient to consider only the number of copies Müteferrika may have sold in his lifetime, for these figures must be related to the market in which they circulated – the book market. In view of any market, and the book market in particular, price is the singularly most important issue, and has great implications for the success or failure of any commercial enterprise. As Osman Ersoy showed, the first printed books were far more expensive than manuscripts and were beyond the reach of even high-level functionaries.³⁶ This confirms de Saussure's remark that Müteferrika was unable to sell books because of their exorbitant prices. This apparently led the first Ottoman printer to reduce the initial prices, sometimes even twice, as Holdermann (in 1730),³⁷ Müteferrika himself (in 1733 and 1734)³⁸ and Edvard Carleson (in 1735)³⁹ pointed out. The probate inventories of the time confirm such discounts of Müteferrika's printed books.⁴⁰ It is worth noting that the prices of some of Müteferrika's editions such as the Vankulu dictionary and Raşid Efendi's *Tārīh* were discounted twice, but subsequently recovered in the late 1740s. Such discounts may have been a commercial ploy that Müteferrika implemented as a sort of 'promotion offer' to induce the sale of his books, which would later be priced at what had initially been set. Thus, the relatively high prices of Müteferrika's printed books must have affected their sales negatively, which were evidently less promising than expected. We may safely conclude that Müteferrika's enterprise was established at a high price for the printer himself. The commercial success of his business, while not disastrous, was also not staggeringly successful.

Aside from quantity of sales, we need to address yet another issue in evaluating the success of the printing press, and that is the quantity of printed books relative to the reading public's market. Osman Ersoy has opined that İbrahim Müteferrika could hardly have hoped for commercial success because the total print runs of his editions were so insignificant – not even 'a handful of sand thrown to the sea' or 'a teaspoon of water given to a sick man dying of thirst'.[41] To treat this issue, one needs to consult the appropriate source documents and apply a reasonable methodology. Thus far, Turkish researchers of Ottoman printing history have been unreasonably critical. They point out that the total print runs of the first Ottoman printed books were much lower than those in western Europe during the first half of the eighteenth century. Such a synchronic comparison, so to speak, is not very reliable because we are confronted with two identical processes but at different stages of development. One should not forget that Müteferrika's effort represented *the very first* introduction of the printing press in Ottoman society, while in other parts of Europe at that time print culture was already centuries old. In my opinion, an accurate comparison would be between the initial stages of European (fifteenth century) and Ottoman (eighteenth century) printing respectively. This would represent a diachronic comparison between two processes that developed in different ages and contexts but that are in fact similar enough to warrant comparison. In applying such a methodology, one could reach a more objective assessment of the real achievements and importance of the beginnings of Ottoman printing.

In this respect, comparing the average print runs of Müteferrika's editions with those of European incunabula, one can see that they are identical. Early printing houses in Europe tended to print between 150 and 1500 copies of a book and a considerable number of presses failed after only one or two books.[42] It is thus not only unfair but also incorrect to claim that Müteferrika's print runs were too low. After all, the print run of a given book should relate to its number of potential buyers and readers.

Some insights into the Ottoman Muslim reading public can be gained by exploring probate inventories that include titles of books, but this approach is problematic for several reasons. First, the documentary basis for such a study is selective because, under Islamic inheritance laws, the registers of deceased persons only required inventories if the deceased person had left children under age, if there was a dispute over the inheritance, or if there were no heirs at all and the state treasury (*beytülmāl*) would thus sequestrate the property. Second, the inventories reflect the situation at the time of death, so it is difficult to ascertain whether the deceased had had more books before the time of his or her death. Some book owners may have sold, given, or donated some or all of their books. Third, the number of book owners found in the probate inventories does not cover the number of actual readers, for many potential readers may not have owned books, like the *medrese* students who usually made use of public *waqf* libraries. Fourth, not all the registers survive. Even though the number of preserved registers is quite considerable, it is not possible for a single researcher to undertake the huge project of consulting all the available material.[43]

Given the many problems in the sources, the best that a researcher can do is to limit the scope of his or her study in terms of chronology, geographical span and items studied. Having this in mind, I sought to look for book owners in probate inventories at the time of the first Ottoman printing press, limiting the range to the probate inventories of Istanbul. I chose to consult inventories related to people who enjoyed *askeri* status and who had left at least four manuscripts or printed books among their possessions when they died. The reasons I chose this sample are as follows: first, since these individuals lived in Istanbul, where the press was established, they must have seen or heard of it; second, as individuals belonging to the *askeri* class they were the most likely to have been able to afford such relatively expensive books; and third, as individuals who possessed more than three books, they were probably more interested in books than those who owned fewer than three. In the *askeriye* collection of the Mufti Archives of Istanbul, I was able to track down roughly 335 deceased persons with more than three books registered during the period between 1724–26 (1137–38) and 1747–48 (1160–61), namely from the years when Ottoman Turkish printing started to the years when its first stage came to an end. This figure does not, of course, refer to the real number of persons of *askeri* status who were book owners because, as I pointed out in the previous paragraph, the inheritance registers do not include the inventories of all deceased persons. Another caveat regarding the sample at hand is that the book market was not limited to Istanbul, but given that it is the imperial capital city, one would still expect to have the largest concentration of the reading public. Having said this, the figure of 335 book owners with more than three books found in Istanbul probate inventories implies that as a whole, both in absolute and relative terms, the Ottoman reading public seems to have been more or less limited. De Saussure narrates that 'the literate Turks are not so many in numbers; they are not fond of reading and they do not enjoy reading.'[44] Holdermann made the same observation in 1730.[45] The print runs of even poetry collections, a favourite topic of urbane Ottomans, and the textbooks printed in the 1840s and 1850s by the order of Istanbul book sellers (*sahhāf*) were usually 1200 copies.[46] It was rare for the print run of an edition to reach 2000 copies.[47] In this respect, the allegation that Müteferrika's 'handful of sand thrown to the sea' seems to be incorrect. Given how limited the Istanbul reading market was in the eighteenth century, and the rather small demand for books, even in the middle of the nineteenth century, Müteferrika's output was not at all insufficient, but actually a bit on the ample side considering the potential of the Ottoman book market.

Special attention should be paid to the social and professional profiles of the people who bought Müteferrika's printed books. A cursory glance at the same Istanbul probate inventories in this regard is necessary. While I found Müteferrika editions in only 16 probate inventories, it was immediately apparent that the first printed Ottoman books appeared in probate inventories very soon after they were printed. Thus, their high initial price seems not to have been a problem for many potential buyers, and the same seems to hold for probate inventories held in the provinces.[48] It is remarkable that those who owned such printed and expensive books were not only Ottoman military and bureaucratic officials but also religious functionaries. This is significant because it has been alleged that religious functionaries were the traditional opponents of the printing press.

In view of the contemporary reading public's taste and preferences, it is important to contextualize Müteferrika's print production. The majority of the book owners I studied, which included five booksellers, possessed predominantly religious literature, mainly in Arabic, and samples of poetry in Persian, Arabic and Turkish. Among the religious books the most popular were, naturally, the Qur'ān, a small collection of the most popular Qur'ānic chapters (*sura*) entitled *En'ām-i Şerīf* after the sura *En'ām* (the Camel), the religious poem *Muhammediye* written by Yazıcıoğlu Mehmed in 1444, a biography of the Prophet Muhammad in verse, as well as Mehmed Birgivi's sixteenth-century *Vasiyetnāme*, a book on religious dogma and practice. The latter two writings belonged to Ottoman Turkish authors and their popularity was due largely to the accessibility of the language in which they were written. In history and geography the most popular books pertained to Islamic history, especially the *History of al-Tabari* recounting the life of Muhammad and the emergence and development of the early Islamic state,[49] and travelogues written by pilgrims to Mecca.[50] Old Persian epics such as *Şāhnāme* and *Hamzanāme* were also among the favourites. Dictionaries, on the other hand, are seldom listed in these inventories, even in those of the five booksellers I came across. As for the constitution of the reading public, it was mainly men of religion (*ulema*), both scholars and students, administrative and military officials, and sometimes traders and craftsmen. In terms of gender, men considerably prevailed over women as readers.

Given such a reading public and taste in books, İbrahim Müteferrika definitely filled a gap by printing dictionaries first. Vankulu's Arabic–Turkish redaction of *Sihāh* became a bestseller. However, in his editing policy Müteferrika was much more inclined to print historical and geographical books: nine of the sixteen editions are related to history, two others (*Tuhfet* and *History of West Indies*) combine history and geography, while the most eminent product of his printing house was Kātip Çelebi's geographical work *Mirror of World*. Müteferrika, however, printed texts, which were not in line with the traditional religious or epic literature popular at the time. By printing Ottoman maritime history or the political history of Persia, the caliphate and the Ottoman empire, as well as geographical books, Müteferrika seems to have attempted to provide books that would be useful to those involved in government by offering historical works of didactic value. Indeed, as William Watson states, İbrahim's printing philosophy seems to have been completely utilitarian.[51]

On the other hand, it is noteworthy that except for one title (*Calendar of Histories*, in Persian) all the books Müteferrika printed were in Ottoman Turkish and thus more accessible to potential readers. These books could be read not only by Muslims but also by Turkish-speaking non-Muslims. In this way the printer practically exceeded the scope of the traditional Ottoman Muslim reading public. Moreover, by providing secular and utilitarian knowledge, he challenged the traditional Muslim concept of knowledge and learning, which placed the emphasis on religious matters.[52] A. Ubucini claims that printing brought to the Ottomans new branches of learning that played a significant role in their progress.[53]

Was the first Ottoman printing press a success or failure? İbrahim Müteferrika's probate inventory shows no evidence that he had failed in his undertaking. While unsold copies of books he had printed constituted a large part of his assets, that is probably normal for a tradesman and enterprising person.

By the end of his life İbrahim Müteferrika was able to sell about 70 per cent of the books he printed: quite a sufficient reward for his enterprise. Indeed, he seems to have been luckier than Johann Gutenberg, who lost his printing house through a debt to his sponsor Johann Fust. As Sigfrid Steinberg remarked, most early European printers seem to have been better printers than businessmen. They had limited commercial success because they were unaware of one important feature of printing: it requires significant advance investment and the turnover is necessarily slow.⁵⁴ In fact, de Saussure seems to have been aware of these requirements in that he expressed concern that the Müteferrika enterprise might cease with the printer's death because of the Turks' impatience with and lack of enthusiasm for delayed long-term returns.⁵⁵

Sigfrid Steinberg's remark raises the question of if we accept that the first Ottoman Turkish printing enterprise was not a commercial failure, why did it cease production immediately after Müteferrika's death to revive sporadically just for one edition in the mid-1750s and then only in 1784 to continue along a more stable path? Is previous scholarship incorrect in claiming that the first Ottoman Turkish printing press was a failure rather than a success? Perhaps, the hitherto negative assessments of Müteferrika's printing press come from an impression that the invention of printing in the West was a sweeping revolution that took place in a short period of time. In her famous book, Elizabeth Eisenstein put forward the idea that the printing press was an 'agent of change' that resulted in a 'communications revolution' in which the print culture replaced the traditional scribal culture.⁵⁶ In response to criticism, Eisenstein explains her use of the term 'revolution'. Her particular notion of revolution is inspired by Raymond Williams's oxymoronic expression 'long revolution'⁵⁷ in the sense that it is not about a fast change due to a single act, but a continuous, irreversible process, the effects of which gradually become visible in the course of its development.⁵⁸ Not everyone, however, shares Eisenstein's 'revolution' theory. Robert A. Houston, for example, agrees with Eisenstein that printing undoubtedly changed ways of thinking and played an indirect role in economic, social and political development in early modern Europe (1500–1800), but he qualifies Eisenstein's thesis by stating that the impact of the printing press 'was neither immediate, nor direct, nor certain'. The changes were slow and contingent on various social, economic and political contexts, and the printing 'was arguably not fully developed until the eighteenth century'.⁵⁹ Jacque le Goff also stresses that, upon its introduction in Europe, the printing press met the needs of only the literate elite, and it was not until the counter-reformation that this technology was used to educate the public.[60] Finally, Brian Richardson concludes that 'the transition from manuscript to printed book was in some respects, then, a process of evolution.'[61] Indeed, some recent scholars in book history have been re-evaluating Eisenstein's theory in radical[62] and moderate ways.[63] Some criticize her non-contextual approach by positing that print culture existed side by side or competed with manuscript culture well into the eighteenth century.

With respect to printing in the Islamic world, most scholars are inclined to think that the same 'print revolution' should have happened.[64] However, there are a few who think that the printing press gave rise to a cultural 'evolution' in the Ottoman empire and Islamic world in general.[65] So, was Müteferrika's printing enterprise an 'agent of change'? Earlier scholarship answered this question by referring to the supposed commercial failure of his enterprise, which was suspended after his death. But, in my opinion, İbrahim Müteferrika was an 'agent of change', though not an 'agent of immediate change'.

Indeed, the transition from scribal to print culture was a slow, gradual and arduous process. In Brian Richardson's words, old habits die hard.[66] But at what stage in the development of printing could one speak of a 'print culture'? This leads us to the question of how to define a print culture. So-called traditional 'print-culture scholarship' considers printing technology with movable type to be the beginning of print culture. However, for a print culture to dominate a scribal culture there needs to exist a social conviction in the necessity of printed 'agents' of knowledge and information. Thus, the establishment of a printing house is certainly a starting point in the formation of a print culture, but the spread of a print culture is contingent on the particular social context.

It seems that the cursive nature of the Arabic script, which was in general use in the Islamic world, was not particularly suited to, and subsequently led to a reluctance to adopt, printing with movable type. It was through the personal strife and effort of people like Müteferrika, and not socio-cultural demand that Muslim printing came into being. In fact, unlike many other innovations of European origin, such as cannons and firearms, the Ottomans did not apparently really need the printing press. However, once introduced, it attracted attention and left traces in Ottoman cultural history.

İbrahim Müteferrika's printing enterprise became possible because he was a confident bearer of the already developed European print culture and was probably well skilled in its arts. He was eager enough to undertake such an enterprise in an Ottoman milieu where calligraphy was esteemed and printing considered inappropriate for the Arabic alphabet. In a letter of 1737, de Laria, an interpreter at the French embassy in Istanbul, provides a noteworthy detail about İbrahim Müteferrika's habits. According to him, although İbrahim was a Hungarian convert to Islam, he was not particularly observant. In the light of such accounts, one could assume that İbrahim was in fact a good example of a cultural dichotomy or symbiosis. In other words, he never forgot his Christian past and never became a real Muslim – he could never negate his background, which was familiar with the print culture, and could never become a 'traditional' Muslim for whom manuscripts were pretty enough. This explains why he was a quite adventurous 'agent of change'. He succeeded in establishing a new enterprise and in putting in place the beginning of a long-term process of forming an Ottoman print culture.

But when was Ottoman print culture formed? Jale Baysal suggests that an important step was made in 1803 when for the first time a religious book, Birgivi's *Vasiyetnāme*, was printed in Istanbul and thus the Muslim reading public could get access to this rather popular text in printed form.[67] According to her, during the period from 1869 to 1875, when the first Ottoman Turkish novels and plays were being written and printed, printing could adequately meet the expectations and tastes of the Muslim reading public and hence 'was already accepted by the society'.[68]

During that period, however, another major step made it irreversible – the printing of the Qur'ān, first lithographically in 1871 and then with movable types in 1874.[69] Apparently, only in the 1870s did Muslim society get ready to have its holy text in printed form, having waited a long enough time to be persuaded by the advantages of printing technology. The probate inventory of a certain Hadice, daughter of Hacı Ömer Ağa from Salonica, dated 1878 and including two printed Qur'āns,[70] suggests that printing was still not fully accepted as late as 1844 when, according to Charles White, Istanbul booksellers saw manuscript copyists as deserving to go to paradise and the printing press as made of the poisonous oleander (zakkum) plant.[71]

It seems that the 1870s were indeed a turning point in the development of Ottoman print culture. Intellectuals like Münif Pasha (1830–1910) and Celal Nuri were concerned that printing with movable type did not meet the specificities of the Arabic cursive script.[72] But this did not deter the Ottomans from experimenting with printing with movable type. Quite the contrary, in 1879 the Council of Public Education (Meclis-i Ma'arif-i Umumiye) appointed a special committee to revise the Arabic script in order to make it incursive precisely for printing purposes, but the committee was unsuccessful.[73] Later, however, in 1914 the so-called 'Enver Pasha's orthography' (Enver Pāşā imlāsı), divided Arabic characters (in other words, made it incursive) and tested it in printing.[74] Of course, what marked the end of all these problems was the introduction of a Turkish version of the Latin script in 1928.

So, by the 1870s the Ottomans seem to have become accustomed to having their books printed and the problem of the cursive Arabic script solved. If İbrahim Müteferrika could have seen these later developments he would have been very satisfied. Though we can never be certain if he died a happy or a desperate man, as in Jale Baysal's play, Nevres's consoling words are at least full of historical optimism. 'Probably the next [generations] will read [your printed books] … as well as the generations after them. Did you not pave the way?'[75]

THE FIRST OTTOMAN TURKISH PRINTING ENTERPRISE

## Appendix

Publications of the first Ottoman printing
1. Tercümetü's-Sihāh-i Cevheri [Lugat-i Vānkūlu] (Kostantiniye, 1141/1729)
2. Tuhfetü'l-Kibār fī Esfāri'l-Bihār (Kostantiniye, 1141/1729)
3. Tārīh-i Seyyāh der Beyān-i Zuhūr-i Ağvāniyān ve Sebeb-i İndihām-i Binā-i Devlet-i Şāhān-i Safeviyān (Kostantiniye, 1142/1729)
4. Tārīhü'l-Hindi'l-Garbī el-Müsemmā bi-Hadīs-i Nev (Kostantiniye, 1142/1730)
5. Tārīh-i Tīmūr-i Gurkān li-Nazmīzāde Efendi (Kostantiniye, 1142/1730)
6. Tārīhü'l-Mısri'l-Cedīd li-Süheylī Efendi; Tārīhü'l-Mısri'l-Kadīm li-Süheylī Efendi (Kostantiniye, 1142/1730)
7. Gülşen-i Hulefā li-Nazmīzāde Efendi (Kostantiniye, 1143/1730).
8. Grammaire turque ou Méthode courte & facile pour Apprende la Langue turque. Avec Recueil de Noms, de Verbes, & des Manières de Parler les plus Nécessaires a Savoir. Avec Plusieurs Dialogues familiers (Constantinople, 1730)
9. Usūlü'l-Hikem fī Nizāmi'l-Ümem (Kostantiniye, 1144/1732)
10. Füyūzāt-ı Mıknātısiyye (Kostantiniye, 1144/1732)
11. Kitāb-ı Cihānnümā li-Kātip Çelebi (Kostantiniye, 1145/1732)
12. Takvīmü't-Tevārīh li-Kātip Çelebi (Kostantiniye, 1146/1733)
13. Tārīh-i Naʿīmā (Kostantiniye, 1147/1734)
14. Tārīh-i Rāşid Efendi (Kostantiniye, 1153/1741); Tārīh-i Çelebizāde Efendi (Kostantiniye, 1153/1741)
15. Ahvāl-i Gazavāt der Diyār-i Bosna (Kostantiniye, 1154/1741).
16. Lisānü'l-ʿAcem [Ferheng-i Şuʿūrī] (Kostantiniye, 1155/1742).

**Figure 3.1: Sale percentages of *Tercümetü's-Sihāh-i Cevheri* [*Lugat-i Vānkūlū*], 1141/1729**

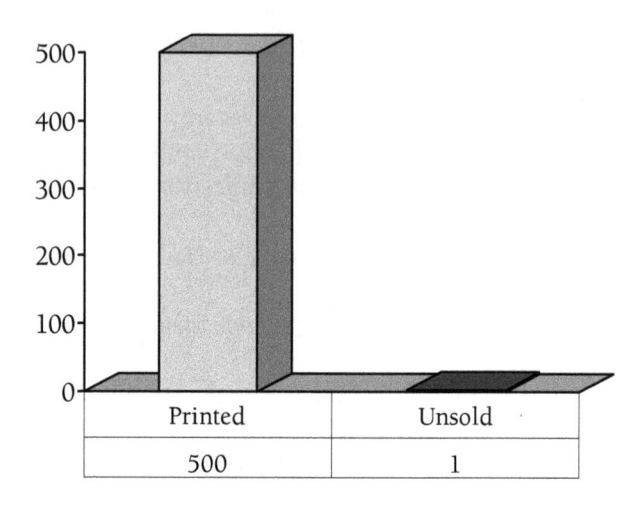

| Printed | Unsold |
|---------|--------|
| 500     | 1      |

**Figure 3.2: Sale percentages of *Tuhfetü'l-Kibār*, *Tārīh-i Seyyāh*, *Hindi'l-Garbī*, *Tārīh-i Tīmūr*, *Tārīhü'l-Mısır*, 1141–42/1729–30**

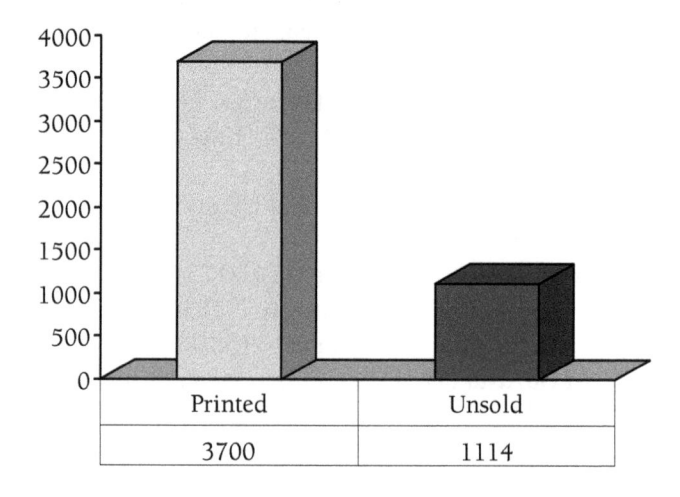

| Printed | Unsold |
|---------|--------|
| 3700    | 1114   |

**Figure 3.3: Sale percentages of *Gülşen-i Hulefā*, 1143/1730**

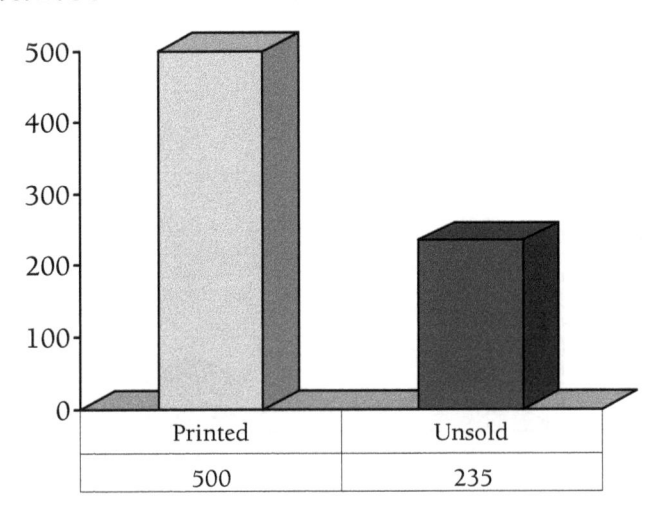

| Printed | Unsold |
|---------|--------|
| 500     | 235    |

**Figure 3.4: Sale percentages of *Grammaire turque*, 1730**

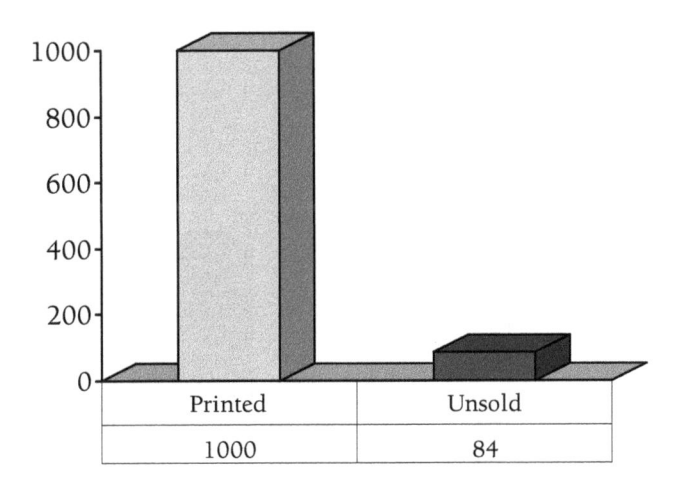

| Printed | Unsold |
|---------|--------|
| 1000    | 84     |

*Figure 3.5:* **Sale percentages of *Usūlü'l-Hikem, Mıknātısiyye*, 1144/1732; *Ahvāl-i Gazavāt der Diyār-i Bosna*, 1154/1741**

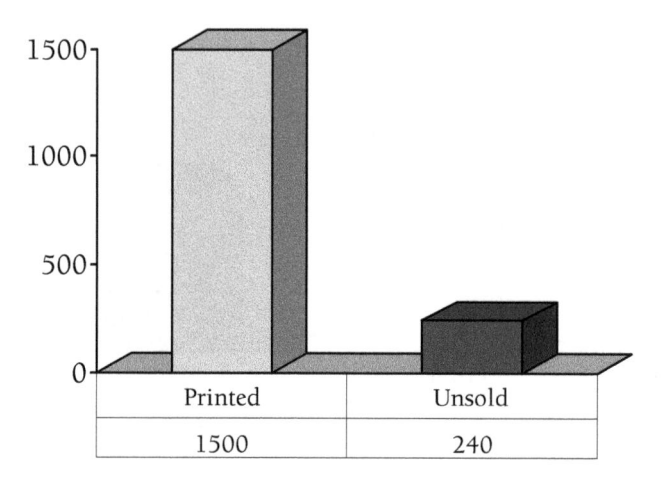

| Printed | Unsold |
|---|---|
| 1500 | 240 |

*Figure 3.6:* **Sale percentages of *Kitāb-ı Cihānnümā*, 1145/1732**

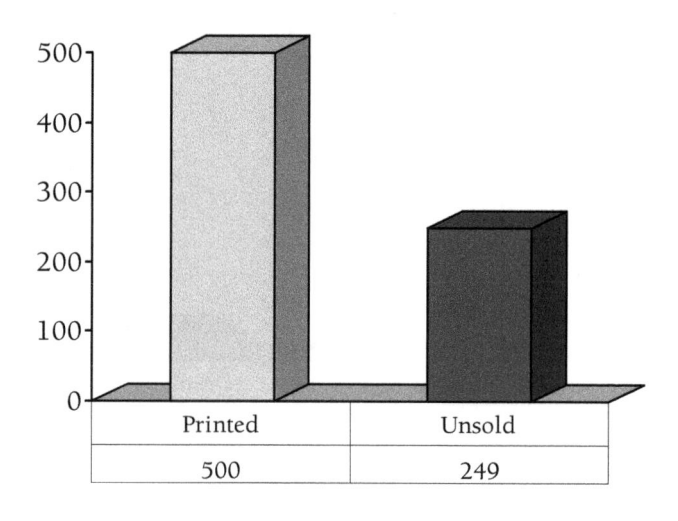

| Printed | Unsold |
|---|---|
| 500 | 249 |

**Figure 3.7: Sale percentages of *Takvīmü't-Tevārīh*, 1146/1733**

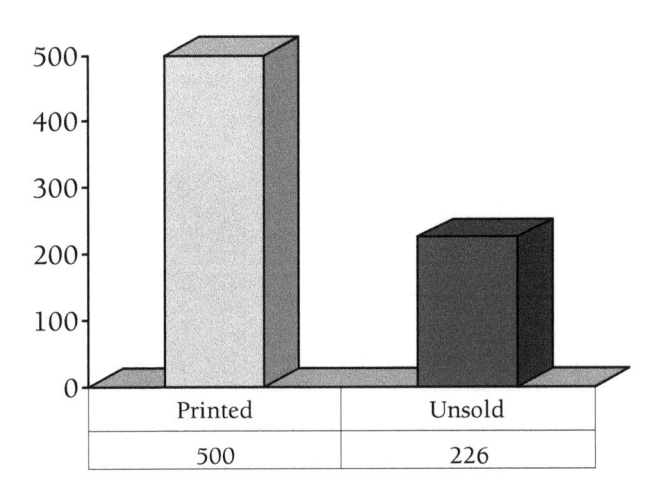

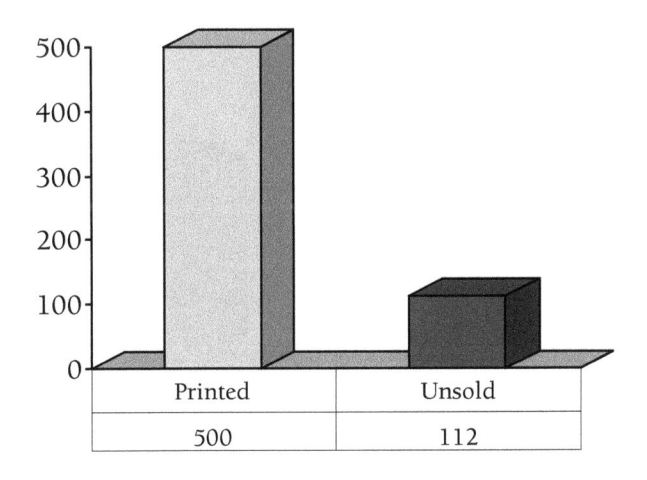

| Printed | Unsold |
|---------|--------|
| 500 | 226 |

**Figure 3.8: Sale percentages of *Tārīh-i Na$^c$īmā*, 1147/1734**

| Printed | Unsold |
|---------|--------|
| 500 | 112 |

**Figure 3.9: Sale percentages of *Tārīh-i Rāşid Efendi*, *Tārīh-i Çelebizāde Efendi*, 1153/1741**

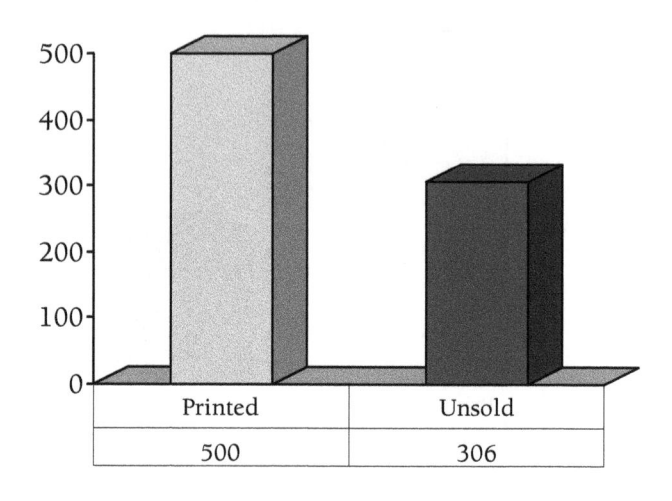

| Printed | Unsold |
|---------|--------|
| 500 | 306 |

**Figure 3.10: Sale percentages of *Ferheng-i Şuʿūrī*, 1155/1742**

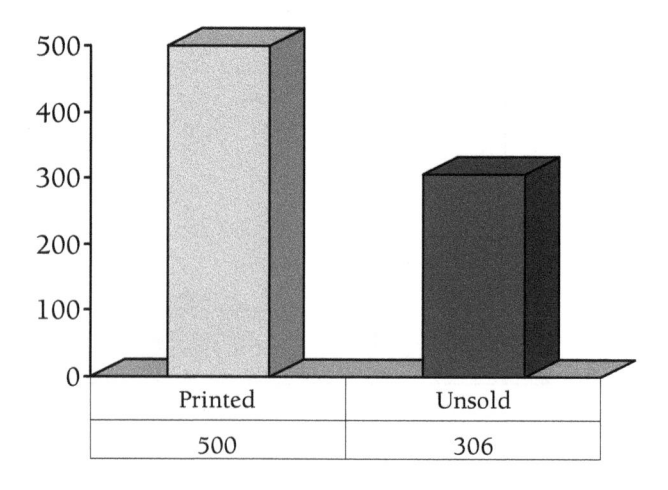

| Printed | Unsold |
|---------|--------|
| 500 | 306 |

## Table 3.1: Book sales and sale percentages of the Müteferrika Press

| Title | Total Print | | Unsold | Sold | % Sold |
|---|---|---|---|---|---|
| Lugat-i Vānkūlu | 500 | | 1 | 499 | 99.8 |
| Tuhfetü'l-Kibār | 1000 | 3700 | 1114 | 2586 | 69.9 |
| Tārīh-i Seyyāh | 1200 | | | | |
| Hindi'l-Garbī | 500 | | | | |
| Tārīh-i Tīmūr | 500 | | | | |
| Tārīhü'l-Mısır | 500 | | | | |
| Gülşen-i Hulefā | 500 | | 235 | 265 | 53.0 |
| Grammaire turque | 1000 | | 84 | 916 | 91.6 |
| Usūlü'l-Hikem | 500 | 1500 | 240 | 1260 | 84.0 |
| Mıknātısiyye | 500 | | | | |
| Diyār-i Bosna | [500] | | | | |
| Takvīmü't-Tevārīh | 500 | | 226 | 274 | 54.8 |
| Cihānnümā | 500 | | 249 | 251 | 50.2 |
| Tārīh-i Naʿīmā | 500 | | 112 | 388 | 77.6 |
| Tārīh-i Rāşid/Çelebizāde | [500] | | 306 | 194 | 38.8 |
| Ferheng-i Şuʿūrī | [500] | | 409 | 91 | 22.2 |
| Total | 9700 | | 2976 | 6724 | 69.3 |

# Chapter 4
# Nahils, Circumcision Rituals and the Theatre State
## Babak Rahimi

In his seminal study of the Ottoman state, *Formation of the Modern State*, Rifaᶜat ᶜAli Abou-El-Haj identifies the seventeenth century as a period of intense and dramatic socio-economic and political changes in Ottoman society and its state apparatus. What constituted this critical juncture in such deep-seated sociopolitical transformation, he argues, is the possession of semi-private lands by the wealthy families and high-ranking officials previously controlled by the Ottoman state. Beginning in the seventeenth and continuing well into the eighteenth century, changes in state taxation led to the development of semi-autonomous provincial ruling classes, which collected taxes on behalf of the central state and, consequently, steadily gained power in the provincial regions of the empire. State power was decentralized as large tracts of land, in the form of private property (*mülk*), were distributed among provincial officials in regions in the empire, creating 'semi-autonomous local dynasties'.[1]

More importantly, in *Formation of the Modern State*, Abou-El-Haj shows how the major social and economic upheavals that brought such far-reaching changes in Ottoman society in the seventeenth century were in fact symptoms of internal or indigenous processes.[2] Because the centralized Ottoman state that emerged in the fifteenth century under Sultan Mehmed the Conqueror derived most of its income from caption tax paid by the peasant population (*reaya*) of the empire, there were almost continuous uprisings by Ottoman subjects in the seventeenth and eighteenth centuries. These internal displays of resistance to the state's form of revenue extraction, which at times resulted in waves of uprisings, marked crucial changes in relations between the state and society, particularly the state's privatization of public property, which changed the *reaya*'s relationship to the land.[3]

Ariel Salzmann's study of the eighteenth-century Ottoman political economy substantiates the above observation by showing how, as a result of various privatizing fiscal policies and decentralization processes, the Ottoman state underwent a major structural transformation in the eighteenth century. While various patterns of administrative devolution of power were evident prior to the eighteenth century, the long-term institutional decentralization of the early modern Ottoman state, in complex social and economic relational settings between a centre and its many peripheries, led to provincial power building and reasserted the state's central significance as the distributor of rights and official duties.

For the most part, an increasing tendency to accumulate revenues through dispersed holdings in the private sector characterized the eighteenth-century Ottoman state. The expanding power of the upper strata of the Ottoman gentry and the privatization or '*Malikānization*' of state capital for new entrepreneurial ventures further accentuated the decreasing authority of the state. This marked the emergence of new state–society relations that underlined the general 'expansion of all sectors of the Ottoman economy during the first three-quarters of the eighteenth century'.[4]

Abou-El-Haj and Salzmann invite us to reconsider the eighteenth century as an era of dramatic changes in the economic and political life of Ottoman society. They show us how the transformation of the Ottoman elite, accompanied by a greater display of intra-elite political struggle and increasing decentralization of authority, can be seen as 'a change in social formation'. If approached in a comparable and commensurable manner, this would also highlight the features that other 'early modern' (mainly European) state-building processes have in common. In this sense, the transformation of the Ottoman state in the seventeenth century should be recognized as having emanated from changes in the Ottoman societal structure that were similar to those that occurred in Western Europe.

In similar vein, the present historical anthropological study can be seen as an invitation to look at the Ottoman state as part of an ongoing process extending from the early modern political transformation to the eighteenth century. My argument here is that, along with a series of socio-economic transformations, a peculiar set of socio-cultural changes occurred that marked a critical moment in the political transformation of relations between the Ottoman state and society. This transformation will be demonstrated in the cultural sphere of ritual performance, particularly in the development of the political rituals surrounding imperial circumcision festivals from the late sixteenth to the early eighteenth centuries.

These celebrations are crucial because they show the ritual ways in which changes in the enactment and representation of power occurred at the symbolic level during the so-called 'Tulip Age' (1718–30). Focusing on the ritual object of *nahil,* the wooden poles displayed during public and court festivals when a prince was circumcised, the circumcision celebrations of 1720 served as an important cultural event in the spectacular 'theatre state' of Ahmed III's Ottoman regime.[5] The early eighteenth century version of the *nahil* identifies the formation of a type of ritual that represents and embodies state power as erect, inconsumable and solid, in other words permanent and absolute. In a sense, the presence of the symbolic association of fertility and consumption in the ritual object of the *nahil,* apparent in the 1582 circumcision rituals, is replaced with the growing pomp of state power versus societal forces, namely guild associations, in the 1720 ceremonies.

What follows is divided into three sections. In the first I focus on the historical formation of Ottoman circumcision rituals and the evolution of *nahil* as a ritual object of great symbolic significance. In the second, in which the concern is more conceptual, I offer an interpretative examination of the political relevance of the *nahil* in the ritual body of the circumcision ceremonies. This will be done by considering how such a fertility symbol, in its close association with the body of the male sovereign, provides various dramatic spectacles in the representation of state power. Finally, in an attempt to emphasize common features in the cultural reproduction of state power manifested in ritual processes across regions and histories, I shall present a brief comparative theoretical study of the imperial ceremonies with the Safavid Muharram rituals.

## The Ottoman theatre state and imperial circumcision rituals

By 'theatre state' I refer specifically to a set of invented or reconstructed ceremonies aimed at enacting and representing power through ritual performance. Such political rituals tend not only to represent power in dramatic ways, but also to conceal tensions of authority and political power, in particular by displaying more harmony than may actually exist in a particular society. In the words of Clifford Geertz, based on his observation of Balinese rites of power, 'the dramas of the theatre state, mimetic of themselves, were, in the end, neither illusions nor lies, neither sleight of hand nor make-believe. They were what there was.'[6]

In other words, ritual enactments of symbols do not imitate social reality as much as they reproduce themselves, their symbolic features, in the ritual process of spectacles and in the dramatic display of images for the sake of power itself. The theatre state involves the repeated enactment of symbols, myths and allegories that evoke imageries of a permanent state in lineage with an eternal past and continuous future, as something that transcends the lives of the individuals who participate in the ceremony and are members of an immortal entity.

In early modern European history, the phenomenon of theatre state formation was mainly accompanied by patterns of statism that saw the emergence of more territorially defined and militarily monopolized processes in the consolidation of monarchical authority. New developments in military technology changed not only patterns for preparing and engaging in war but also the ways states were governed. The rise of 'absolutist states' in western Europe marked the proliferation of organized military institutions that reflected a gradual increase in the integration of territorial boundaries (territorialization), tied in simultaneously with the expansion in the monopoly of organized violence.[7]

In the first place, war and preparing for war involved the advancement of large armies and military technologies for domination in the interstices of competing empire-states.[8] At the second level, the deployment of military coercion followed the centralization of royal authority as the masculinization of monarchical courts from semi-feudalistic towards more territorially bounded states advanced the absolutist conception of royal sovereignty.

Between the late fifteenth and eighteenth century, the Ottoman state shared with political states elsewhere in Europe (most notably in western regions like France, England and Spain) similar features of territorial statism. These included further territorial assimilation, increases in taxation, a rise in military spending, superior military forces and greater regularization of institutions and official administrations. But one feature these states also shared with the Ottomans was the need to devise cultural strategies for constructing collective identities with a view to building and stabilizing individuals capable of interacting with each other in a productive manner, thus creating territorially bounded and stable communities under the hegemony of the state. An increase in the number of festivals and the introduction of elaborate political ceremonies in the early modern period marked an integral feature of the new territorial states in bolstering claims to authority and evoking a cohesive imagery of state power in the minds of the individuals participating in spectacular festivities.

These rituals, in a sense, also produced the knowledge of a total order to which all levels of the social stratum belonged, though to different degrees and separately from other political orders. State power was affirmed through the production of images and symbolic enactments of authority that involved experiences of submission of self and other participants to a transcendental authority present here and now on earth.

The Palm Sunday processions at the Kremlin during the reign of Ivan the Terrible in the mid-sixteenth century and the coronation of the young Louis XIV in the mid-seventeenth century (1654), with their peculiar display of both popular carnivalesque and courtly processions, serve as interesting examples of theatre states. These public spectacles produced a set of visual and iconographic emotions that aimed to generate vivid mental pictorial images and emotive symbols drawn from the repertoire of religious or political schemata. They fostered feelings of collective incorporation and solidarity in which individuals imagined and experienced the presence of a transcendent community of shared emotions and ideals.

Viewed in this comparative sense, the Ottoman circumcision celebrations also serve as an intriguing example in the development of an early modern theatre state. Similar to other European state processions, like the Elizabethan royal ceremonies of the early seventeenth century in which medieval customs of kingship allowed royalty to travel around the kingdom and enjoy 'the hospitality of their subjects, moving from one castle to another and making their power known across the land', the Ottoman circumcision rituals provided a mobile public stage on which, with the circumcision of a young prince as the future sultan, the sacred body of the sultan became a symbolic object of celebration.[9]

Accompanied by days of festivity and celebration – ranging from ten days in 1365 and 1530–1539, to 15 days in 1675 and 1720, and even at times to 55 days in 1582 – the imperial circumcision feasts (*bayram*) marked an honourable occasion during which royal princes, along with hundreds of the sultan's subjects' boys, were blessed by the ceremony of circumcision. These events, which a festival chief (*sur emini*) would supervise, included ceremonial receptions, a variety of communal feasts, athletic games, impersonations of mock battles on castles, fireworks displays, or water features like illuminated models being sailed down the Golden Horn. The participation of foreign performers from Egypt and Persia and various displays of exotic animals like elephants and giraffes gave the ceremonies a more cosmopolitan flavour.[10]

Along with the illumination of the capital city, Istanbul, with torches and lamps (known as *donanma*), the circumcision feasts included the decoration of public buildings, like the Topkapi Palace, Hippodrome and Yali Köşk; banquets for various foreign and state dignitaries; and public displays of animal sacrifices in the course of rich and spectacular pageantries. Interesting features of these dramatic ceremonies also included a circus and musical performances, along with displays of *tableaux vivants* in the shape of dragons and carriages exhibited on the Bosporus.

While many court ceremonies (especially the actual circumcision of the royal prince) took place within the walls of the sultan's palaces at Istanbul (1582) and Edirne (1674), the whole capital city and (at times) the provincial towns as well were involved in the large display of artisans and guild pageantry, which proceeded in an hierarchical processional pattern beginning with the farmers and ending with the tavern associates.[11] Many guilds created *tableaux vivants* and elaborate devices, like a glass furnace surrounded by working glass blowers.[12] Other guild members displayed goods produced by artisans, which were later sent for consumption to the palace or army. Walking alongside the guilds, some non-guild groups, such as the dervishes and various Sufi sects, along with the Greek communities, joined the guild processions, highlighting the ethnic-religious urban feature of these ceremonies.[13]

Drawn on carts or carried through the streets on the artisans' shoulders, the guilds exhibited their technical skills by displaying pieces of work or usable goods on a moving stage.[14] In some guild pageants, there were also processions of state officials, which included *shaykh*s and the supreme commander of the Janissaries (*ağa*) depicting, in Suraiya Faroqhi's words, 'Ottoman society in general, orchestrated by the sultan's official', watching the proceedings from a grand pavilion.[15] For the most part, the participation of guilds underlined the urban social dimension of the Ottoman circumcision rituals, which provided an opportunity for all members of Ottoman society to participate in an official event sponsored by the imperial court, 'so that even the poorest of the workers could have a sense of belonging and recognition'.[16]

*From stage to street: the transformation of a political ritual from 1582 to 1720*
As described in various manuscripts or festival books (*Surnameh*) illustrating the accounts of the circumcision ceremonies, most notably the *Surnameh* of Lokman (1582) and Vehbi (1720) preserved in the Topkapi Palace Museum, circumcision rituals underwent significant change from the late sixteenth to the early eighteenth centuries.[17] By and large, a significant shift of symbolic and performative focus occurred in the course of the ceremonies with their appearance as a full-blown dramatic stage-based spectacle in 1582 to a more street-level carnivalesque processions in 1720.

*The 1582 festivals*
The ceremonies celebrated in the capital city, Istanbul, for the circumcision of Prince Mehmed in 1582 consisted of various festivals and parades before the sultan, who watched them from an elevated pavilion. The *surname* describing the events mentions elaborate paraphernalia with the enhancement of realistic, fanciful and at times comical representations of foreign enemies (mainly Safavid Persians), along with a skirmish between the Janissaries and cavalry of the Porte.[18]

A series of dramatic spectacles performed in unprecedented ways, with the apparent aim of enhancing the power and prestige of the Ottoman state, particularly since the 1530 and 1539 circumcision processions, was central to these ceremonies. A significant development in the celebrations under Murad III was the provision of a ceremonial *stage* on which to mount the spectacles during the course of the rituals. That the 1582 festivities were held on a much larger scale than before was mainly a result of the territorial expansion of the Ottoman state. In these festivals, state pomp was structured to portray the expansion of Ottoman territorial power as a theatre state. The construction of the splendid model of the Süleymaniye mosque, for instance, which was for the first time put on display and carried through the streets of Istanbul, marks the increasing significance of images and symbols of grandeur that depict the greatness of the imperial power through models of buildings and public sites.[19]

Correspondingly, the artisan parades and guild processions first appeared in the 1582 imperial ceremonies. According to the account of a European traveller, artisans took part in the parades and various shows, mainly during the morning hours of the festivities.[20] With more than 150 guilds or *esnaf* participating in the ceremonies, many of their spectacles were displayed in the week before the circumcision,[21] with guild processions continuing for 22 days in the course of the ceremonies and attracting wide audiences. The sultan, especially, enjoyed the rivalry between different guilds as each association tried to make their procession more spectacular as they vied for greater public admiration.[22]

The development of guild pageantry as an emerging feature of the festivals highlights the growing presence of Ottoman associational networks in the increasingly spectacular nature of the festivities surrounding the state's ritual ceremony. This increase in carnivalesque features, which Derin Terzioğlu identifies, signifies both an expansion of mid-sixteenth century state-building in Ottoman society and an accumulation of wealth by the urban guilds.[23]

It is not surprising, therefore, that the carnivalesque feature of the rituals is most prominent in the guild processions. This is mainly because of the way the ceremonies apply certain features of an 'upside down world' in which official culture is defied through acts of misrule and grotesque performances. The expansion of the spectacularity and carnivalesque features of the ceremonies demonstrated a greater potential for disarray or misrule in the 1582 processions as elites and various urban sectors of Ottoman society competed and, at times, fought each other (like the cavalry–Janissary battles) to bolster their social status and claim greater authority in the ritual forum.

## The 1720 festivals

The Ottoman theatre state that found its greatest display of power in the 1582 festivals saw a series of developments in its aesthetic splendour and elaborate paraphernalia in the late seventeenth and early eighteenth centuries.

First, the 1720 festivals, in honour of Ahmed III's three sons, demonstrate a remarkable continuation in the presence of the guild parades, reflecting the prominence of the guilds as autonomous institutions that acted between the artisans and the state in the early eighteenth century. The prominence of guildsmen in the processions is something that can also be detected in the 1675 festivals at Edirne, during the circumcision and wedding celebrations held by Mehmed IV, as described by Evliya Çelebi. According to Çelebi, ceremonies in the second half of the seventeenth century were dominated by the guilds, though apparently the presence of male and female non-artisans increased as well in ways unprecedented in previous festivals.[24]

The guild street processions for the 1720 festivals, which were led by gold embroiderers, blacksmiths, cloth weavers and makers of *seraser*, involved several centres because, unlike the 1582 celebrations, there was no central staging space.[25] Also, with the increase in processional ceremonies held in the streets, along with the gradual decline (though still a prominent feature of the ceremony) in the mounting of performances at major public sites like the Hippodrome, the 1720 festivals took place at numerous centres where spectators and performers gathered, intermingled and together enjoyed the festivities and commotion. As an offshoot of the guild parades, an increase in elaborate displays and images in the artisans' ceremonies can be detected in the 1720 ceremonies, which were barely visible in the 1582 ones. The 1720 display of a three-dimensional model of a bath by Istanbul artisans, for instance, testifies to this pattern of dramatic development in the rituals.[26] The processional display of gold turban ornaments, called *sorguç*, of jewelled ornaments representing the goldsmith guilds, and wagons roasting coffee beans in large ovens representing the merchants of the flea market, highlights the significant role of the spectacular and exotic in the ritual body of the imperial ceremonies.[27] But such theatrical techniques also identify a significant development in the dramatic spectacular facet of the ceremonies, further highlighting the consolidation of the Ottoman theatre state as a result.

In an important way, the appearance in the 1720 festivals of punishment spectacles suggests an increase in state anxiety over turmoil in the market and the intrusion of urban sectors in the organization of the ceremonies. In a direct challenge to the guilds, state punishment of artisans who violated market regulations was a frequent feature of the 1720 ceremonies, reflecting the emergence of an increased threat to the state from the growing power of the empire's urban sector, mostly represented by the guilds.[28] Also, the absence of guilds headed by religious elders or sheikhs in the 1720 ceremonies, which was a common feature of fourteenth-century Anatolian urban organizations knows as *akhis*, signifies the putative link between the market and urban organizations, independent of religious affiliation and state control.[29]

*The nahil in the 1582 and 1720 festivals*
The *nahil*, the central ritual object of imperial circumcision ceremonies, is a large pyramid-shaped wooden pole laden either with real or artificial flowers or with edible objects like fruit or sweets. The *nahil* would be carried at the head of a procession that included a number of Janissaries who would eventually place it beside the yet to be circumcised prince. *Nahil* processions were usually performed alongside various consumption-related activities like the distribution of sweet pastries, sweet drinks and

*sherbet*, and at times a sacrificial animal would be brought along to be slaughtered on behalf of the circumcised prince and royal family. Making *nahils* required products like 'paper, charcoal for heating and for the foundry furnace, flax, willow twigs, flowerpots and wooden pails'.[30] By and large, however, the main symbolic makeup of a *nahil*, in its representational form, included banners, decorative sets of colorful flowers, fruits and candles, which were lit at night.[31] These decorative patterns were consistent symbolic features of *nahil* ceremonies from the sixteenth to the eighteenth centuries, though its construction became more expensive in the later period.

The name *nahil* is derived from the Arabic word for the date palm tree. In the commemorative ceremonies of Muharram, celebrated to mourn the martyrdom of the Prophet's beloved grandson, Husayn, for instance, the *nakhl* (used here in its Arabic terminology) represents a symbolic coffin for the holy imam and his children martyred on the plain of Karbala. This symbolic artefact depicts the stature and courage of Husayn; it represents the sacred death of a male figure symbolically displaying his youth, as well as the way he fought and ultimately became a martyr for the cause of justice.[32]

In Ottoman circumcision rituals, the *nahil* symbolizes birth, the blossoming of life, fertility and regeneration. It is an Ottoman Turkic symbolic object used for weddings and circumcision ceremonies. With possible origins in central Asiatic animistic religious practices, which are absent in non-Turkic regions of the Islamic world – at least prior to the migration of the Turkish tribes to the Islamic world during the Middle Period – the *nahil* represents male strength or, as von Hammer-Purgstall describes it, 'symbols of virile force and fecundity'.[33] The cultural significance of the *nahil* in Ottoman society cannot be overestimated. As a popular symbolic artefact, an entire Ottoman guild association specialized in making *nahil*s, at times building them so large that it required hundreds of slaves to carry them.

In its physical form, built with wax and wire, a *nahil* was covered with fresh flowers and sprouting foliage. *Nahil*s were also decorated with symbols of birds, plants and animals of various kinds, representing fertility and the renewal of natural virility embodied in a symbol of erect vitality.[34]

In the historical development of circumcision ceremonies, the *nahil* remained in a stationary position, mostly within the palace walls. In the 1582 ceremony, when the size and number of *nahil*s exceeded those of previous festivals, the pyramid constructions remained in the Old Palace, from where dockyard slaves and 80 Janissaries would later carry them outside for the prince's procession.[35] In the 1720 festivals, a *nahil agasi* arranged and set up the *nahil*s at the Eski Saray (Old Palace) nine days before the ceremonies began.[36] Along with the candy gardens, which were also an important feature of the ceremonies, the floral decorations at the Eski Saray appear to have been guarded by special guard units from the palace, as illustrated in Levni's *surname*. In a symbolic sense, the four *nahil*s, representing each of the four princes to be circumcised, remain erect and protected within the palace (the domain of purity and royal vitality) and away from the city (the realm of pollution and the ordinary populace).

The *nahil*s are later carried out of the palace and paraded through the city streets by the Tersane Corps, who carry them on portable platforms and parade to the tune of the musicians.[37] Sur Emin Halil Efendi and the deputy commander of the Tersane Corps march in front of the *nahil agasi*.[38] While the *nahil*s are being carried through the streets and alleys, the carpenters who built the gigantic floats demolish any public sites that could obstruct the passage of the *nahil* carriers, as if ceremonially further emphasizing the absolute virility of these ritual objects representing the yet to be circumcised princes.[39] Towards the end of the festivities, once the princes have been circumcised, the *nahil*s are apparently brought back to the palace where they are returned to their stationary position at the sultanate domain.[40]

An important change in the production and development of the *nahil* can be detected in the ensemble of consumable items used for decorating the ritual objects. In the 1582 festivals, the *nahil* was made partly with coloured wax ornaments and partly with sugar. In 1720, this practice continued except that the sugar used to decorate the *nahil* was mixed with other decorative objects, hence making it toxic and inedible. As Faroqhi explains, 'when one considers how expensive and rare a commodity sugar was until the nineteenth century, it becomes clear that these gardens represented conspicuous consumption.'[41] But this, however, remains highly unlikely because, as Faroqhi herself correctly notes, many of the substances used to colour the decorations were toxic, and hence non-edible.

Unlike the pre-1582 festivals, during which the *nahil* was an object of ritual consumption insofar as the decoration and sugar used were edible and distributed to the crowd at the end of the procession, the eighteenth-century makeup of the *nahil* consisted of non-edible substances. In fact, in the eighteenth century the *nahil* pageantry became less sophisticated in its decorative appearance and simpler in its spectacular features, for it was created mainly from gold and silver, which are clearly inedible. Here, there is a clear progression in the making of *nahil*s from being ritual articles for ceremonial consumption to being processional theatrical objects to display for spectacular purposes.

Why did this happen? What does the development of the *nahil* from an edible to a non-edible decorative object signify in the context of the change that took place in the imperial circumcision ceremonies? What political symbolic implications does it entail? And how does this transformation at the symbolic core of the circumcision ritual highlight changes in the Ottoman theatre state in the late seventeenth and early eighteenth centuries?

## From blessing to solidarity: a symbolist interpretation of imperial circumcision rituals

In *Purity and Danger,* Mary Douglas focuses on pollution in an intriguing analysis of food taboos.[42] Religious symbols, she argues, provide a sense of identity, the production of a sense of communal solidarity. This is attained through enacting symbolic and performative activities that are related to concrete aspects of collective demeanour in everyday life, constructing crucial boundary makers in determining who could belong to a particular communal group, while excluding others in the process. Among the most fundamental and significant of these is the communal act of consumption – the culture of the production, preparation and consumption of food.

According to Douglas, the prohibition of food consumption is directly linked to spiritual pollution. This means that spiritual impurity cannot be understood detached from a system of symbols, ideas and values that are linked to social boundaries defining purity and identity. Purity, in this regard, can be defined as an attribute of something that can facilitate a perceived unitary, universal order of existence. Whatever disturbs that order of perceived coherence is at odds with it, and hence causes impurity best embodied in the form of 'dirt' (taboo); and whatever objects or creatures meet the stipulated requirements of their respective categories in the cosmos of order are identified as pure and spiritually clean.

Combining features of central Asiatic (animistic and shamanistic) and Irano-Mesopotamian (Islamic) cultural practices, the Ottoman circumcision ceremonies highlight a fascinating case of production and reproduction of purity and blessing through the public display of the future sultan's body, most notably his most sacred male entity, his phallus, symbolized in the form of a handsomely decorated wooden pole, the *nahil*. It can be argued, albeit in the absence of ethnographic evidence, that the Ottoman circumcision *nahil* ostensibly represents an uncircumcised phallus. As the processions begin at the Eski Saray, where the sweetened gardens are also placed, the *nahil*s remain erect, beautifully ornamented with sugar and decorated with animals and plants representing the purity of the young prince and his reproductive power to renew life prior to his ritual circumcision.

The first point I want to make is that in a number of ways the symbolism of the event occurring at the Old Palace marks an initial process in which the symbolized (uncircumcised) phallus of the prince, though potentially a source of power, still lacks royal strength and virility; its power needs to be actualized through the sacred initiation rite of circumcision, in which the young, uncircumcised prince is transformed into a mature sultan. This perhaps explains why royal guards continue to protect the four *nahils*. The reason to protect the *nahils* is not because of any actual threat to the symbol of sultanate virility, since it is hard to imagine that the wooden poles at the royal palace would be under any danger from outside the court. It appears that such protection is provided mainly for symbolic purposes.

The guards protect the *nahils*, the purist and vital part of the future sultan, as the prince awaits the inevitable act of circumcision. The protection of the *nahil* marks the eventual promise of victory of the supernatural strength of the ancestor sultanate body over the world of nature, symbolized by the consumption of natural products (sugar and the symbolic display of animals) decorating the *nahil*. What is more, there is a striking temporal connection between the presence of the physical domestic realm (royal palace), where the *nahils* are kept in the maternal domain of the *valide sultan*, the mother of the young prince, and the eventual expectation of an outward journey to an outer world (city spaces), as the wooden poles are paraded in the streets outside of the palace.

As in 1582, the *nahils* are taken out of the palace nine days before the ceremony is due to begin. During this period, the ritual objects are sweetened for both eating and decorative purposes in preparation for the dynastic male figure's journey from the domesticated court to the public civic sphere. The initial ritual processions involve a series of ceremonial preparations for taking the young prince away from the world of women and introducing him to the outer world of the public, where, after the royal surgeon or *jerah* has performed the violent operation of circumcision, he will have to share the strength of the sacred royal domain with others. In many ways the link between the royal palace and public domain seems crucial to the circumcision rituals because such a link would also enable the Ottoman public to participate in the act of removing the young prince from the field of matrilineal vitality to masculine virility, and receiving his blessing for the first time.

By and large, the Old Palace also identifies the domain of ancestral authority. The use of sugar for the *nahil* is not just to signify a festive event, as in the case of wedding ceremonies (another purity ritual), but to represent a type of performative ritual of purity that in a stationary position indicates the royal ancestral vitality of the Old Palace, where the spirits of the sultans, the paternal ancestors of the young prince, continue to dwell and maintain a boundary between themselves and the world of the outside populace. But it is with the mix of the future sultan's purity and power, embodied in the *nahil*, that the public too expects to receive a blessing from the royal court, the sacred domain of the sultan and his ancestors. The festivities, in the form of the *nahil* processions, can be seen not merely as a masquerade performed with great shows of ecstasy, but also as a celebration of the ancestral blessing that the act of circumcision would bring to the community at large.

Here, the symbolism of descent plays a crucial role in the circumcision procession. This is because descent is the display of the total social unit, a transcendental force that extends beyond the here and now. The *nahil* represents more than the symbolic union between the ancestors and the living young sultan, depicted in its stationary and erect form. The image of generational shift through the process of individual biological ageing undergoes an identical transfer of blessing for all descent-group members, including those living outside the royal palace. It is in this sense that the Old Palace, partly representative of personalized maternal virility, must be left in order for the prince to obtain maturity and royal strength. This must be done so as to ensure an important ancestral transition from the inside (domestic) to the outside (public) world, where an individual prince will mature and gain virility by becoming part of the depersonalized outside realm of the public. Inherent in the domestic domain is the ambiguous maternal–paternal guardianship as a source of ancestral authority over the yet to be circumcised prince.

## NAHILS, CIRCUMCISION RITUALS AND THE THEATRE STATE

The following description of an odd ritual in the course of the 1582 circumcision celebration of Murad's son Mehmed by Joseph von Hammer-Purgstall highlights the ambiguous ancestral nature of the Old Palace.

> The musicians of the sultana, widow of Sokolli, put on a kind of mythological pantomime; accompanied by the harmony of cymbals, lutes, and violins, a hired assassin approached a young child disguised as Cupid, and tried to seize him, at first using flattery, then force; but a young girl, armed with a javelin like a nymph of Diana or an Amazon, intervened at the moment, drove off the audacious aggressor, and saved the young child. [43]

This performative display, where a female protector defends and rescues a young boy from an immediate threat, underlines the authority of the young prince's female guardians, who are acknowledged as significant carriers of ancestral authority, housed in the Old Palace, in the course of the ceremonies.[44] This dramatic representation was sponsored by Ismihan Sultan, the prince's aunt, and indicates that the female elders of the court play a special role in the orchestration of the festivals, as protectors of the dynasty's heir as he enters public life. The maternal feature of the dynastic life is reassured when circumcision finally occurs and the young prince's foreskin is carried to his mother on a gold plate.[45] The foreskin symbolizes a new beginning in the prince's life, as the maternal guardian or the *valide sultan* now receives a disjointed bodily part of the prince, representing the uninitiated life of the prince embodied in the spiritless foreskin – a prince who no longer lives under the protection of his mother.

When the hypothesis of purity and danger, as defined by Douglas, is applied to imperial circumcision rituals, the *nahil* can be seen as a symbolic act of ancestral blessing. By this I mean that the ways in which this pyramid-like ritual object embodies the purity of the sultan's body at its most basic and elementary –

sugary and sweet, a source of strength – binds the eternal soul of the sultan's ancestral authority, shared by the prince's mother and father, to the profane world of the public. Symbolically, it is the sultan's essential male body part that the *nahil* represents, signifying his chivalric status as the male figurehead of the community.

How ideology is produced through the circumcision festival has been illuminated by Victor Turner in his famous study of the ritual process, though Turner reaches a different set of conclusions from the interpretation I am applying to this case. According to Turner, a rite of passage can be seen as a movement or process from structure to anti-structure, and back once more to structure. The anti-structural or *liminal*, 'betwixt-and-between', identifies a middle stage in an initiation ritual that is indefinable and consists of aspects of both purity and profanity. The structural, when a ritual process begins, identifies the orderly though a yet to be actualized identity of an individual or community that undergoes a process of subjective transformation. The movement away from the liminal towards the structural, however, reassures the system of ranks, offices, organization and hierarchy used to order society in a more enhanced form. The final point of a ritual process, its end journey, then is the reaffirmation of a society's power structure and of the ideals of a given community.[46]

While a lack of ethnographic data and textual evidence make it impossible to deal with the sequence of the ceremonies in detail here, there are three aspects of these ceremonies on which I would like to comment briefly. First, as mentioned earlier, the *nahil*'s stationary position at the Old Palace can be recognized as a structural medium through which the phallus of the sultan, in its most purified, though untouched (uncircumcised) form, is set up and prepared (even protected) for the upcoming ceremonies. Second, the days of the ceremonies (both in the 1582 and 1720 versions) include a *nahil* parade that lasted for an entire week. Much of this period can be seen as an act of blessing in that the participants in the ritual are celebrating the continuity of the community in ceremonial ways that show the power of the future sultan, with the promise of virility in the shape of a phallic-like object, displayed and paraded in the festival grounds and streets of the capital city, where people celebrate and cherish its presence with carnival festivities.

The third final stage, the super-structural phase, includes a period in which the *nahils* are returned to the palace from where the processions originally began. This is to suggest a moment of return, a homecoming to which a community blessed by the sultan's virile power embodied in the *nahil* can now enjoy the presence of a yet to be circumcised prince and symbolically participate in the making of a new sultan. The consumption of the *nahil*, as it is paraded through the streets, serves to demonstrate how the sultan's body in its most blessed and yet elementary form can be shared by the community and consumed (internalized) by other members of the community during the processions. This is also indicative of how sacred vitality can be transformed to other members of the community, to the royal subjects of the sultan and to the upper strata of the court, with the sultan's body embodying elements of a permanent institutional structure upon which Ottoman society depends.

This two-way process, an outer and inner movement, culminates in a final violent event, the circumcision of the young prince within the native, domestic domain, governed and controlled by the prince's mother, namely the royal palace (as evident in both the 1582 and 1720 cases). Though a pre-Islamic institution, throughout Islamic history circumcision rituals have been performed either to signify the purification of the young or as an initiation rite, a reception into a religious community of believers.[47] Adulthood is attained by committing an act of violence on the body and, more importantly, the fertile and most 'private' part, the foreskin of the phallus in the case of boys and genital mutilation in the case of girls.

As Arnold van Gennep explained, features of fertility in circumcision rites underline the reason why the ceremonies show a striking similarity with bridal processions. The use of *nahil* for both circumcision and bridal processions, as in the case of the 1539 circumcision festivals, suggests strong symbolic reference to fertility and biological reproduction in the course of the two distinct types of initiation rites.[48] For this reason circumcision was also a fertility ceremony for the Ottomans, an event of regeneration, in terms of a 'wedding of the soul', with overtones of rebirth of life and resurgence of vitality.[49]

A striking feature of the ceremony, and indicative of the public significance of the performance, is that a number of ordinary (non-royal) boys are circumcised along with the young prince. This collective performance of circumcision highlights the union the sultan and his sons make with the (future) Ottoman society, personified in the common boys, a union that involves an initiation ceremony or rite of passage towards creating a more unified collectivity and affirming communal solidarity. In these rituals, the political underlines a type of ritual process in which collective identity is constructed through the symbolic performance of collective violence (public circumcision).

The most fascinating feature of the *nahil* symbolism is the use of animals and flowers to decorate the phallic object. The symbolic display of flowers and animals is indicative of the virility of the young prince, which through the performance of circumcision blossoms, so to speak, a new, strengthened form of vitality. The symbolism of such natural objects is crucial to the rituals, since it highlights the symbolic conquest of natural vitality for the strengthening of supernatural virility promised for the young prince and shared by the community.

The significance of such symbolism can be recognized in a 1582 official invitation letter to Ottoman dignitaries, poetically identifying the young prince as a 'new plant' and blossoming 'flower'. Consider the following passage from the invitation:

> We have consequently resolved to accomplish the precept relative to the act of circumcision, the person of prince Mehmed our well beloved son; of this prince who, covered with the protective wings of celestial grace and divine

assistance, believes in felicity and in good grace, in the glorious path of the imperial throne ... of this prince who is the most beautiful of the flowers of the garden of equity and of sovereign power; the most precious sprout of the garden of grandeur and majesty; the pearl of the most fine pearliness of monarchy and supreme felicity; finally the most luminous star of the firmament of serenity, calm, and of the public happiness. Thus the august personage of this prince, the plant of his existence, having already had some happy enlargements in the garden of virility and force, and the tender shrub of his essence making already a superb ornament in the vineyard of prosperity and grandeur, it is necessary that the vine-trimmer of circumcision work his sharp instrument on this new plant, on this charming rose bush, and that he direct it towards the vegetative knob which is the chief of the reproductive faculties, and the bud of precious fruits and fortunate sprouts in the great orchard of the Caliphate and of supreme power.[50]

There are two salient ideas present in the above letter that deserve analysis. First and foremost, the metaphoric use of the terms 'plant', 'rose bush', 'precious fruits and fortunate sprouts' is clearly symbolic of the inherent purity of the young prince, which the act of circumcision aims to reinforce or further purify for the 'garden' of the sultanate (ancestral authority), which is 'already a superb ornament in the vineyard of prosperity and grandeur'. In other words, the young prince requires a 'vine-trimmer' so that his purity based on royal birth can be ensured as he matures and grows older. Second, the act of directing the circumcision 'towards the vegetative knob' is meant to signify the regeneration of virility in gaining the ancestral fertility depicted in the 'great orchard of the Caliphate'.

Here blessing and reproduction remain inseparable. Accordingly, the metaphoric use of natural objects is crucial to the way the ceremonies are described, since they highlight the symbolic embodiment of natural vitality for the expansion of 'sovereign power' in terms of supernatural protection ('celestial grace') promised for the young prince, ensuring the extension of royal blood for generations to come. The symbolic ritual extension of royal virility remains central here.

But this symbolic ritual feature appeared to undergo a dramatic transformation between the late sixteenth and the early eighteenth centuries. As I indicted earlier, the *nahils* of the 1582 ceremonies were most likely to have been made of edible objects, mainly sugar and fruits, which the greater population would have been able to consume. This, I suggested, brings to light the earliest formation of the Ottoman theatre state, in which the royal subjects can participate in the vitality of the sultan by consuming a personal part of his body, symbolized in the form of a wooden pole. The 1720 *nahils*, however, appear to be made of non-consumable components. This, I argued, testifies to the expansion of the Ottoman theatre state into an impersonal repertoire of ceremonial pageantry in which the sultan's son and his symbolized body in the form of a *nahil*, had to be kept apart from the populace. Though paraded in the public streets, signifying the affirmation of power embodied in the yet to be circumcised prince and a future sultan, the 1720 *nahils* solidly remained a property of the palace, inedible and detached from the community, the urban domain.

With the continuing presence of guild processions in early eighteenth-century pageants, it is most likely that the growing authority of Ottoman society also contributed to this ritual symbolic development. For the most part, the eighteenth-century version of the ceremony represents a political ritual that involves greater state pomp amid the presence of the guild parades, representing communal authority in the course of a sultanate state ritual. What the *nahil* of the 1720 ceremonies identifies is the symbolized version of the sultan's power, paraded alongside a powerful social sector of Ottoman society, the guild associations.

With the transformation of the elaborated *nahil* into a more simplified gold and silver object, the imperial circumcision processions reflect increased impersonalization of the Ottoman theatre state, a ritual process that performatively dramatizes state power in distinction from societal performances of guild pageantry. To what extent the popularity of the royal circumcision rituals faded during the late eighteenth and nineteenth centuries is not clear. They definitely lost the prominence they once had in earlier centuries. For the most part, though, one can claim that the eighteenth century saw significant changes in state and collective identity formation processes of Ottoman history in the ritual symbolic medium of the *nahil*, where power was both *enacted* and *represented* to affirm state authority and social solidarity.

*A comparative note on the Ottoman and Safavid theatre state*
As Abou-El-Haj correctly suggested, to overcome the notion that the Ottoman state and society were unique, it is crucial to engage in a comparative study with other histories. Although the rise of the early modern European absolutist monarchies maintain an important point of comparison, the development of the Safavid state, a neighbouring Muslim empire to the east of the Ottomans, in the seventeenth century deserves serious comparative analysis.

Consider the Muharram rituals performed in commemoration of the martyrdom of Muhammad's beloved grandson Husayn on the plains of Karbala in 680. These commemorative ceremonies, consisting of various ritual activities including self-mortification and lamentation processions, began to spread rapidly in Iran under the Safavids in the early sixteenth century. The declaration by Shah Isma'il I (1501–24) of Imami Shi'ism as the state religion of Iran in 1501 put into effect a systematic attempt by the new regime to introduce what John R. Perry calls the 'territorialization of a state cult'.[51] Built as it is around the symbols of martyrdom and a militant ethos of fortitude, the state patronage of the rituals introduced a new dimension of public procession, *shabih*, initiating radical transformations of the ceremonies in the form of political performative events.[52] Muharram ceremonies became increasingly sophisticated as a public representation of political power towards the mid-sixteenth century with the expansion of the Safavid state under the reign of Shah Tahmasb (1524–76). The ceremonies then became associated with the state, shaping the Safavid theatre state in the early seventeenth century.

The most interesting development in the ceremonies is the state introduction of camel sacrifice rituals in the early seventeenth century. These rituals consisted of a ceremonial procession in which a camel was walked around the city for nine days, then taken to the outskirts of the city and slaughtered. The public procession takes place in the presence of the shah and his officials and with their direct involvement. The ceremonies end in the public display of ritual battles between urban religious guilds during which the winning team places the head of the camel in the ceremonial Tower of Skulls in the centre of Isfahan, where all the hunted heads of animals are kept, forming a high of tower of skulls.

As I have argued elsewhere, these processions identify a three-stage ritual: an allegorical hunting game, emerging from the realm of the sacred (city); then proceeding towards a violent assault against the purity of the shah lost in the camel and the pollution embodied in the animal; and finally ending with the slaughter and consumption as conquest over an imagined adversary (notably the Ottomans) in terms of expansion into aggression and war. On the two dimensions of spatial and temporal development, the sacrificial rituals reveal a significant political symbolism in which the participants regain a relinquished vitality in the performance of ritual consumption, a practice that ultimately affirms the immortality of the state as a transcendent entity.[53]

But how can we compare the development of *nahil* in Ottoman circumcision rituals with the cultural practices of the Safavid state in camel sacrifice ceremonies? There is a fascinating common symbolic element in these two rituals. As in the case of Safavid Muharram camel rituals, the meat of the animal is ritually consumed by the guilds as an indication that the sacred vitality of the shah is distributed among (both male and female) members of the community. Ambiguously, the camel represents not only the shah (in the initial phase of the ritual process), but also an imagined adversary (in the second and final stage of the ritual process), notably the Uzbeks and Ottomans, in which the act of slaughter and consumption finally affirms a complete victory over the enemy. As in the case of Ottoman circumcision rituals, the *nahil* too represents royal (sultanate) authority in its purist form. The consumption of the *nahil*'s decorative sugar and fruit parts signifies how the sultan's vitality is internalized by the (mostly male) members of the community. The *nahil*, like the camel, manifests royal sacredness in its most corporeal features: the phallus of the sultan (in the case of *nahil*); the bride of the shah (in the case of the camel as a sacrificial animal).

Both ceremonies also indicate the ceremonial ways in which state power can be put on display through consumption rituals and fertility symbols. In a sense, it is interesting to note here that the camel, like the *nahil*, also represents a fertility symbol. The only difference though is that the female camel used for the Safavid Muharram ceremonies undergoes a process of pollution as it leaves the city (Isfahan), whereas the *nahil* ritual objects in Ottoman circumcision festivals not only retain their purity, but also increase their purifying and regenerative power once they are returned to the palace.

The key issue here is the way ritual plays a central role in the production of Ottoman and Safavid theatre state from the late sixteenth to the early eighteenth centuries. Both states represent and enact power in diverse symbolic ritual mediums, as the royal authority grows increasingly powerful and detached from societal urban sectors. The transformation in the dramatization of symbols used in the Ottoman circumcision and Safavid Muharram rituals highlights the increasing theatrical aspect of the two territorial states in the late seventeenth and eighteenth centuries.

*Conclusion*
The above interpretation of the circumcision rituals is intended to show how Ottoman state power expanded in a complex set of cultural practices. The development of the *nahil* from the late

sixteenth to the early eighteenth centuries underlines this expansion in its apparent symbolic transformation from an edible to a non-edible ritual object. This, I argued, underlined changes in relations between the Ottoman state and society, in which an increase in the use of non-edible materials in making the *nahil* in the 1720 version of the ceremony signified a separation of the sultanate theatre state from Ottoman society, represented by the guild sector. The eighteenth century identifies the consolidation of the Ottoman theatre state in the dramatization of its symbolic repertoires in its inconsumable manifestation, through which the representation of power is enhanced in terms of a symbolic segregation of royal power from the urban populace in the course of the ceremonies.

In broad theoretical terms, therefore, by focusing on the imperial circumcision ceremonies I have aimed to show how ritual drama and ceremonial performance can be seen as a major cultural site in the production (and reproduction) of state and society relations. At the historical level, I stressed how the study of early modern Ottoman state-building should also entail a study of ritual transformations, in which power is ultimately represented and enacted in complex symbolic ways. The early eighteenth-century circumcision rituals, therefore, serve to illustrate how the Ottoman theatre state experienced considerable transformation through the ritual expansion of state power amid the bustle of civic societal life.

## Chapter 5
# Janissary Coffee Houses in Late Eighteenth-Century Istanbul
*Ali Çaksu*

Recently, serious attention has been paid to the institutions of the Ottoman coffee house and of the Janissaries, but to the best of my knowledge there is no separate study on *Janissary coffee houses*.[1] Given the importance of both institutions in Ottoman history – the Janissary in the military and political life of the empire, and the coffee shop in its public and cultural life – the Janissary coffee house is an important aspect of Ottoman history that is yet to be explored. It would be interesting to see how the institutions of the Janissary and the café, the former military and the latter primarily civic, came together, not in opposition, but to reinforce one another.

This chapter constitutes a preliminary enquiry into Janissary use of the institution of the coffee shop and the multiple roles the café performed for this military group. I suggest that beyond the usual repertoire of activities that took place in civilian coffee shops, such as entertainment, gossip, political discussions, literary exchanges and concerts (all of which also took place in Janissary coffee shops), the Janissary coffee shop seems to have functioned as a site for other seemingly irreconcilable activities like policing, racketeering, Sufi rituals and even the provision of lodgings. Given that Janissaries ran a significant number of Istanbul's numerous coffee shops, it is not enough to understand the role of the coffee shop without looking into its uses by the Janissaries, and it would be impossible to understand the Janissaries in the late Ottoman period without exploring one of their most important haunts.[2] While I do not claim that this study is definitive, I do hope that it will spark further research into this important topic.

Before exploring the various functions of the Janissary coffee shop, I shall present a brief history of the Janissaries in the early modern period to show how this once elite military corps, famed for its formidable military skill, discipline and organization, came to be involved in such an earthly and mundane enterprise as the business of coffee shops.

Despite their small numbers, for a long time the Janissaries formed the backbone of the Ottoman empire's armed forces.[3] Their discipline, efficiency and unique contribution have left an indelible mark on both Ottoman and European history.[4] Generally of slave origin, most members of the Janissary had been recruited as children from the non-Muslim populations of the empire through what is called the *devşirme* system. They would be isolated from the urban civilian populace and given special training in the art of warfare and the precepts of the Islamic religion. They were the sultan's elite troops and he was considered their head. Although in principle they were kept in relative isolation from the rest of the population, about 31 of the 196 Janissary *orta*s (battalions) were assigned duties that brought them into contact with the urban populace of Istanbul through, for example, security, law and order or other municipal tasks in the city.[5] Each *orta* would be assigned to one of the capital city's districts and would operate out of a *kolluk*, which corresponded to a modern-day police station. Often, a Janissary café would be situated next to a *kolluk*, and sometimes an existing café would even double as a *kolluk*.[6] Thus, even before the collapse of the *devşirme* system, which will be dealt with presently, the Janissary did have contact with the urban civilian population and, like them, used the coffee house as a primary site of sociability.

When the *devşirme* system finally came to an end in the eighteenth century, the institution suffered a breakdown in discipline and vigour and began to lose its original elite status.

Meanwhile, the worsening economic situation, which entailed a significant decrease in Janissary salaries, forced the previously self-sufficient soldiers to engage in income-generating activities that fell outside their military functions. At this point, the Janissaries were no longer subject to the original rules of the corps, such as celibacy and non-engagement in regular civic trades. Therefore, not only did Janissaries begin to get married and have families, for which they had to provide, but they also obtained permission to engage in several kinds of civilian services, trades and businesses, which rendered them eligible to join the urban *esnaf*, or guilds. However, this 'esnafization' of the Janissaries was not a one-way process; it opened the door for the 'Janissarization' of the *esnaf*, whereby members of the guilds started to acquire military status and the privileges that went with it.[7] The increase in membership to the corps inflated the number of Janissaries to 200,000, which was far too many to accommodate in the barracks. Consequently, many Janissaries took up lodging in bachelor rooms, inns, coffee houses and public baths.[8] Not unexpectedly, it was roughly around this time that Janissaries became more heavily involved in the coffee house business.[9] This new situation had a significant impact on the socio-economic life of the capital as well as on the Janissary corps. Not only did Janissaries become very involved in the social and cultural life of the city, but they also continued to meddle in the affairs of the state.

Armed and generally discontented, Janissaries, as we shall see later in this chapter, were involved in several rebellions; they became a thorn in the side of the state and were seen as the most seditious element of the urban population. Some modern scholars have suggested that in the seventeenth and eighteenth centuries the Janissaries' political activities constituted a sort of counterbalance in favour of the people against the arbitrariness of state power, and that they became a formidable social force that provided a check against absolutism.[10] This view was also expressed earlier, only a few decades after the state finally disassembled the corps: 'It was the sight of thousands of Janissary bodies rotting in the Golden Horn which have made our people unable to speak their mind since the Vak‛a-i Hayriyye [the event when the Janissary corps was dismantled], for the Janissaries provided a countervailing force to the oppression of officials.'[11]

However, while the Janissaries reflected and represented the urban population's concerns and complaints, they also felt no inhibitions about intimidating and bullying people if they felt so inclined. Through their engagement in all kinds of illegal and criminal activities, some of which we see treat later in this chapter, the population's attitude towards the Janissaries was, at best, ambivalent. So, while the Janissaries mitigated state despotism in favour of the people, their integration in, and acceptance by, the populace was never complete.[12]

Given the relentlessness of the Janissaries' political disturbances and intimidation of the population, the ruling elite became convinced that no amount of reform could transform the Janissary corps into an effective military defender of the empire in the modern world.[13] Therefore, in 1826, in an event official Ottoman historiography terms the 'auspicious incident' (Vak‛a-i Hayriyye), the corps was finally and tragically dismantled.[14] The Janissaries' coffee shops, which as we shall see shortly functioned as the headquarters of Janissary political and criminal activities, shared the Janissary corps' inauspicious fate at the hands of the 'auspicious incident'.

Janissary coffee shops in Istanbul varied in size.[15] Some were so luxurious and opulently furnished and decorated that they became the subject of poetic praise.[16] They were generally established in places that had the best views; many of them were built on the city walls overlooking the sea or on columns erected in the sea. Some of these coffee houses, which resembled palace *divanhânes* (reception rooms), were built by renowned architects of the time and furnished by master carpenters.[17] For instance, we are informed that the Janissary coffee house at Çardak İskelesi (Çardak Wharf) was designed by an architect from the famous Ottoman Armenian Balyan family.[18] Sometimes one *orta* might own a few cafés, or one Janissary officer might have more than one coffee shop.[19] What marked Janissary coffee houses was the insignia (*nişân*) of the *orta*, which would be placed above both the entrance to the coffee house and the hearth. Janissary coffee house customers were usually Janissaries of various ranks and their associates.[20] According to some sources, non-Janissaries also visited these cafés and, in fact, the owner sometimes *made* them visit so that the latter's income might increase.[21] In some coffee houses, at least at the famous Çardak coffee house, visitors of various ethnic and religious origins frequented the place.[22]

It is difficult to know exactly why the coffee house business was so popular with Janissaries, but I can venture a few suggestions. First, as a business, running a coffee house was not too demanding; it required no particular skills, training or apprenticeship, so anyone with sufficient capital could open a café. Second, since coffee houses did not impinge on, or meet the objections of, businesses that were associated with well-organized guilds, the guilds allowed the coffee shop business to mushroom. Third, the café offered an appropriate place in which the *orta* spirit (regiment solidarity) could survive and flourish, which was of utmost importance to Janissaries in an environment outside their natural habitat – the barracks. Finally, and most importantly for this study, the café provided an adaptable place in which to house and absorb multiple activities. Beyond the 'regular' coffee shop activities usually associated with the cultural and social life of an urban civilian populace, like literary or musical exchanges and other forms of entertainment,[23] the Janissary coffee shop also housed activities that fell within the Janissaries' specific cultural requirements, such as the practice of Bektashism, and official duties like policing and market inspections. Furthermore, the coffee shop was also an ideal place in which to organize and carry out activities that 'exceeded' both 'regular' functions and official duties and that fell within the domain of the seditious, the intimidating and the unlawful. The following is an exposition of some of the functions of the Janissary coffee house as they are related to activities specific to the Janissaries.

## Functions of the Janissary coffee house

*As a centre of rebellion and 'sedition'*
Perhaps the most important role of the coffee house in general, and the Janissary café in particular, was in the sphere of politics, which rendered them a target of the authorities. 'Devlet sohbeti', literally 'state talk', is the term used in the sources to refer to the political discussions that by and large took place in coffee houses. Such 'talk' disturbed officials who regarded it with suspicion and, due to its potential impact on the people, perceived it as a threat to the existing order.[24] These political discussions included rumours ranging from the corruption of a certain pasha, changes in the cabinet to the possibility of war. In an age when illiteracy was rife, rumours were a very important means of communication, and they had a capacity to influence and orient public opinion, when the public was not supposed to have an opinion, about political matters. The authorities would habitually close down coffee shops, often using some non-political excuse. The famous court historian Na'îmâ's complaints about the coffee shop are a good example of official disdain for such establishments. He states that coffee houses are places where people assembled to criticize men of rank and invent false rumours about state affairs, appointments and dismissals. Lest such gatherings lead to conspiracy, Murad IV patrolled the city day and night, keeping smokers and coffee drinkers under close scrutiny. His displeasure extended even to ordering coffee houses to be torn down.[25] When coffee was first introduced in the sixteenth century, it was 'considered harmful for political reasons and *fetva*s were therefore issued against it'.[26] In 1826 Mehmed Dâniş Bey made a similar complaint in his *Netîcetü'l-Vekâyiᶜ*. According to him, coffee houses (and incidentally barber shops) were places of 'false rumours', 'baseless talk' and 'various news regarding serious state affairs' and therefore they often had to be closed down. Nevertheless, they invariably reopened and became so popular and widespread that in some districts their numbers began to exceed those of the houses and other shops.[27]

Although political discussions were not confined to Janissary establishments, Janissary coffee houses were particularly seditious and politically volatile places, simply because Janissaries possessed the means of coercion and could put words into action. As an armed urban force with a clear sense of group identity, the Janissary constituted a might to be reckoned with. Cemal Kafadar has demonstrated that the very existence of the Janissaries as a substantial physical force in the capital meant that parties struggling for political power would invariably try to form an alliance with them.[28]

The insufficient salaries they received from the state was a particular source of resentment among Janissaries. Although some Janissaries found other means of earning an income, the salary of a senior Janissary 'was not enough to take a bath in a public bath' or rent a room, let alone provide a livelihood.[29] Members of newly established units like Nizâm-ı Cedîd received high salaries, by contrast, which made the Janissaries look upon them with envy and resentment.[30] This created an atmosphere of mutual distrust and hatred, and facilitated the circulation of 'conspiracy theories' by both the Janissaries and the elites, some of which were spun in coffee shops.[31] Thus, dissatisfied and resentful of being replaced by new troops, the Janissaries were prone to sedition and rebellion. And their plots were often hatched in coffee shops.

The connection between Janissaries, sedition and coffee shops is not confined to discontent and political plotting; it includes also the presence of yet another subversive element, the immigrants who took refuge in Janissary coffee shops and bachelor rooms and who ultimately became members of the corps.[32] It was not 'coincidental that bachelors' chambers in the city were either owned by the Janissary coffee house proprietors or built nearby these coffee houses'.[33] According to a study by Ahmed Yaşar, Janissary recruitment of migrants from rural areas was an important cause of city banditry.[34] Following their relatives or fellow townsmen, these migrants shared ethnic or regional origins, took up the same jobs and resided in or visited the same cafés.[35] Thus, occupational, regional and ethnic solidarity were forged among new immigrants. Together with the pre-existing *orta* spirit, this social cohesion probably made migrants, Janissaries and migrant-Janissaries act together to promote their common interest and benefit regardless of the laws and norms of the society. Hundreds of incidents recorded in the chronicles testify that these people constituted one of the most seditious groups.[36]

Indeed, not only did Janissary coffee shops embrace marginal newcomers but they also became centres of discontent and grievance. For instance, in the short tenure of the mighty grand vizier Alemdar Mustafa Pasha in 1808, some of those who were beaten and injured by the vizier's bodyguards came to Janissary coffee houses to complain about the incident and the government's general behaviour. The vizier received death threats, and Janissaries finally assassinated him.[37]

Thus, armed and generally discontented, the Janissaries became an especially volatile and threatening force. And, when the mighty 'servitors of the Sultan' decided to rebel, they were not only capable of changing governments and high-ranking officials ranging from grand viziers to their own commander-in-chief (*Janissary ağa*), but also to dethrone the sultan. In the eighteenth and nineteenth centuries, the coffee shop happened to be one of those sites connected to Janissary rebellions. The famous Patrona Halil rebellion of 1730 is a case in point. The rebellion reflected and articulated the resentment of some sectors of society suffering poverty, injustice, corruption and neglect,[38] and it was sparked off in a Janissary coffee house,[39] which the insurgents took as a meeting place where they could find sympathetic support among fellow artisans, street vendors and Janissaries.[40] As it happened, Kahveci Ali Ağa, the closest friend of the rebellion leader Patrona Halil, was the *çorbacı* (head of the Janissary *orta*) of the *kolluk* at Çardak İskelesi. He ran what undoubtedly was going to become the infamous coffee house belonging to the 56th *orta*.[41] Also, in the Kabakçı Mustafa revolt in 1807, Segban Başçavuşu Mustafa Ağa, an active figure in the event, ran a coffee house at Atpazarı. Likewise, Janissary coffee houses were hot spots during the 1826 rebellion and many Janissary coffee house owners or keepers were executed (some even in front of their own coffee houses) because of their active involvement in the events.[42] Yet another example is Canbaz Kürd Yusuf, who was actively involved in the 1826 uprising and was eventually executed. During the uprising he is said to have met Janissaries in a Janissary coffee house at Sepetçiler to exhort them into action.[43] In short, Ottoman official fear of and displeasure with Janissary coffee houses was warranted and well-placed.

As mentioned above, the authorities were extremely disturbed by Janissary coffee shops, but were incapable of getting rid of them.[44] As the nineteenth-century author Mehmed Dâniş Bey informs us, if any of their coffee houses were demolished, sedition would immediately break out.[45] As a matter of fact, from the middle of the seventeenth century onwards, instead of banning all the coffee houses, the state began to close down a few as a deterrent to the others. As Kırlı has suggested in his research on nineteenth-century Istanbul coffee shops, the state's 'compassion', as expressed through 'exemplary punishment' rather than a total ban on cafés, may have been due to its fear of political opposition at the Janissary coffee houses.[46]

But the state's 'tolerance' of the Janissary coffee shop came to an end. The decisive blow given to the Janissaries in the Vakᶜa-i Hayriyye also targeted their coffee houses. According to Mehmed Dâniş Bey, more than 10,000 coffee houses located in the old city and neighbouring places and on both sides of the Bosporus were demolished.[47] Indeed, the state understood that to dismantle an institution it also had to destroy its supporting structures: the coffee shop, which had provided the social cohesion and public discourse that allowed the perpetuation of the Janissary ethos, was finally destroyed.

## As a centre of Bektashism

Although Hacı Bektaş Veli, the founder of the Bektashi Sufi order, may not have even met a Janissary (he may even have died before the establishment of the Ottoman state), Janissary legend had it that he personally had established the Janissary corps and served them soup from the 'holy cauldron' (*kazan*). Both the name of the corps and some of its garments, such as its headgear (*börk*), are also linked to Hacı Bektaş.[48] In an age when almost every occupation and art had a *pîr* (patron-saint), for the military corps a Turcoman *gâzî*, Hacı Bektaş seemed to be the appropriate patron-saint.[49]

With the passage of time, the Janissary corps and Bektashi order became so inextricably linked that they were indistinguishable, so much so that both suffered the same fate. When the state dismantled the Janissary corps, the Bektashi order was abolished, and many of its members were exiled or killed. Like the coffee houses, Bektashi *tekke*s (dervish convents) were closed down and sometimes demolished or converted into other kinds of facilities.[50] Bektashism was not only simply the official order of the corps, but the corps was informed by Bektashi Sufism on all ethical, religious, ritual and even literary matters (the figures of speech used by Bektashi poets entered into the forms and ceremonies of the Janissary).[51] The connection between Janissaries and Bektashis is widely accepted and need not delay us.[52] But, it is the Bektashi presence in Janissary coffee shops that concerns us here.

From early on in the life of the institution, Janissaries were exposed to Bektashi education and culture. Given the role and place of the Bektashi order in the corps, it is not surprising to find very strong Bektashi influence in the coffee houses where Bektashi rituals and symbols had an important place. Bektashi hymns, among others, were often sung. On the walls there were framed inscriptions of Bektashi sayings or prayers. Thus, some even suggest that Janissary coffee houses functioned like Bektashi *tekke*s.[53]

In fact, the Janissary coffee house almost 'embodied' the Bektashi order. Not only did it physically reflect the primacy of the order in the corps by reserving a special sofa inside the coffee shop for the *baba* (head of the order), but the rituals surrounding the opening of a Janissary coffee house were very much a joint affair between the Bektashi order and the Janissaries, thus, confirming the interdependence of the two.

The opening of a Janissary coffee house was marked by a parade that started at Ağakapısı at Süleymaniye, where the Janissary *ağa* had his office.[54] All the members of the *orta* to which the coffee house owner belonged joined the parade, and they were accompanied by the Bektashi *baba* bearing a Sufi axe, a *nefir* (a horn) in his girdle, and a *keşkül* (boat-shaped cup) on his arm. Behind the *baba*, walked an officer of the *orta* who carried the *orta* insignia to the coffee house above his head. On either side walked young barber apprentices and coffee servers, followed by the other members of the *orta*; various high-ranking officers accompanied them. Upon arrival, the Bektashi *baba* would sit on the sofa reserved for him in the coffee shop, and would be fed and served well. The *baba* would spend the night there. When the time came for him to sleep, all the candles would be extinguished in the Bektashi manner except for one, which would continue to burn until morning.

Thus, the old connection between the Bektashi order and Janissary corps was retained and carried over to the coffee house, which became a site where Bektashism not only continued to be practised, but actually thrived.

*As a business office*
Some Janissary duties in Istanbul were directly related to the economic life of the city. As I mentioned earlier, the 56th *orta* was in charge not only of policing the area around Yemiş İskelesi, but also of regulating the distribution of all foodstuffs entering the capital, including fresh fruit and vegetables, which were unloaded at Çardak İskelesi, right next to the *kolluk* of the 56th *orta*.[55] The *orta* was also officially responsible for supervising the market for timber and other construction materials and fuel for heating. Naturally, the *kolluk* was designated as the *ihtisâb* office – the office responsible for supervising prices and the proper functioning of the market, trade and business. However, what is of note is that the famous Çardak coffee house, or Ellialtı Kahvesi, situated right next to the *kolluk* of the 56th *orta*, was also assigned as an *ihtisâb* office.[56] Thus, the coffee shop was not only near, but at the heart of trading activities and municipal duties.

The location of coffee houses at the nodes of business, trade and commodity distribution allowed some Janissary members not only to oversee the market, but also actually to participate in it and this enabled some of them to become powerful local and international traders. Indeed, 'a large part of foreign commerce, particularly the coastal trade to Syria and Egypt, was in their [Janissary] hands.'[57] It is remarkable that some of these Janissary international traders were also coffee shop owners. The case of a certain Hacı Hâfız, a Janissary trader and coffee house owner at Unkapanı, is an interesting example. He had a dispute with the admiral, Seydi Ali Paşa, who claimed to be the owner of a small-sized merchant ship that Hacı Hâfız had recently bought. The admiral ordered the ship to be returned to the maritime arsenal. When Hacı Hâfız heard about the order, he gathered together some fellow members of his *orta*, took the ship by force and brought it to Unkapanı, where he tied it up in front of his coffee house.[58] Kahvecioğlu Mustafa Ağa was another example of a café owner cum trader. He was a man of great political influence and he owned a whole fleet of trade ships, which he had acquired through his former post as Tersane Başağası (chief *agha* of the maritime arsenal).[59] One can imagine that the coffee houses owned by traders doubled as business centres where deals were negotiated, contracts drawn up and labour forces recruited.[60] If the coffee house could function as a market inspection office, why not as a business centre?

Janissary involvement with trade and business is obvious. And it is also clear that many of those Janissaries who dealt with trade and business also owned coffee houses. One, therefore, may surmise that in addition to providing an extra income to their owners, they provided Janissary traders with a location from which to manage their business activities.

*As a 'mafia' club*
Let us start with the rather cliché statement that Janissaries were famous for being 'bullies'. They were no longer the choicest of the sultan's servants, but they still held posts (such as policing and

commodity distribution) that allowed them some control. This unique position, coupled with the fact that they were armed, meant that the Janissaries were able to intimidate and coerce the urban populace. Known as *zorbas*, some Janissary members led 'gangs' from among their fellow *orta* members. These *zorbas* seem to have found it useful to own coffee shops, for they doubled as 'mafia clubs' from which to conduct their 'business' – and there were many examples of such coffee shops (see appendix).[61]

While, as we have seen above, some distinguished Janissary officers were quite rich, and thus able to establish luxurious coffee houses with marble hearths, richly decorated ceilings and coloured ornamentation, others were less well off.[62] The question is how did the former afford to establish such lavish cafés? The answer is that it was often by unlawful means.

One method of establishing and financing a Janissary coffee shop was through forced 'contributions'. The *zorba* would simply note down the names of the rich and well-known figures (Muslim and non-Muslim) of the district where the coffee shop was to be established, along with the items needed for the new coffee house. A messenger would then be dispatched to the named residents to 'convey greetings' and announce the expected 'gift'.[63] The named resident would then have to send the requested item without hesitation or delay, sometimes personally bringing the item to the coffee house.[64] Furthermore, the cost of the upkeep of the Janissary coffee house would sometimes be provided by forcing all the residents of the area (both rich and poor) to pay racket or protection money.[65] The residents had no choice but to comply because refusal may well have resulted in the person's house being burnt down.

Another method of financing the establishment and maintenance of a coffee house was to raise money through the practice of 'axe-hanging' (*balta asma*). When an axe (*balta*), carrying the insignia of the *orta*, was placed or hung on a commodity or property, it announced 'rightful' proprietorship by the *orta*. Thus, axe-hanging was sometimes plain extortion or wrongful seizure of a commodity or property, and at other times a means of imposing the Janissary's terms and conditions on a business. To cite an example, if a person wanted to build a house in Istanbul, he would need to bribe the *zorba* of his district.[66] If he failed to do so, the *orta*'s axe would be hung on the construction site announcing 'who was in charge', thereby scaring away the construction workers hired for the job, who would be afraid to continue working without the *zorba*'s sanction.[67] Collecting protection money through axe-hanging was a standard method used to establish and maintain Janissary coffee shops.[68]

Such 'mafia'-like activities were not only used to open and maintain coffee shops, but they were also directed *from* these selfsame coffee houses. Thus, *zorba* cafés situated near Istanbul's ports, especially those in the Galata area, were located there precisely to enable the *orta* to survey the movement of trade ships for the purposes of either collecting protection money or establishing a monopoly over the relevant trade or business. Incoming ships would be 'axe-hung' until such time as the terms of the *zorba* had been met.[69] From time to time the state prosecuted those who were involved in this practice and, in spite of fierce opposition from the Janissaries, would have all the 'axes' removed from the ships in order to clamp down on the Janissary's 'mafia' activities at the port.[70]

Another form of 'mafia' activity that involved coffee house owners was debt collection. For example, we have the case of a priest in Istanbul who was unable to collect a debt, so sought the help of Yetimoğlu, a naval officer and coffee house owner. The latter collected the debt and took a 50 per cent cut. Due to a certain misdeed and defiance of official orders, Yetimoğlu was arrested in his coffee house at Sandıkçılar, Galata and taken to the admiral's ship where he was executed in 1811.[71]

Although friendly relations between the members of different *ortas* were not uncommon, competition between the different messes over trade and service monopolies and the 'right' to extortion would cause disputes, and often fierce clashes.[72]

While the great *zorbas* tried to restrict their involvement and activities to particular areas, territorial delimitation sometimes did not meet consensus and would result in the parties concerned having to 'fight it out'.[73] For instance, if an axe hung by an *orta* was removed by another *orta*, then that would immediately trigger a fierce battle in the city between the two gangs, which no authority could prevent.[74] These bloody skirmishes would cause loss of life and, perhaps, the elimination of one or other of the warring parties.[75]

As one might expect, in these wars over monopolies, money racketeering and 'axe-hanging' rights, one of the main sites that were targeted for attack was exactly the *place* that *enabled* the *orta*'s access and control: the Janissary coffee house.[76]

## Conclusion

The economic and political changes that took place in the eighteenth century forced the once elite and relatively isolated Janissary corps out of its barracks and into the city, where it found refuge in the institution of the coffee house. The coffee house business, which was in and of itself easy to establish, not only allowed Janissaries to integrate into the fabric of urban civilian life, but it also enabled them to gain access to and control over the city's markets, businesses and trade. The coffee shop was capacious enough to accommodate the wide range of activities the Janissaries conducted beyond the call of their military duties. In it, not only were they able to engage in the usual repertoire of social, cultural and political activities that took place in 'regular' coffee houses, but they were also able to service their own specific cultural needs and requirements, often associated with promoting the '*orta*-spirit' and practising Bektashism. They were able to continue to perform their policing and market-inspection duties and, above all, to engage in various activities that went beyond the legal and cultural norms set or accepted by the state and society. While the Janissary coffee house was a place in which to drink coffee and smoke tobacco, it was also a cultural salon, a rebel headquarters, a police precinct, a Sufi lodge, a business office and a mafia club all rolled into one.

Table 5.1: *Some Zorba proprietors and their coffee houses*

| Zorba's name | Zorba's coffee house |
| --- | --- |
| Kahvecioğlu Burunsuz Mustafa[77] | Kuledibi Coffee house |
| Darıcalı İbrahim Çavuş[78] | Hendek C. |
| Galatalı Hüseyin Ağa[79] | Çardak İskelesi C. |
| Tiflisli Ali[80] | Toygar Tepesi C. |
| Kız Mustafa | Balaban İskelesi C.[81] |
| Babadağlı[82] | Esir Pazarı C. |
| Sarhoş Mustafa[83] | Hasanpaşa Hanı C. |
| Turnacı Ömer[84] | Irgat Pazarı C. |
| Nahılcı Mustafa[85] | Coffee house at Kumkapı |
| Sekban Başçavuşu Mustafa Ağa[86] | Coffee house at Atpazarı |

## Chapter 6
## The Heart's Desire: Gender, Urban Space and the Ottoman Coffee House
*Alan Mikhail*

A well-known Ḥadīth reported by Ibn Ḥibbān states that 'happiness has four elements: a good wife, a spacious house, a good neighbour, and a comfortable riding beast'.[1] While perhaps this statement by the Prophet Muhammad never crossed the minds of most Ottoman urban residents or coffee house patrons, it points to a relationship between women, the home and the neighbourhood that the Ottoman urban neighbourhood café helps us to elucidate. I argue in what follows that Ottoman urban cafés were important spaces in the geography of Ottoman cities because they serve to highlight and challenge the complex nature of urban space and conceptions of gender in the Ottoman world. Attempting to move beyond café histories that posit the Ottoman coffee house as primarily a site of political subversion, I seek to understand the café as a cultural space of socialization that served multiple functions within the city beyond representing simply a space in which Janissaries could gather and discuss politics.[2] It should be noted at the start that I am concerned mainly with urban neighbourhood coffee houses (*mahalle kahvehaneleri*) rather than with Janissary or guild cafés or with those in small towns or in large commercial complexes known as *khāns*.[3] In other words, I am interested in those cafés in urban quarters of Istanbul, Cairo and Aleppo that were mainstays in the lives of neighbourhood residents, where men would often go to see their friends and to relax in a space near their homes.[4]

When first approaching the Ottoman urban neighbourhood café, we should take care to note that we really have no vocabulary for discussing urban space as it was understood by Ottoman city residents. As Cem Behar notes in his study of one Istanbul neighbourhood, 'It remains that the interface between the public and the private domains in Ottoman cities, and its evolution and its relationship to Ottoman urban culture in general is a topic not yet sufficiently investigated.'[5] We do not know what kinds of spaces were thought of as 'public' or 'private', but it seems clear that these words and the notions they represent prove a hindrance rather than an aid in describing Ottoman cities. Indeed, in her work on the harem, Leslie Peirce shows 'that a dichotomy of public/commonweal/male and private/domestic/female does not work for early modern Ottoman society'.[6] She suggests instead that we centre our discussions on the concepts of inner and outer, or the interior and exterior. The relevant terms in Ottoman Turkish are *iç* or *içeri* for inner or interior and *dış* or *dışarı* (or *taşra*) for outer or exterior.[7] Suggestive also are Gabriel Piterberg's descriptions of the Ottoman usages of 'the garden' and 'the wilderness' as signifiers of Istanbul and the provinces respectively.[8] Alternatively, perhaps we could think in terms of the city in opposition to the palace. Walter Andrews proposes that we examine the 'closely related oppositions of *smooth/striated* space, and *nomadic/royal* approaches to human behaviour'.[9] My goal in raising these differing conceptions of space in the Ottoman empire is not to suggest that we must find a definitive spatial vocabulary. Instead, I want to make the point that these various ideas of space within the Ottoman world existed in concert with one another, and to suggest a rigid conceptualization of space within the Ottoman empire would in all likelihood prove ineffective in describing the vast multiplicity of spaces that made up the Ottoman world. Indeed, we can go even further and posit that no single dichotomization of space could accurately reflect Ottoman urban realities. Building on the ideas of Ottoman space mentioned above and hoping to move beyond simple notions of 'public' versus 'private' or 'male' versus 'female', I seek to show in this chapter how the Ottoman coffee house was a space of overlapping functions in which a spectrum of ambiences and affects fluidly combined to form a complex realm of social interaction.

I should state at the outset that while perhaps initially appealing to historians of coffee houses in the Ottoman world – or anywhere else for that matter – Habermas's arguments about the public sphere prove a hindrance rather than an aid in thinking about Ottoman cafés and their many roles in Ottoman cities.[10] The reason I raise this point at all and offer my own critique of Habermas's formulations is that many Ottoman historians continue to attempt to salvage some form of Habermas's arguments in discussing Ottoman cafés.[11] Habermas's goal in his study is to understand how the conversations of individuals become bases for political action.[12] He thus traces the emergence of a bourgeois public sphere from its beginnings in the meetings of groups of educated and propertied European men through its expansion in the form of large-scale social organizations – such as print media and coffee houses – to its demise. Habermas grounds his arguments firmly in the context of the relationships between capitalism and the state in the seventeenth and eighteenth centuries offering us an alternative way of thinking about the interactions between state and society during this period.

What proves highly problematic in Habermas's account and what is most important for my own arguments in this chapter is Habermas's incessant insistence on 'the line between public and private', which separates the public world of cafés and the market from the private space of the home and family.[13] He writes that 'the model of the bourgeois public sphere presupposed strict separation of the public from the private realm.'[14] What I seek to show in this chapter is that Ottoman coffee houses help to explode this dichotomy between 'the public' and 'the private' (or whatever vocabulary we choose to talk about Ottoman space) proving that this distinction is not tenable in the Ottoman world. Ottoman cafés were at differing moments domestic spaces, places of business and leisure, an extension of the street or market, a venue of entertainment, a space of courtship, an arena of communication, a place in which to read and a realm of distraction. We should not think in terms of lines and boundaries when conceptualizing the Ottoman spaces of which coffee houses were an integral part, but in terms of layers and multiplicity.[15]

Habermas's rendering of the European public sphere and its relations to the early modern coffee house also holds important consequences for women and the relationships between gender and modernity. He writes:

> Critical debate ignited by works of literature and art was soon extended to include economic and political disputes, without any guarantee (such as was given in the *salons*) that such discussions would be inconsequential, at least in the immediate context. The fact that only men were admitted to coffee-house society may have had something to do with this, whereas the style of the *salon*, like that of the rococo in general, was essentially shaped by women.[16]

On the exclusionary mechanisms at work in this account that eliminate from the public sphere women and the lower classes, one commenter writes, 'when women are shut out of the coffee-house they are also, in the terms of this analysis [Habermas's], shut out of a constitutive role in the development of the intellectual and political self-consciousness of the bourgeoisie, the emergence of characteristically modern literary forms and of a reading public, the initiation of democratic forms of participation in society.'[17] As Habermas would have it then, the coffee house was a male institution of the public realm where men with a vested interest in and control over their own caffeinated futures debated rumour, politics and society. Much scholarship on the Ottoman world continues to uphold both the idea of a Habermasian split between 'public' and 'private' and the notion that this 'public' is male. Take the following for example: 'as we try to imagine the social context of culture in the early modern period both in the Ottoman empire and elsewhere, we must keep in mind that public space at the time was male space.'[18] Again, I argue below that Ottoman coffee houses stand in almost complete opposition to these ideas since they were spaces in which men gossiped (perhaps, as I shall show below, more than they rumoured) and, more importantly, in which notions of male *and* female gender were essential to the socializations taking place within them. Through a discussion near the end of this chapter of Ottoman poetry and its representations of coffee and coffee house servant boys, I show how the female was a complicatedly important aspect of the masculine world of the Ottoman coffee house.

Instead of Habermas's strict world of dichotomies, I propose that we think of Ottoman coffee houses in terms of what Michel Foucault calls a *heterotopia*, or a space 'capable of juxtaposing in a single real place several spaces, several sites that are in themselves incompatible'.[19]

For Foucault, heterotopias are places connected to specific known cultural referents that are able to rearrange and combine these familiar signs in a new and useful way. In his own words, heterotopias 'have the curious property of being in relation with all the other sites, but in such a way as to suspect, neutralize, or invert the set of relations that they happen to designate, mirror, or reflect'.[20] Ottoman coffee houses did just this as spaces with connections to the neighbourhood, home and market that made them at once familiar but contemporaneously novel in the way that men could gather within them as spaces of layered functionality and a multitude of ambiences.

The association of coffee and its consumption with a place of socialization is one that emerges almost from the very beginning of coffee's entrance into the Muslim world. Exactly when coffee first appeared in the region is, however, under some dispute. Ralph Hattox places coffee's beginnings in the Middle East in the middle of the fifteenth century.[21] Others claim that there is no mention of coffee in any sources before the sixteenth century.[22] As to when coffee first arrived in Istanbul, again we do not know exactly, although it was some time during the middle decades of the sixteenth century. The Ottoman historian İbrahim Peçevi writes that before 1554 coffee and coffee houses did not exist in Istanbul, but in that year two men – Hakem from Aleppo and Şems from Damascus – brought coffee to Istanbul and quickly opened the city's first coffee house in the neighbourhood of Tahtakale.[23] According to Kātip Çelebi, coffee first arrived in Istanbul in 1543.[24] The historian Mustafa Âli, for his part, claims that coffee houses first appeared in Istanbul and 'in other regions of the Well-Guarded State' some time in 1552 or 1553.[25]

Nevertheless, what is important for our present purposes is not the exact date of the arrival of coffee in the Middle East, but the fact that the places in which it was consumed and the social rituals constructed around this consumption became more significant than the actual drink. Commentators have noted that coffee houses became an inseparably synergistic component of the meaning of coffee in the Muslim world.[26] At the linguistic level, we note that coffee houses are usually referred to as simply *kahve* in Turkish or *qahwa* in Arabic. These words literally mean the drink, coffee, but their use to signify coffee houses suggests a nearly equivalent relationship imagined between coffee and the places in which it was drunk.

Coffee houses were not only intimately linked to the caffeinated libations that patrons consumed in them, but they were also integral parts of Ottoman urban geography. Soon after coffee's arrival, coffee houses could be seen all over the major urban areas of the Ottoman empire. Writing at the turn of the seventeenth century, Mustafa Âli claims that in Cairo 'thousands of coffee houses are in operation'.[27] Later he comments, '[Remarkable] is the multitude of coffee-houses in the city of Cairo, the concentration of coffee-houses at every step, and of perfect places where people can assemble.'[28] At the end of the eighteenth century, the British traveller to Aleppo Alexander Russell notes that 'coffee-houses naturally attract the notice of a stranger, more than any of the objects he meets with in rambling over the city. They are found in all quarters of the town, and some of them are spacious and handsome.'[29]

In sixteenth-century Istanbul a few decades after coffee came to the city, Katip Çelebi writes, 'They were opened everywhere, freely: on every street-corner a coffee-house appeared.'[30] Peçevi notes that cafés became so popular in the sixteenth century that there were often no places to sit or stand because they were so crowded. It reached the point where no one was going to the mosque any more.[31] The historian Cengiz Kırlı asserts that at the beginning of the nineteenth century one out of every seven or eight businesses in Istanbul was a coffee house. The neighbourhood of Beşiktaş alone had 22 cafés out of a total of 108 coffee houses situated in neighbourhoods along the Bosporus.[32] Writing about the same period, the nineteenth-century British traveller Charles White estimated that Istanbul was home to no fewer than 2500 coffee houses.[33]

Part of the reason for the ubiquity of cafés in urban locales was the important fact that they were opened almost immediately whenever a new neighbourhood of a city was developed or when new economic configurations seemed promising for café business. Indeed, along with homes, coffee houses were some of the first structures to appear in newly constructed neighbourhoods. In 1771, in the area of Cairo along the Nile known as Būlāq, ᶜAlī Bey undertook a project to construct a *khān* complex complete with residential areas, a mosque and storage facilities. The project was so huge that it extended into the Nile and the flow of the river was actually diverted in order to reclaim land for the city. Residents of Cairo quickly moved to this newly available land and, as narrated by the Egyptian historian of the eighteenth and early nineteenth centuries ᶜAbd al-Raḥmān al-Jabartī, the first two structures built on this land were houses and cafés.[34] Coffee houses were also some of the first businesses opened in any complex devoted to commerce. When the construction of all the stores in a certain Cairo *wakāla* was complete, the first thing to be added to the complex before its opening was a coffee attendant's (*qahwajī*) stand.[35] Likewise, when Ismāᶜīl Bey opened a large business complex (*qayṣariyya*) in 1787, he was sure to include a coffee house along with his 21 shops so that customers would not have to leave the area to drink their coffee.³⁶ Interestingly, during the French occupation of Egypt, local Egyptians took the presence of the French in their midst as a business opportunity to open up coffee houses around the French military's living quarters.³⁷

As one of the most visible trappings of Ottoman culture, coffee houses emerged wherever humans went. The Amīr Qāsim Bey Abū Sayf, who had a certain flare for architecture (*kāna lahu malaka wa fikra fī handasat al-bināʾ*), built a huge palace complete with a very ornate garden of running water, myrtle and willow trees, and all sorts of shaded areas. He opened this garden to the general public and it immediately became a very popular place in which to stroll and escape the heat. As soon as people began frequenting this garden in significant numbers, Amīr Qāsim Bey Abū Sayf decided to open a coffee house there. Al-Jabartī speaks almost in the same breath of the increasing numbers of visitors to this place and the opening of a café in the garden as if the latter were a requisite of the former.³⁸

As a backdrop to this discussion, we should remember that serving and consuming food was of the utmost importance to the social life of the Ottoman city in the eighteenth century.³⁹ Around this basic element of life revolved numerous rituals of socialization, leisure and politics. Eating in this world was most closely associated with the family and home, for there was no such thing as a culture of restaurants and eating out was rare.⁴⁰ When people did eat outside their own homes it was usually in the home of a friend or family member.

The question of whether or not families had kitchens in their homes is obviously an important factor in assessing the culture of eating in the Ottoman world, but it is an enquiry that has not yet received a definitive answer. Nelly Hanna estimates in her study of seventeenth and eighteenth-century homes in Cairo that only 14 per cent of medium-sized homes included kitchens.⁴¹ This relatively low number though does not mean that only 14 per cent of Cairene families cooked in their homes. As Hanna explains, families utilized a *kānūn* (a portable grill) to cook meat in or near their homes, since this mobile cooking apparatus could be shared by many different households on the basis of need.[42] In the case of eighteenth-century Aleppo, Abraham Marcus suggests that almost all homes – including those that cost as little as eight piasters – contained kitchens.[43] Marcus's findings though stand in contrast to the work of Antoine Abdel-Nour who asserts that only a fifth of all homes in Aleppo in the seventeenth and eighteenth centuries contained kitchens.[44]

In seventeenth-century Jerusalem, Dror Ze'evi's study of inheritance records indicates that most families had knives (but no forks and spoons) in their homes along with pots, pans and various sorts of plates.[45] This of course suggests that families ate in their homes, but does not necessarily mean they cooked in them. While the question of the role of the kitchen in the Ottoman home remains unanswered, the consensus in the above scholarship is that families usually ate at home.

One of the most important parts of Ottoman culinary life in this domestic setting was the recognized and celebrated tradition of the dinner party.[46] These dinner parties of course included much more than just food as they were also leisure events to be enjoyed with friends and family. Smoking, chatting, playing backgammon or other games, gossiping and drinking coffee were all requisite parts of a fine evening. One exception to the general rule that residents of Ottoman cities only ate or drank in their homes was the coffee house. Indeed, the coffee house was the one place outside the home where people could share in all the revelries of an enjoyable dinner party without the presence of a meal.

Another important social change ushered in by the widespread emergence of Ottoman urban coffee houses was that they served as places of nocturnal socialization outside the home.[47] The Englishman John Fryer, writing of his visits to seventeenth-century Persian cafés, states that 'at night here are abundance of lamps lighted, and let down in glasses from the concave part of the roof, by wires or ropes, hanging in a circle.'[48] When the sun set and the streets emptied, people were usually either at home or in their local café.[49] Indeed, al-Jabartī relates that during the month of Ramaḍān, people in Cairo spent their nights either at home or in coffee houses.[50]

Coffee's association with the night-time machinations of its consumers contributed to official apprehensions about coffee houses during the sixteenth and seventeenth centuries. Nevertheless, 'conquering the night' was both a source of pride and excitement for urbanites and a way for local authorities to show their control over an area.[51] When the French were about to invade Cairo in 1798, tensions arose in many neighbourhoods throughout the city about the impending danger. In an effort to comfort the city's residents, local authorities ordered all markets and coffee houses to open at night and requested that lanterns (qanādīl) be hung throughout these areas to dispel gloom from people's hearts and to gain a semblance of society and companionship (dhahāb al-waḥsha min al-qulūb wa ḥuṣūl al-istiʾnās).[52] Later we read that during the celebration of ʿArafa (the ninth day of the pilgrimage month), coffee houses and businesses were opened to create a mood of joy and delight (al-faraḥ wa al-surūr).[53] Both these examples reveal the important associations between coffee houses and the joy derived from their night-time patronage.

Coffee extended the day for its male imbibers well beyond dusk and this meant that they were often out of their homes and apart from their families for longer periods than was previously observed. Coffee was, moreover, a beverage consumed by all, and members of all social classes frequented coffee houses, even though the rich could afford to drink it at home. The nineteenth-century British traveller, Charles White terms coffee both 'the solace of the rich and the principal sustenance of the poor'.[54] Peçevi, writing in the seventeenth century, notes that those men of high standing who were not prominent functionaries of the state (eşḥāb-ı menāṣıbdan gayri kibār) had no choice but to come to cafés since they were all the rage.[55]

Nevertheless, the association between coffee and the poor and destitute is repeated over and over again by chroniclers and contemporary observers alike. Commenting on the poverty of the people of Cairo at the end of the sixteenth century, Mustafa Âli writes, 'The pious and the poor of the country live in perpetual abstemiousness. Most of them are content with coffee as a liquid and roasted coffee-beans and one or two dry biscuits as solid food.'⁵⁶ Later he describes café goers as 'a bunch of parasites ... whose work consists of presiding over the coffee house, of drinking coffee on credit, [and of] talking of frugality'.⁵⁷ Al-Jabartī describes the management of coffee houses as one of the lowest or most menial forms of labour (one of *al-ḥiraf al-danīʾa*) akin to fish frying or pastry selling.⁵⁸ In sixteenth-century Ottoman Jerusalem, we learn that what Ottoman authorities termed 'wickedness, mischief, perniciousness and refractoriness' often accompanied the economically destitute café patrons of that city leading to official fears about the spread of coffee houses as the meeting places of such rabble.⁵⁹

Considering how poor many of the men who went to cafés were, how might we explain their frequent patronage given the associated costs?⁶⁰ To begin answering this question we must first locate the coffee house in the social world of the Ottoman city and specifically within the context of the city neighbourhood (*mahalle* in Turkish, *maḥalla* in Arabic).⁶¹ Coffee houses were sprinkled throughout the various neighbourhoods of Ottoman cities. During his travels in Egypt, Evliya Çelebi describes more than 40 neighbourhoods in Cairo, and almost every single one of them, regardless of its size, had at least one coffee house. In the neighbourhood of Kefri Cedid, for instance, Evliya Çelebi informs us that there were 200 homes, a mosque and a coffee house. In Kefri Nahe, a neighbourhood of 1000 homes and a mosque, there were no shops, *ḥammāms*, or *vekāles*, but there was a café. He writes of all kinds of coffee houses in all kinds of neighbourhoods terming some cafés Arab *kahvehaneleri* and others *fellāhīn kahvehaneleri*.⁶² From Evliya Çelebi's account, we get a sense of Cairo as a city made up of many different neighbourhood parts, in each of which the local café was a central hub worthy of mention.

Like most cities at this time, Ottoman cities were relatively small, stretching at most for two or three miles from one end to the other. Within this compact space, however, was a densely packed network of roads, many different kinds of houses, businesses, religious institutions, coffee houses, ḥammāms, waqf complexes, public fountains and a whole range of other kinds of spaces. Within the official Ottoman mental mindscape, the city stood in opposition to the palace. Whereas the latter was sophisticated and learned, the former was vulgar, common and uncouth. Mustafa Âli, for example, ascribes the disgusting habits of 'someone of inferior quality' to that person's 'city nature', which he employs as a foil to the manners observed in the company of 'great men'.[63] Elsewhere, he differentiates the palace from the city by likening the former to a pearl hidden 'in the depth of the oyster shell'.[64] This imagery eloquently accentuates the absolute authority vested in the sultan and his palace as the centres from which all imperial power emanates. Leslie Peirce suggestively terms the courtyard of the inner palace 'the all-male harem', pointing again both to the spatial and symbolic impenetrability of this space and to its seclusion from other sections of the palace and from the city.[65]

Within the city the majority of urban residents spent most of their lives in one neighbourhood, rarely venturing beyond their local sphere of activity because all their daily needs could be met in their immediate social surroundings. The neighbourhood was therefore the self-sufficient axis around which urban life revolved for most Ottoman city dwellers. It was, in other words, 'the most intimate social unit outside the family'.[66] In each neighbourhood there was a small market for daily goods, perhaps a small mosque, a butcher shop, fruit vendors, and other institutions providing vital social services.

The residents of these tightly woven communities necessarily saw one another quite regularly, and this fostered a distinctive sense of local neighbourhood identity, which often took on the characteristics of an extended family.[67] Since everyone in these neighbourhoods knew their neighbours, strangers were immediately noticed. This level of intimacy was not, however, all in the spirit of camaraderie and goodwill; it also produced a social milieu in which people regularly talked about others, about what they were doing in their homes and about how they interacted with others within the community and elsewhere. Regular meetings in the streets of a neighbourhood, at the local vendor, or near the public fountain meant a constant atmosphere of gossip, prying and general curiosity about one's neighbours.

Nonetheless, these neighbourhood communities seem to have observed a set of unwritten rules about social interactions, the use of space and the spirit of the neighbourhood.[68] Urban residents could use space as they pleased as long as they did not infringe on the privacy, health, safety or comfort of their neighbours, or of the community as a whole. The popular Arabic saying 'al-jār qabl al-dār' (the neighbour [comes] before the house) embodies this notion of the wellbeing and security of the local whole over the interests of the individual. Practically, this meant that issues such as the construction of new buildings, extensions or add-ons to existing structures, water usage and the maintenance of streets and thoroughfares were negotiated and regulated by and among neighbours with a shared interest in their common spaces.[69]

Space within Ottoman neighbourhoods was fluid and overlapping and should not be understood in terms of divisions and distinctions. How, for instance, do we interpret the fact that neighbourhood affairs that affected the community as a whole were controlled by private individuals jockeying with one another for their own advantage? Interiors of homes were reserved for the eyes of family members and invited guests only, yet the noise of the neighbourhood and its gossip travelled freely in and out of houses, onto the street, into shops and back again. Often what the eye could not see the ear could hear.[70] Moreover, there were numerous kinds of spaces within Ottoman neighbourhoods where domestic life spilled out onto the street or where the affairs of the neighbourhood came into the home. As an example of the former, we should remember that dead-end streets shared by a few families provided an extra space in which to do chores or store excess supplies of wood and other necessities for the home.[71]

Those whose houses did not border this space or who had not

explicitly been invited by members of these families were often not allowed to enter the area at all. This space then was in some senses an extension of the home outside its physical boundaries.[72] As Cem Behar explains with reference to the Istanbul neighbourhood of Kasap İlyas, 'The Istanbulites, in their public life, often saw their *mahalle* as a direct extension of their untouchable individual private space, of their inner personal domain.'[73] We shall return to these issues of space and the city below, but suffice it to say for now that this is a rough sketch of the urban world in which the Ottoman coffee house flourished.

As neighbourhood institutions catering to regulars who lived nearby, coffee houses thrived in this fluid world of local communities where spaces played multiple and overlapping roles not adequately described by terms like 'public' and 'private'. I would like to suggest that neighbourhood cafés in the poorer sections of Ottoman Istanbul, Cairo and Aleppo might be better understood by looking for clues within rather than away from the home. By this I mean that urban cafés offered their male clientele a substitute for a *selamlık*, the name given to the section of the house reserved for the men of the family to greet and socialize with their guests.[74]

A great many families in these cities could not afford large houses with separate *selamlık* and *haremlik* (the comparable space of female socialization) and therefore could not entertain guests in their homes given the traditionally-observed separation between male and female guests in the home.[75] As Dina Khouri notes in her work on Mosul, separate domains for men and women within the household become less and less common as one moves down the economic social ladder.[76]

Contrasting the homes of Ottoman urban residents with the villas, gardens and orchards of the wealthy, Mustafa Âli had this to say: 'there exists another gloomy prison for downcast people who are tight, silent, and afflicted, and which is narrow like the hard heart of the miser, a torturesome and grief-inflicting gathering place entirely enveloped in torment and misery and suffering.'[77] Though perhaps an exaggeration, Âli's description makes the point that most Ottoman houses were rather small and cramped spaces. The coffee house then gave poorer men a chance to have their own sort of communal *selamlık* in which to 'take up residence', in Âli's words, with their friends and associates while at the same time affording women their own autonomous zones of conviviality in the space of the home refashioned as a *haremlik*.[78]

For the lower and middle classes, the price of constructing separate male and female spaces within the home was prohibitive, yet women were still able to maintain autonomous areas within the home. Although all members of the family, whether female or male, shared this section of the home, known as the *bayt*, it 'was rarely divisible and appears to have been the only truly private space of the women and their children'.[79] Thus, women shaped the hierarchies and relations of their homes and households because it was the home more than any other institution or structure in the Ottoman city that constituted the bulk of most people's personal wealth.[80] Nevertheless, when one looks at the dwellings of the poor majorities of Ottoman cities, any divisions between male and female are hard to find given that most of these houses consisted of a large common room where family members sat together, ate, socialized and slept. Some lower-class families we should note were able to afford a house with a small courtyard and a room for storage, but this seems to be quite rare and was only possible after a long period of saving money or after acquiring a large inheritance or some other similar increase in income. The majority of the population, therefore, did not have domestic spaces within their homes in which males or females could gather together without the other to entertain friends, conduct business, eat, relax or host guests.

It is this absence of a domestic *selamlık* and *haremlik* within poorer households that leads me to identify the coffee house as the crucial Ottoman institution that allowed men and women their autonomous zones of socialization. On this subject, Mustafa Âli observes that 'indigents and poor people go there [to the café] because they have no home or shelter. For indeed the poor have neither cash nor worldly goods enabling them to gather anywhere else. This is the reason they are in constant attendance at coffee houses.'[81]

Ehud Toledano makes a similar point when he writes that 'the Ottoman-Egyptian elite socialized mostly at home, as the male section (*selamlık*) of most elite houses could accommodate visitors quite comfortably. So it was for those with modest homes, or no home at all, that the coffee house was ever so important.'[82] Ottoman *mahalle* cafés offered the neighbourhood's men a place in which to gather with their male companions in a sort of communal *selamlık* while at the same time affording women the home as an autonomous, albeit temporary, female space.

Coffee houses were, of course, not the only reasons men left their homes. Indeed, like places of work and worship, Ottoman cafés allowed for two similar processes to occur simultaneously. On the one hand, with men out of the home, women temporally made their domestic space into a place of gathering, a quasi-public space in which non-kin and friends could assemble to discuss neighbourhood affairs, conduct business, gossip and relax with one another. At the same time, men engaged in a similar sort of socialization in coffee houses. We might suggest then that the café was a space that had more in common with the domestic world of the home than it did with the city, its streets and public thoroughfares. Likewise, we might view the home as an occasional space in which women gathered to converse and perform their socializations. Commenting on this former phenomenon while completely ignoring the latter, the scholar of coffee houses Ralph Hattox mentions 'the occasional transferal of the act of hospitality from the home to the coffee house'.[83] Indeed, if the coffee house was to serve as their *selamlık*, men had to have the sense that they were in a familiar space, a space that might be taken as their home even though it was not. To get a better sense of exactly how this temporary imagining of the coffee house as the home took place, it is instructive for us to enter the physical realm of the Ottoman café to see what its men saw and to feel what they felt.

Before actually setting foot in the coffee house a customer often had to remove his shoes and place them in a small container near the door called a *pabuçluk*.[84] This custom of removing one's footwear before entering the café was most common in Anatolian coffee houses and of course immediately reminds one of the practice observed when entering a mosque or the home. Importantly, in all these places, the removal of one's shoes symbolizes the crossing of a threshold between the outside world of dirt, the street and the city on the one hand and the comfortable familiarity of the home, mosque or coffee house on the other.

*Mahalle* coffee houses were usually single-storeyed wooden structures with wooden floors, although some café floors were covered with carpets. A coffee house was most often located in a small square at the meeting point of several streets near shops, the mosque and fountains. The cafés in these *mahalle* centres of gravity were often surrounded by small gardens or clusters of trees.

Upon entering the coffee house, one would first find oneself in the large common area known as the *orta* or *meydan*, which took up most of the café interior. This area was similar to the living room of a house, into which guests are greeted when they first enter and, like that part of a house, this was where most café patrons spent most of their time sitting on small wooden chairs or slightly raised *divan*s with their coffee and waterpipe. One corner of the café housed the equivalent of a kitchen where *fincan*s and coffee-making equipment were stored. More importantly, this was also where all the coffee was brewed on a small furnace known as an *ocak*.[85]

In the corner opposite the *ocak* was the *başsedir*, the top *divan*, where local notables and distinguished men of the neighbourhood sat. The *başsedir* was the spatial pinnacle of the coffee house social hierarchy. It was from this elevated point that neighbourhood elders, imams and important tradesmen made announcements, disseminated neighbourhood news and sometimes gave lessons or told stories. Again, this café social order and its physical manifestations remind one of the situation prevailing in the home where the kitchen was usually on the side of the house opposite the entrance and where the father's favourite seat occupied an important position within the household hierarchy.[86] The café built in the *waqf* complex of İpshîr Mustapha Pasha in Aleppo provides one of the most striking examples of the resemblance between a coffee house and an individual home. According to Evliya Çelebi, who visited Aleppo in 1671, the city was full of cafés; in fact there were 105 in all.[87] The *waqf* complex of İpshîr Pasha, located in the northern suburb of Aleppo, was the largest charitable endowment built in the city during the seventeenth century, and one of its most socially and architecturally important features was its large coffee house.[88]

The İpshîr Pasha coffee house consisted of a courtyard, originally centred around a pool, and a hall covered with domes forming a cruciform. This courtyard resembled the summer reception areas of the luxurious private homes of Aleppo's wealthier residents in that both were centred around a pool and contained an *īwān*. Likewise, the covered portion of the coffee house corresponded to the cruciform domed winter reception halls of wealthy urbanites. Moreover, the simple decoration of the café courtyard and its *īwān* and the ornate façade of the covered hall also correspond to the decorative traditions associated with summer and winter domestic architecture.[89] In his study of İpshîr Pasha's *waqf*, Jean-Claude David writes that 'le café est un véritable prolongement de la maison'.[90] Thus, again in Aleppo, we observe that Ottoman coffee houses and the home were not the worlds apart they are often imagined to be.

Because the male world of the coffee house shared so many characteristics traditionally associated with an Ottoman home, we might go so far as to assert that 'the coffee-*house* is so named with reason, instituting a public imitation of a private home'.[91] While acknowledging the intimate similarities – linguistic, imaginary, architectural and otherwise – between the coffee house and the home, there is one crucial structural and functional difference between the two spaces. As noted earlier, Ottoman *mahalle*s were highly protected spaces that allowed only the familiar in and kept everything else out. Individual homes were even more highly protected spaces, for their interiors and the women and children inside them were meant never to be seen by those not immediately sanctioned by the family. People's houses were usually down narrow streets and alleys and did not have much traffic going past them.

Coffee houses, by contrast, were in central areas of the neighbourhood and were usually open structures into which one could gaze and out of which one could look. 'The kahweh [coffee house] is, generally speaking, a small apartment, whose front, which is towards the street, is of open wooden work, in the form of arches.'[92] Many café patrons sat outside the built structure of the café on the street in full view of passers-by. Peçevi writes that during the reign of Sultan Murad III at the end of the sixteenth century coffee houses were no longer allowed to spread out onto the street. He refers specifically to 'koltuk kahvesis' (literally chair coffee houses), which presumably blocked the flow of street traffic with their array of chairs, waterpipes and patrons.[93] The point here is that café patrons could see the street and what was going on outside or around their coffee house and that, more importantly, people could see into the café.

The coffee house of the *waqf* complex of İpshîr Pasha in Aleppo again offers us a good example of how Ottoman cafés challenged traditional strictures against vision – and specifically against seeing interiors – within the city. The İpshîr Pasha coffee house opened onto the street rather than towards the interior courtyard through a series of windows surrounded by elaborately decorated façades. This represents the one break in the seamless exterior wall enclosing the complex and, as Watenpaugh asserts, 'the degree of decoration of the façade correlates with the expected degree of interaction [between the street and the interior].'[94]

The coffee house was therefore not completely separated from the exterior streets beyond the walls of the *waqf* complex. Indeed, it interacted with its outside as those passing by could see into the café and patrons of course could look back at them. This visual back and forth correspondence between the interior of the café and what was outside it made the coffee house in some ways a transparent space of performative socialization where patrons had always to be aware of who might be looking in from the street.[95] This is of the utmost importance because of all the built spaces in the city – mosques, homes, shops, hospitals, soup kitchens and so on – the coffee house was one of the few – if not the only – into which and out of which one could look. Of course there were times when the sides of cafés were closed and their windows draped over, but for much of the year most cafés were open to the breeze and, more significantly, to the gaze.

Historic prohibitions against vision within the Muslim city are grounded in the Qur'ān and in various Ḥadīth traditions that assure urban residents a high degree of visual privacy.[96] For instance, one Ḥadīth instructs that 'he who pulls the curtain and looks into a house before he is granted permission to enter has committed an offence.'[97] Similarly, we read in the Qur'ān, 'O ye who believe! Enter not houses other than your own, until ye have asked permission and saluted those in them. ... If ye find no one in the house, enter not until permission is given to you. ... Say to the believers that they should lower their gaze and guard their modesty.'[98] Both these quotes stress that one must be given permission to look into or enter a home that is not one's own, even if the house is empty of inhabitants.

The scholar of Islam, Yūsuf al-Qaraḍāwī, summarizes the prohibitions against visual intrusion in Islam by saying that 'what we do not see should not be probed into.'[99] The Prophet Muhammad instructs that if a person ever peeps at someone without his permission, then the offended party may put out the transgressor's eye without fear of being counted a sinner.[100] In practice, these proscriptions against uninvited vision into the home meant that Islamic domestic architecture developed in such a way as to eliminate, to as great a degree as possible, all visual corridors between the home and what was external to it – other homes and the street.

One of the fullest and most sustained studies of building principles in the Islamic world is the fourteenth-century Tunisian

Mālikī scholar and master builder Ibn al-Rāmī's *Kitāb al-iʿlān bi-āḥkām al-bunyān*, which loosely translates as *The book for communicating building solutions*.[101] For Muslim jurists like Ibn al-Rāmī and others, the two most worrying features of the built environment were doors and windows. Both Ibn al-Rāmī and another Mālikī, Ibn al-Qāsim, instructed that doors were not to be constructed across from one another for fear that upon exiting one's home one might be able to see into the domestic space of the home opposite if its door were by chance open.[102] Ibn al-Rāmī though asserted that doors could be constructed across from one another as long as the space between them – usually the street – was sufficiently wide and the traffic heavy enough so as to hinder direct sight lines between the two doors. Ibn al-Rāmī further refined his notion of visual penetration through open doorways by stating that if a man standing in an open doorway completely blocked a visual corridor into the space behind him, then this door was deemed too small for visual penetration, and the construction of doors opposite it was allowed. Moreover, if a man standing near the mouth of the door could not be seen because of the lighting conditions or size of the opening, then a doorway could also be constructed opposite this door.[103]

In addition to doorways, windows, as visual conduits into the domestic realm, became the subject of much distress for Muslim jurists. Indeed, windows were of particular concern because, as Ibn al-Ghammāz, a contemporary of Ibn al-Rāmī articulated, unlike doors, which were sites of constant movement in and out, an individual could sit unseen at a window and gaze at his or her neighbour without the neighbour knowing.[104] Upper-storey windows were only to be used to let in light and air, and if they provided one the opportunity to look into another's home, they were to be closed. To determine the proper height of a window from the interior of a structure, Ibn al-Rāmī cites the Caliph ʿUmar Ibn al-Khaṭṭāb who instructs that 'a bed is to be placed underneath the window, and if a man standing on it does not see through it, then the window is allowed to remain, otherwise it should be shut.'[105]

The placement of windows closer to the ground was determined by two factors. First, the window was to be high enough so as not to allow passers-by on the street the opportunity to look into the house. The second stipulation stated that ground-floor windows should not allow one to see from the inside of the house into another neighbouring residence even if this window is above eye level. Similar arguments meant to prevent visual access into the home were also made about the construction of balconies and roofs.

Most of these prohibitions were of course meant to prevent those outside the home seeing interior spaces in which they might catch a glimpse of women and children. Thus, as places where only men gathered, coffee houses escaped most of these traditional strictures against vision in the Islamic city, helping explain why so many were open structures with few visual barriers between the inside and outside.

Furthermore, Ottoman cafés draw our attention to an arguably more important urban sensory experience – audition. By this I mean that in coffee houses what was most important was not what was seen, but what was said and of course what was heard. In other words, in neighbourhood cafés, where the clientele was made up of *mahalle* regulars who returned day after day, the visual effects of the café eventually became simply background in the sense that the familiarity of the place bred a sort of blindness to its detail, especially since most coffee houses had rather unadorned interiors. The place itself and its visual evocations became secondary to what went on inside it and specifically to what was said in it. Another way to make the same point is to remember the common proverb that is still found in many Turkish coffee houses: *'gönül ne kahve ister ne kahvehane, gönül sohbet ister, kahve bahane'* – The heart desires neither coffee nor a coffee house. The heart desires conversation. Coffee is simply an excuse.

Significantly, Ibn al-Rāmī instructs that while visual penetration of the home was to be guarded against, sound was allowed to travel freely and seemingly unchecked within a city's neighbourhoods. Thus, he sanctioned opening a window that did not overlook a neighbour's property even though it provided for audible penetration of this space. Likewise, muezzins (those who performed the call to prayer) were not allowed to climb minarets if their elevated positions provided a direct line of sight into a neighbouring home, but their voices were sanctioned and of course encouraged to enter every space in the home.[106] External voices or noise were thus allowed into the home but the visual gaze was not. Indeed, as Mustafa Âli documents, the city was full of unseemly noises: belching, nose-blowing that 'sounds like a horn', whistling and 'the indecent sounds made by crude city boys'.[107] This shift in emphasis from the visual to the audible forces us now to grapple with the historically illusive subjects of speech, rumour and gossip within the city.

Before proceeding, though, we must deal with a problem immediately evoked by conversation and speaking and that is the question of hearing. Specifically, what is at issue here is not the audible perceptions of café patrons but our ability as historians to hear them. In other words, how can we listen to the conversations of coffee house men who lived and died hundreds of years ago? A different way to ask this question and one that has received much attention is Gayatri Spivak's rendering: 'can the subaltern speak?' She of course famously answers her own question with a resounding 'no', claiming that 'the subaltern has no history [in other words no representation in historiography] and cannot speak.'[108] By entreating us to think carefully about those subalterns who have traditionally not received the attention of historians interested in political and economic history, Spivak's essay poses numerous challenges to the historian. Yet, in the end, she overstates her thesis and thereby precludes any possibility of hearing the voices of these subalterns. In her brilliant study of prostitution in twentieth-century Shanghai, Gail Hershatter offers us an important addendum to Spivak's arguments:

> If we replace 'The subaltern cannot speak' (or, what I take to be closer to Spivak's actual argument, 'The subaltern

cannot represent herself in discourse') with 'Many subalterns making cacophonous noise, some hogging the mike, many speaking intermittently and not exactly as they please, and all aware to some degree of the political uses of their representation in that historical moment,' we probably have a closer approximation of the situation confronting historians. If we are lucky, we also have a way out of the 'disappearing subaltern' impasse, in which any subaltern who speaks loses the right to that status. Finally, we have a chance to complicate the picture of one overarching discourse, in which subalterns appear only as positioned by their elite spokespersons.[109]

Hershatter's point is that the subaltern *can* speak and that the historian *can* hear him. Whether she does or not though is another question entirely.

One of the most notable recent attempts to hear subaltern voices is the work of Cengiz Kırlı on Istanbul coffee houses. Through his impressive study of nineteenth-century Ottoman spy reports – *jurnals* as they were known – Kırlı seeks to hear the everyday voices of café men to learn about their experiences, their concerns, and ultimately about the world in which they lived.[110] Kırlı is, in the final analysis though, unable to hear men's voices because he is listening to them with the ears of the state. Apart from one example of a conversation between two men about the relative merits of bathing and cleanliness, all of the coffee house conversations cited by Kırlı are about what we might crudely term political history.[111]

For example, one of the most important topics of the day for the Ottoman state was Muḥammad ʿAlī's invasion of Syria and Anatolia, and much of the space in the *jurnals* at this time was devoted to this topic. Other issues covered by these reports were taxation, state appointments and Ottoman state relations with Greek and Armenian communities in the face of conversions and European machinations. After a reading of these reports then, we come away with the sense that nearly all men's talk in coffee houses was about politics and the economy.¹¹² Of course, as Kırlı notes, these were reports by government bureaucrats hired by the state to get a sense of the political mood of its subject citizens, and it should therefore be no surprise that most of what we get from these *jurnal*s is about the politics of the Ottoman state.¹¹³

The problem of hearing and of hearing Ottoman coffee house men, though, is not simply one of sources.¹¹⁴ While historians are of course limited by their source material, it is instructive here to remember that gossip is not rumour. While both are talk about others or events not immediately present in one's field of vision, rumour is usually considered to be talk that matters to a political entity – idle chatter's version of *realpolitik*. Rumour is about the world of state politics – a realm in which important *men* make important decisions about war, taxation and so forth. Rumour is critical of the establishment, can lead to rebellion and is therefore of concern to those with a vested interest in upholding the existing social structure.¹¹⁵

Al-Jabartī refers to rumour at one point as curiosity, talk and clamour (*al-fuḍūl wa al-kalām wa al-laghṭ*) that stirs up feelings of enmity (*mimmā yuhīju al-ʿadāwa*).¹¹⁶ In the Ottoman empire, this type of talk was known as *devlet sohbeti* (state talk) and it became an issue worthy of state attention, thus motivating the spy reports of the nineteenth century.¹¹⁷ Gossip, on the other hand, was for the state far more benign.¹¹⁸ It did not lead to rebellions, regicide or strikes. It was talk of the neighbourhood, politically meaningless stories about one's neighbours, or simply the idle babble of the masses.¹¹⁹ Mustafa Âli calls this chatter 'urban affection of speech and nonsensical talk, grounded in allusions, ambiguous phrases and untruths'.¹²⁰ As long as there was social stability and taxes were being paid on a regular basis, the Ottoman state did not care about the politics of gossip in its numerous urban *mahalle*s. Why should it become involved in what was considered to be the petty bickerings of its subjects?¹²¹

Important also are the truth claims associated with each of the two categories of speech. Rumour tends to have a more tendentious relationship with the information it supposedly relays than gossip. Rumours are more likely to be lies – what Mustafa Âli calls the 'snakelike-winding sweet lies that clash with the facts'.[122] Both types of conversation also imply a level of trust between parties and even a degree of friendship. Admittedly, the distinction between rumour and gossip is a slippery one for which I can offer only tentative interpretative suggestions. In addition to the terms mentioned above, there are a number of ways in Ottoman Turkish in which to think about rumour and gossip.

The Ottoman terms used to denote things about which people are talking include *ishāʿat*, spreading, diffusing or disclosing; *shāʾiʿa*, a rumour or generally-known news; and *shāʾiʿ olmak*, spread or commonly talked about. Other words include *namīme*, which can mean whispering, making mischief or telling tales, but also includes 'the sound of a pen when writing', suggesting an interesting relationship between the spoken words of gossip and rumour and their written counterparts.[123] The originally Persian word *lāf* for talk, chatter or boasting, gives us the expression *lāf ü güdhāf*, which Redhouse translates as 'empty words'.[124] Şemseddin Sami offers the following synonyms for the expression *lāf ü güdhāf* – *boş lāqırdı* (empty conversation or, more idiomatically, nonsense or idle talk) and *saçma söz* (nonsensical word).[125] We also have the expression *qīl ü qāl*. Whereas Redhouse translates this as 'tittle-tattle',[126] the late seventeenth-century lexicographer Franciszek Meninski defines it as 'much conversation'[127] or 'loquaciousness, garrulity'.[128] Şemseddin Sami includes *qīl ü qāl* under his entry for the word *dedikodu*, the most common word in modern Turkish for gossip.[129]

The relative differences in usage and understanding of these terms are not easily ascertained, but I offer them as examples of the type of vocabulary Ottomans used in discussing ideas similar to those of rumour and gossip. As with the conceptions of space in Ottoman cities mentioned above, ours is largely a problem of vocabulary when attempting to express the subtle distinctions between rumour and gossip in the Ottoman world. How would Ottomans, for example, have described rumours about social issues, familial life or neighbourhood corruption? What words would they have used to describe gossip about the politically damaging drinking habits or sexual life of a certain judge? How, in short, did Ottomans describe the ways they talked? The point I wish to stress here is that historians have been overwhelmingly concerned with rumour – precisely because of the state's engagements with it – rather than gossip. Rumours are, to put it simply, much easier for historians to hear than gossip.

Thus, the *jurnal*s Kırlı studies deal solely with rumour and almost completely ignore gossip because the latter was not important for the state to hear. In fact, Kırlı does not distinguish between gossip and rumour, and clearly, though seemingly unwittingly, privileges the latter as a means of reading state power. He writes that 'rumour and gossip were the most important media in Ottoman society.'[130] Yet, he more clearly restates his opinion with the following: 'Rumour constituted the single most important medium in the Ottoman empire. ... Its mobilizing capacity as a vehicle of dissent made it an object for the state to control and suppress. In the eyes of the state its uncontrollable nature made it a formidable threat against the social order.'[131] Kırlı's preference for rumour over gossip as the most significant form of communication in the Ottoman world is I think an exaggeration that at best reifies the power of the Ottoman state and at worst blinds us to the realities of Ottoman life.

In other words, I think we can say with some confidence that most conversations in Ottoman coffee houses were not about Muḥammad ᶜAlī or the conversions of Armenians to Islam. They were about men's families, their problems at work, troubles with their children, a new purchase, gossip about their neighbours or about their hopes for the future.[132] Indeed, scholars of gossip describe the dialectical nature of this performative mode of expression as a constant tension between the social need to maintain friendship networks and the ideals of familial privacy.[133] Thus the everyday conversations of cafés were precisely about the everyday lives of men, not the political goings-on of the Topkapi Palace or elsewhere. In the words of one nineteenth-century European traveller to Istanbul, coffee houses were 'the headquarters of gossipry, and news, and enjoyment' where 'time is suffered to slide by as carelessly as though it might one day be redeemed'.[134]

Mustafa Âli describes coffee house conversations as 'nonsensical speech' filled with gossip, backbiting and slander.[135] Elsewhere, he terms the men frequenting coffee houses 'captives of companionship ... who love to sit and talk with their friends for hours on end'.[136] To assume that what café patrons talked most about were the political intrigues we find in *jurnal*s is to short-change the experiences of these men as those of purely enlightened political actors. Moreover, it gives I believe an incorrect view of the coffee house as a completely public realm devoted to the affairs of state – a kind of local imperial *divan* dedicated to political debate.

To move beyond accounts like Kırlı's, which depict the café as *the* male public institution of rumour and political intrigue, we must acknowledge, as noted above, that the Ottoman coffee house was not, as Habermas suggests, the paradigmatic institution of the bourgeoisie's public sphere. Again, the distinction between 'public' and 'private' – and the corollary dichotomy of 'male' and 'female' – are a hindrance in thinking about Ottoman neighbourhoods and their coffee houses.

Instead of looking for divisions, we should – recalling Foucault's notion of the heterotopia – stress the idea of multi-layered or overlapping spaces within the city where different places were constantly infused with fluidly changing meanings. Certain homes, for instance, functioned as spaces of communal, quasi-public gathering for groups of poor women who were unable to afford separate *haremlik*s in their own houses. Likewise, the neighbourhood sometimes took on an interior character by virtue of women who did domestic and familial chores in spaces outside the physical structures of their homes, thereby symbolically transforming 'public' spaces like the street into 'private' spaces.[137] As noted above, the coffee house was just such a space because it offered its patrons a physical space similar to that of the home, complete with *divan* and kitchen, yet in the setting of the neighbourhood and the street.

The seventeenth-century Ottoman state historian Mustafa Naima, writing about 'a crowd of good-for-nothings', spoke in the same breath of their meetings in coffee houses, barber shops and private homes, thus indicating the rotation and overlap of these three places as spaces of gathering.[138] Because the café was convivial and offered men a chance to be with their peers and friends, it functioned as a kind of *selamlık* for the poorer men of Ottoman cities. Moreover, what Richard Sennett terms 'the mark of friendship', created an environment in the café conducive to feelings of comfort, camaraderie and trust.[139] The coffee house was thus an institution outside the home that offered men many of the same comforts traditionally associated with that domestic space.

The focus on the multiplicity of coffee-house functions and affects is not only about space but also about gender. Whereas the world of coffee houses, *devlet sohbeti*, rumour and politics has traditionally been portrayed as the domestic realm, the home has been gendered female as a place of innocuous gossip and chatter. Dina Khoury provides an example of the female gendering of gossip with reference to the following popular Mosuli proverb. 'If I tell my neighbor [the female *jāra*], the neighbor will tell another neighbor [again the female *jāra*], and if I keep it in my heart, my gallbladder will explode.'[140] Thus, at least in the Mosuli popular imagination, gossip seems to be the domain of females. Important also is that the female gossipers are neighbours. This points to the spatialized imagining of the neighbourhood as a place where, like a lingering smell, gossip wafted in and out of homes, out onto the street and through the minds of *mahalle* residents.

If, as this Mosuli proverb suggests, gossip was the business of women, how then do we account for the fact that Mustafa Âli and other writers make it clear that coffee houses allowed men the space to wile away their hours in idle gossip and chatter? For example, Charles White relates that coffee house regulars would 'curl up their legs, and remain in listless enjoyment from one prayer hour to another', adding that 'here the gossips and quidnuncs of the quarter assemble to discuss private as well as public affairs.'[141] For the English case, one scholar suggests that 'the coffee-house transformation of manners renders its public space a more private and sentimental arena (the "home" or "neighbourhood"). The structural privatization of the public sphere into the division of the "neighbourhood" is managed according to a model celebrating values associated with and derived from the construction of *femininity*.'[142]

Another commentator goes so far as to say that the coffee house 'ushers private, "feminine", practices into the public domain.'[143] The overlapping senses of meaning expressed in the space of the Ottoman coffee house show us that dichotomies of female/male, masculine/feminine, and public/private in their traditional Habermasian senses with all their social and political associations are inadequate conceptual tools with which to analyse Ottoman cities. By getting past these conflations of 'the public' with men and 'the private' with women, I think we come to a fuller understanding of Ottoman neighbourhood life where what was meant by 'male' and 'female' and 'public' and 'private' was constantly changing and flowing between the home, the coffee house and the neighbourhood.

To interrogate further this relationship between gender and coffee houses in the Ottoman world, it proves instructive to explore the genderings of coffee itself in this social milieu. An initial question then is, did coffee have a gender in the Ottoman world? The Arabic word for coffee, *qahwa*, from which the Turkish word *kahve* is derived, is feminine. Alan Kaye surmises that 'since *khamr* "wine" is feminine, *qahwah* [feminine] was chosen over the hypothetical masculine counterpart *qahw*.'[144] Kaye's explanation relies on the early association of coffee with wine as both were thought to lessen one's appetite for food.[145]

Thus, at the level of language we observe a latent association between coffee and the feminine. Moreover, Katip Çelebi associates coffee with those of 'moist temperament', by which he means women. He writes, 'especially to women, it is highly suited. They should drink a great deal of strong coffee. Excess of it will do them no harm, so long as they are not melancholic.'[146] More importantly, in Ottoman homes preparing and serving coffee was considered to be the responsibility of women. They drank it themselves in the *haremlik* and gave it to their guests. Wealthier families employed women whose sole function was the preparation of coffee for the household, and in these upper-class homes, 'a curious old custom, still observed, requires that while the coffee is served all the slaves and attendants shall enter the room and stand at one end with folded arms.'

Coffee also played an intimate role in betrothal and marriage customs. According to one European travel account, a prospective bride's ability to make good coffee was an important factor in weighing the relative merits of the woman as a future wife. Coffee also functioned as the warm and familiar mediator between the bride and her bridegroom during their first moments alone together.[147] All this suggests that coffee was indeed gendered female in the Ottoman world. It was associated with the domestic labour of women and came to be a sign of female hospitality within the home. Thus, we could read the coffee house as an extension of the feminine (in the form of coffee) into the public sphere in the same way that women's domestic chores were often performed outside the physical confines of the home.

This female gendering of coffee becomes significantly more complicated when one turns to Ottoman poetry.[148] As I have been arguing throughout, coffee houses are important sites in the Ottoman world precisely because they complicated and confused our traditional notions of space and gender. To understand the meanings of coffee and gender in Ottoman poetry, we must first examine the role of wine in the Ottoman poetical tradition.[149] Since its beginnings in the Muslim world, coffee was considered to be a close associate of wine. Before coffee houses, coffee drinkers enjoyed their beverage in wine taverns.[150] Moreover, the effects of coffee were thought to be similar to those of wine, for both impaired judgement, made the blood race and stimulated the mind and heart. Take for instance Mustafa Âli's description of the similar physiological effects of wine and coffee: 'the bitter drink of tenebrous temperament which they call "coffee" is exceptional in that it cuts off sleep and lust. Over indulgence in it certainly leads to the affliction of excessive passing of urine. The same applies to the best of the bunch, red wine.'[151]

In Ottoman poetical traditions, wine often comes to symbolize love or the beloved.[152] Consider the following from the eighteenth-century poet Nedim: 'at the gathering of desire you made me a wine-cup with your sugar smile.'[153] Figani, a sixteenth-century poet, muses 'my tears mirror your lip, red as blood-coloured wine.'[154] While wine-inspired imagery infuses descriptions of the beloved, we should not too quickly assume that the beloved is a woman. Indeed, more often than not precisely the opposite is the case. With regards to Ottoman Arabic poetry, Khaled El-Rouayheb writes that 'it is illegitimate, in light of the predominance of masculine word-forms in love-poetry and the frequency of gender-markers indicating that the portrayed beloved was male, to assume without further ado that the Arabic love-poetry of the period usually portrayed a woman.'[155]

In our present context, the usual referent in this type of poetry is the male *saki* (wine server). Ottoman wine parties took place in gardens and were usually all male affairs among friends in which male *saki*s and other servants were on hand.[156] Thus, we read, 'The wine party is a rose-garden in which the *saki* is the garden watchman/The curl of the beloved on her cheek is the garden watchman of the garden of paradise.'[157] In a similar vein, the eighteenth-century poet Sheyh Galib writes, 'Oh Saki, you filled my cup with tears of blood, it glows scarlet like the dawn/On the morning after the wine-party, if I'm still drunk, it is because of you.'[158] In sum, then, the tradition of Ottoman lyrical poetry identifies wine as a suitable symbol of the beloved, who is usually the young male *saki*.

A poem written during the reign of Süleyman helps us to see how these images of wine and the beloved changed once coffee came to replace wine as the most important social beverage in the Ottoman empire. The poet Beligi recites that:

The qualities of coffee are not like those of rosy wine
But that black-faced one's blood will warm a person
Does it have a like or equal in heating up its customer
When its face it seen all heated up, everyone wants it. ...

It travelled through Egypt, Damascus, Aleppo on its way to Turkey
That disruptor of the world, took the cup/power[159] from wine
He is attracted to money, he walks around and collects *akçes*
I don't know if he's a whore, that coffee house owner's boy.[160]

This poem is useful for numerous reasons. First, it refers to the history of coffee and specifically to its importation from Egypt through Syria and into Turkey. More importantly, Beligi's poem mentions that coffee, 'that disruptor of the world', replaced wine as *the* important drink in Ottoman life. This phrase 'disruptor of the world' (*cihan fettanı*) attaches great significance to the advent of coffee in the Ottoman world and suggests not only coffee's importance but also its character as a temptation or source of evil since *fettan* can refer to one who habitually tempts another, to Satan, or to a fiendishly flirtatious courtier.

This line – the sixth of the poem – is also important because of the idiomatic expression *ayak almak*, which has a double meaning in this context. *Ayak* means both foot and cup and *almak* simply means to take. Thus the expression could be translated literally as 'to take the foot', which idiomatically translates as 'to undercut' or 'to take the prestige or power of'. One meaning of the line then is that coffee appeared suddenly to displace the importance of wine. Alternatively, if we take *ayak* to mean cup, then the phrase suggests that the cup was physically taken away from wine to be filled with coffee. On this same point, the poet Sani writes, 'The jugs are broken, the goblet empty, wine is no more/You've made us prisoners of coffee, alas destiny alas.'[161]

In terms of the importance of this poem for what it tells us about gender and its relationship to coffee, two points stand out. First, coffee is personified in the poem through the image of bleeding, a trope also used in describing wine (as 'tears of blood' for instance).¹⁶² Thus the literal 'bleeding' of the coffee bean as it transforms into a liquid evokes images similar to those used when describing wine: the beloved's 'blood-coloured' lips or the pumping of the blood as the heart races with passion. Furthermore, the notion of 'heating up its customer' suggests both a literal and an erotic meaning. The following line – line four – about the heated face again plays a double function: the heating of coffee and the warm rosy cheeks of the beloved.

Mustafa Âli uses similar language to describe guests at wine parties as their heads heat up and soften with the 'flames of fire'.¹⁶³ Another related issue of importance raised by this and other poems is the symbolism of roasting or carbonization. Often we read that the heart of the melancholic lover burns to the point of blackness.¹⁶⁴ Figani for example in a poem cited earlier writes that 'my sad heart is burnt black in the fire of my breast.'¹⁶⁵

This link between carbonization and the sorrow of unreciprocated love should also inform our reading of Beligi's poem about coffee and its cooking. 'When its face it seen all heated up, everyone wants it,' but perhaps if heated too much to the point of roasting, the fire will overwhelm the prospective lover leaving his heart burnt black. We should also remember that the carbonization of coffee was one of the reasons given by religious jurists for why coffee was considered illegal and therefore forbidden. Katip Çelebi refers to *fatwa*s promulgated against coffee for this very reason.¹⁶⁶

Peçevi also notes official religious opposition to coffee because of its carbonization, but he writes that once coffee and cafés became sufficiently popular to be beyond the point of any possible prohibition, religious officials then changed their decision claiming that coffee did not actually get completely carbonized. Coffee, they asserted, was therefore legal and Peçevi tells us that from among the ulama, sheikhs, viziers and the important members of society there was not one of them that did not drink coffee.¹⁶⁷ Thus, along with symbolizing the burning pain of unrequited love, carbonization and burning also had an air of illegality attached to them.

The second point to be made here is about the issue of the coffee house boy and his representation in Beligi's poem. It was suggested that these boys be allowed only to drink 'simple coffee' – or coffee with no narcotic additives.[168] The genealogy of this position of course harkens back to the role of the *saki* in garden wine parties, and the notion of the café boy as an object of affection or desire is one commented on by numerous observers.[169] Whether or not the coffee house boy was indeed a 'whore' (*kahbe*) with whom one could have sexual relations or merely an attractive boy is not immediately clear from the poem itself. As noted earlier, we do know though that these beardless boys were objects of sexual desire for Ottoman men, and we often read of women and these beardless lads in the same breath as equally suitable sexual objects. In the words of two scholars of Ottoman poetry, Walter Andrews and Mehmed Kalpaklı:

> The beloved is most often male – a young male – and constitutes an ideal of male beauty. Where female beloveds are intended, or where a poem is addressed to a female, there is little, if any, gendered difference in the description of the looks or behaviour of the beloved. ... It is important to remember as well that the beloved of the poetry is ambiguous, androgynous. ... Our topic is a love that does not distinguish the gender of the beloved in any meaningful way.[170]

On the specific topic of beardless boys, Everett Rowson explains that 'the canons for beauty of boys are virtually the same as those for women, a fact underlined by the extraordinary prominence of the question of the beard in homoerotic poetry and anecdote. ... Like women, boys lacked both beards and power, and that they should be assimilated to them as objects of sexual desire as well is hardly surprising.'[171] By way of example, Mustafa Âli states in the sixteenth century that 'the beautiful servant girls and boys ... are usually mentioned as a pair like the houris and male servants of paradise.'[172]

Later, he describes the troops of a certain rebel army doing 'as they please with beardless boys, and the most beautiful and attractive girls, kissing and caressing them'.[173] Similarly, 'hot-blooded young men' are 'fond of drinking and fornicating with women and boys'.[174] Âli condemns any sexual relations between men and boys terming it 'reprehensible to fondle and grope these boys' and instructing – in telling language – that beardless lads should not be used 'as a female animal'.[175] Âli's injunctions, however, made no impact on Ottoman men's sexual wants. He does, nevertheless, go to the trouble of documenting the sexual scheduling required by this Ottoman male desire for both women and boys. Thursday night was reserved for sexual relations with women, Friday night for young men and Friday afternoon for servant boys and beardless youths.[176]

As shown above, Ottoman learned men most often desired these beardless boys more than they did women. Âli complains that 'nowadays there are more dishonorable men who prefer beardless, smooth-cheeked, handsome, and sweet tempered servant boys than there are men who prefer pretty and charming women.'[177]

To explain this phenomenon, Âli suggests that Ottoman men desired boys more than women because women were far too often out of sight, protected by the walls of their homes. It was impossible he said to develop friendships with women. Conversely, a man could travel openly with a boy and be alone with him in the home to develop a meaningful relationship. Âli's complaints thus rest on issues of space, privacy and the home. Since women were at home and difficult to meet and boys were in the market, café and at home, the latter were more suitable companions and friends with whom relations would not seem improper and were more easily established. Coffee-house boys thus again show us how the café challenges and makes more complex traditional understandings of space and gender within the city.

Moreover, the association of coffee with the complicatedly gendered constructions of these young boys, as well as its symbolic link with love and sorrow, help us understand how gender in the Ottoman world was a complex and constantly-negotiated terrain. Again, as Andrews and Kalpaklı state, insofar as the erotic was concerned 'the (elite) male imagination made no practical distinction between boys and girls/ women. The genders blend one into the other. Each one can act the part of the other in an erotic script. Anyone who can be dominated and penetrated can be the object of sexual desire.'[178] Thus, within the gendered power relations of coffee houses, beardless boys – like women – were certainly in positions of weakness as the penetrated objects of men's desire.

We should take care though not to extrapolate this point too far because, 'despite the asymmetry between the sexes symbolized by penetration, neither male nor female homosexual interest or behaviour carries any implications for general conceptions of gender.'[179] Nevertheless, coffee houses, as sites of both coffee – with all its symbolic evocations of the heart and the lover – and coffee-house boys, force us to think of gender in the Ottoman world as a complicated layering of ambiences, identities and desires – a kind of gender-heterotopia. In the Ottoman imagination, the coffee house – like gardens where so many wine parties occurred – is 'a special kind of space, one where the rules of normal (public) space do not apply'.[180]

Moreover, these beardless boys also challenge our ideas of the home and the domestic as exclusive realms of the female, for these lads were not only gendered female but also described in terms that lauded their domestic skills. Commenting on Abyssinian boys, Âli writes that 'if it gets cold in the house, they're everyone's sable fur. One hears that they are especially proficient at taking care of beds – that they adore perfuming the bedclothes with incense and fluffing up and arranging the mattresses and pillows.'[181] Thus, here the young boy is extolled for his domestic and sexual capabilities and praised as an integral part of the household.[182] Thus, if beardless boys disrupt our notions of the Ottoman café as an all-male space where the female did not exist, then they also challenge ideas of the home and the domestic as exclusively feminine zones.

Coffee in the Ottoman world was a material substance infused with various social, religious, cultural, political, medical and economic meanings. For some, it was a religiously forbidden drink that could adversely affect the body, soul and mind of its imbiber. Others saw in coffee an opportunity for financial gain through trade or coffee-house proprietorship.[183] The social manifestation of coffee in the Ottoman world was the coffee house and these institutions, like the drink itself, aroused all kinds of competing emotions and opinions.

My concern here has been to evaluate notions of gender and space in Ottoman cities through an examination of urban neighbourhood cafés. These spaces I believe force us to reassess how we think about Ottoman cities and show how simple distinctions between spaces termed 'public' and 'private' and between notions of 'male' and 'female' are inadequate analytical tools. Ottoman cities were complex places in which gradations of gender and space constantly shifted. Within this continually changing environment, moreover, coffee houses – along with places like public baths and barber shops – existed as heterotopias of overlapping functions and multiple identities.[184] Neither cities nor coffee houses can possibly be understood using simple dichotomies, and to think otherwise is to remain deaf to the Ottoman *mahalle* coffee house.

# Notes

**Chapter 1: Decline, its Discontents and Ottoman Cultural History:
By Way of Introduction by *Dana Sajdi***

This chapter has received more kind attention than it deserves. For their meticulous readings and extensive comments on an earlier version of it, I extend my profound gratitude to Ilham-Khuri Makdisi, Shirine Hamadeh, Mohammed Waked, Farish Noor, Alan Mikhail, Orlin Sabev and Dyala Hamzah. I have also benefited greatly from a lively discussion with colleagues at the Zentrum Moderner Orient, Berlin, where I presented some of the ideas herein. I am also grateful to Shahab Ahmed, who has extended the accustomed encouragement and editorial assistance. This could not have been written without the indispensable help of Rehan Ali, who kindly provided materials that were unavailable to me at the time.

1. Amy Singer, 'Review of *State and Provincial Society in the Ottoman Empire: Mosul, 1540–1834* by Dina Rizk Khoury', *International Journal of Middle East Studies*, 31 (2) 1999, pp. 300–1 (my emphasis).
2. I should make it clear at the outset that this introduction does not aspire to be a survey (for which one for the eighteenth century already exists). Neither does it purport to be comprehensive in its treatment of anti-decline, for the majority of works produced in the past quarter-century have been written in that vein, making the task impossible and imposing selectivity. Last but not least, while it would be instructive to compare the output of the different national and regional academies, for reasons of space this will be devoted mostly to production in the English language. For the aforementioned survey, see Jane Hathaway, 'Rewriting eighteenth-century Ottoman history', *Mediterranean Historical Review*, 19 (1) 2004, pp. 29–53. See also, Karl Barbir, 'The changing face of the Ottoman Empire in the eighteenth century: past and future scholarship', *Oriente Moderno*, 18 (1) 1999, pp. 253–67.
3. See Linda Darling, *Revenue Raising and Legitimacy: Tax Collection and Finance Administration in the Ottoman Empire, 1560–1660* (Leiden: E. J. Brill, 1996), pp. 3–16 (section entitled 'The myth of Ottoman decline'); Cemal Kafadar, 'The question of Ottoman decline', *Harvard Middle*

NOTES FOR CHAPTER 1

Eastern and Islamic Review, 4 (1–2) 1997–98, pp. 30–75; and Hathaway, 'Rewriting eighteenth-century Ottoman history', pp. 30–3.

4. Of course, the locus classicus is Edward Said, Orientalism (New York: Pantheon Books, 1978). For the Ottoman context, see Huri İslamoğlu-İnan, 'Introduction: 'Oriental despotism' in world-system perspective', in Huri İslamoğlu-İnan (ed.) The Ottoman Empire and the World Economy (Cambridge: Cambridge University Press, 1987), pp. 42–7; and Darling, Revenue Raising and Legitimacy, pp. 2–16.
5. Cited above.
6. Albert Hourani, 'The changing face of the Fertile Crescent in the XVIIIth century', Studia Islamica, 8, 1957, p. 91.
7. Halil İnalcık, 'Centralization and decentralization in Ottoman administration', in Thomas Naff and Roger Owen (ed.) Studies in Eighteenth Century Islamic History (Carbondale: Southern Illinois University Press, 1977) pp. 27–52.
8. Abdul-Karim Rafeq, The Province of Damascus (Beirut: Khayyats, 1970).
9. Albert Hourani, 'Ottoman reform and the politics of notables', in W. R. Polk and R. L. Chambers (eds) The Beginnings of Modernization in the Middle East: The Nineteenth Century (Chicago: University of Chicago Press, 1968) pp. 41–68. See the application of the category by Margaret Lee Meriwether, The Kin Who Count: Family and Society in Ottoman Aleppo, 1770–1840 (Austin: University of Texas Press, 1999).
10. Abdul-Karim Rafeq, 'Relations between Syrian ʿulamāʾ and the Ottoman state in the 18th century', Oriente Moderno, 18, 1999, pp. 67–95; and Abdul-Karim Rafeq, 'The Syrian ʿulamāʾ, Ottoman law, and Islamic sharīʿa', Turkica, 26, 1994, pp. 9–32.
11. Thomas Philipp, The Syrians in Egypt (Stuttgart: Franz Steiner Verlag, 1985); Thomas Philipp, 'Jews and Arab Christians: their changing positions in politics and economy in eighteenth century Syria and Egypt', in Amnon Cohen and Gabriel Baer (eds) Egypt and Palestine: A Millennium of Associations (868–1948) (New York: St Martin's Press, 1984).
12. Hourani, 'Changing face of the Fertile Crescent', pp. 91–2. My emphasis.
13. Cornell Fleischer, Bureaucrat and Intellectual in the Ottoman Empire: The Historian Mustafa Âli (1541–1600) (Princeton: Princeton University Press, 1986); Rifaʿat ʿAli Abou-El-Haj's Formation of the Modern State: The Ottoman Empire Sixteenth to Eighteenth Centuries (Albany: State University of New York Press, 1991); Rifaʿat ʿAli Abou-El-Haj, 'The Ottoman nasihatname as a discourse over "morality"', in Abdeljelil Temimi (ed.) Mélanges Professeur Robert Mantran (Zeghouan: Centre d'études et de recherches ottomans, morisques de documentation et d'information, 1988) pp. 17–30; Rifaʿat ʿAli Abou-El-Haj, 'Power and social order: the uses of kanun', in Irene A. Bierman, Rifaʿat Abou-El-Haj and Donald

Preziosi (eds) *The Ottoman City and its Parts: Structures and Social Order* (New Rochelle: A. D. Caratzas, 1991) pp. 77–91. For a less sceptical approach to the *nasihatname* literature, see Cemal Kafadar, 'The myth of the Golden Age: historical consciousness in the post-Suleymanic era', in Halil İnalcık and Cemal Kafadar (eds) *Suleyman the Second and his Time* (Istanbul: Isis Press, 1993) pp. 37–48.
14. Barbir, 'Changing face of the Ottoman Empire', p. 254.
15. H. A. R. Gibb and H. Bowen, vol. I, *Islamic Society in the Eighteenth Century*, part 1 (London: Oxford University Press, 1950). Part 2 of the study came out in 1957 by the same press, but volume 2 never materialized.
16. Norman Itzkowitz, 'Eighteenth century Ottoman realities', *Studia Islamica*, 16, 1962, pp. 73–94.
17. Ibid., p. 81 n.1.
18. Albert Howe Lybyer's *The Government of the Ottoman Empire in the Time of Suleiman the Magnificent* (Cambridge, MA: Harvard University Press, 1913).
19. Itzkowitz, 'Eighteenth-century Ottoman realities', p. 81. It is precisely at this juncture that Itzkowitz adds the footnote for the reconsideration of the decline thesis mentioned in the main text above.
20. 'You'll never plumb the Oriental mind/And even if you do, it won't be worth the toil', ibid., p. 77.
21. Norman Itzkowitz, 'Mehmed Raghib Pasha: the making of an Ottoman vezir' (Ph.D. dissertation, Princeton University, 1959); Thomas V. Lewis, *A Study of Naima*, edited by Norman Itzowitz (New York: New York University Press, 1972); Fleischer, *Bureaucrat and Intellectual*.
22. Roger Owen, 'The Middle East in the eighteenth century: an "Islamic" society in decline? A critique of Gibb and Bowen's *Islamic Society and the West*', *Bulletin of the British Society of Middle Eastern Studies*, 3 (2) 1976, pp. 110–17.
23. Soon afterwards, Thomas Naff along with co-editor Roger Owen published one of the first volumes devoted to the eighteenth century in the vein of post-decline, *Studies in Eighteenth Century Islamic History* (Carbondale: Southern Illinois University Press, 1977).
24. Bernard Lewis, 'Some reflections on the decline of the Ottoman Empire', *Studia Islamica*, 9, 1958, pp. 111 and 111 n.1.
25. Lewis, 'Some reflections on the decline of the Ottoman Empire', p. 112.
26. Bernard Lewis, *The Emergence of Modern Turkey* (London: Oxford University Press, 1962). A third edition was published in 2002.
27. Cited above.
28. Peter Gran, 'Political economy as a paradigm for the study of Islamic history', *International Journal of Middle East Studies*, 11 (4) 1980, pp. 511–26.

29. Peter Gran's *Islamic Roots of Capitalism: Egypt, 1760–1840* (Austin: University of Texas Press, 1979); reissued in paperback (Syracuse: Syracuse University Press, 1998).
30. Gran's book has been reviewed many times by scholars with different expertise, each remonstrating from the point of view of his field. See Charles Issawi, 'Review of *Islamic Roots of Capitalism: Egypt, 1760–1840* by Peter Gran', *Journal of Economic History*, 39 (3) 1979, pp. 800–1; Daniel Crecelius, 'Review of *Islamic Roots of Capitalism: Egypt, 1760–1840* by Peter Gran', *American Historical Review*, 85 (1) 1980, p. 182; Roger Owen, 'Review of *Islamic Roots of Capitalism: Egypt, 1760–1840* by Peter Gran', *Economic History Review*, 33 (1) 1980, pp. 150–1; Donald G. Quataert, 'Review of *Islamic Roots of Capitalism: Egypt, 1760–1840* by Peter Gran', *Business History Review*, 55 (3) 1981, pp. 464–5; and F. De Jong and Peter Gran, 'On Peter Gran, *Islamic Roots of Capitalism: Egypt, 1760–1840*. A review article with author's reply', *International Journal of Middle East Studies*, 14, 1982, pp. 381–99.
31. The book's re-edition in 1998, two full decades after it was first published, is testament to its continued relevance.
32. Huri İslamoğlu-İnan and Çağlar Keyder, 'Agenda for Ottoman history', *Review*, 1 (1) 1977, pp. 31–56. This was later republished in Huri İslamoğlu-İnan (ed.) *The Ottoman Empire and the World Economy*, pp. 43–62. I will use the pagination of the latter.
33. The *çiftlik* estates will become the subject of a debate, see Çağlar Keyder and Faruk Tabak (eds) *Landholding and Commercial Agriculture in the Middle East* (Albany, NY: State University of New York Press, 1991).
34. In response to criticism, İslamoğlu-İnan offered a revised and more nuanced version of the theory's application to the Ottoman context. See her 'Introduction: "Oriental despotism" in world-system perspective' (cited above).
35. Beshara Doumani, *Rediscovering Palestine: Merchants and Peasants in Jabal Nablus, 1700–1900* (Berkeley: University of California Press, 1995).
36. Halil İnalcık, 'The impact of the *Annales School* on Ottoman studies, and new findings', *Review*, 1 (3–4) 1978, pp. 69–96.
37. The most famous of their articles are Ömer Lütfi Barkan, 'The price revolution of the sixteenth century: a turning point in the economic history of the Near East', *International Journal of Middle East Studies*, 6, 1975, pp. 3–28; Halil İnalcık, 'The socio-political effects of the diffusion of fire-arms in the Middle East', in V. J. Parry and M. E. Yapp (eds) *War, Technology and Society in the Middle East* (London: Oxford University Press, 1975) pp. 195–217; and Halil İnalcık, 'Military and fiscal transformations in the Ottoman Empire, 1600–1700', *Archivum Ottomanicum*, 6, 1980, pp. 283–337.
38. A complete list of Suraiya Faroqhi's publications is next to

impossible. Among her more famous book publications are *Towns and Townsmen of Ottoman Anatolia: Trade, Craft and Food Production in an Urban Setting, 1520–1650* (Cambridge: Cambridge University Press, 1984); *Men of Modest Substance: House Owners and House Property in Seventeenth-Century Ankara and Kayseri* (Cambridge: Cambridge University Press, 1987); *Coping with the State: Political Conflict and Crime in the Ottoman Empire, 1550–1720* (Istanbul: Isis Press, 1995); and *Making a Living in the Ottoman Lands, 1480–1820* (Istanbul: Isis Press, 1995).

39. Suraiya Faroqhi, 'Crisis and change 1590–1699' in Halil İnalcık and Donald Quataert (eds) *An Economic and Social History of the Ottoman Empire: 1300–1914* (2 vols, Cambridge: Cambridge University Press, 1994) vol. 2, pp. 469–70. I was first made aware of the model and Faroqhi's utilization of it in Darling, *Revenue Raising and Legitimacy*, pp. 8–10.
40. İslamoğlu-İnan, 'Introduction', p. 19.
41. It should be noted that some of these studies benefited from the seminal article by Mehmed Genç on the Ottoman finance department and the change of land tenure patterns from *timar* (land grants) to *iltizam* (short-term tax farms) to *malikane* (life-long tax farms). See his 'Osmanlı Maliyesinde Malikane Sistemi', in Osman Okyar (ed.) *Türkiye İktisat Tarihi Semineri Metinler/Tartışmalar* (Ankara: Hacttepe Üniversitesi Yayınları, 1975) pp. 231–96. Also, Darling's oft cited *Revenue Raising and Legitimacy* is in the same vein.
42. Published in Albany by State University of New York Press in 1991 and in Syracuse by Syracuse University Press in 2005.
43. Abou-El-Haj, *Formation of the Modern State*, p. 29.
44. Ariel Salzmann, 'An ancien regime revisited: "privatization" and political economy in the eighteenth-century Ottoman Empire', *Politics and Society*, 21 (4) 1993, pp. 393–423.
45. Ibid., p. 409.
46. Karen Barkey, *Bandits and Bureaucrats: The Ottoman Route to State Centralization* (Ithaca: Cornell University Press, 1994), p. x.
47. Published by Oxford University Press in 1993.
48. See Hathaway's evaluation of the utilization of law court records and central state archives as sources for Ottoman history, 'Rewriting eighteenth-century Ottoman history', p. 36. For a good introduction to the variety of Ottoman sources, see Suraiya Faroqhi, *Approaching Ottoman History: An Introduction to the Sources* (Cambridge: Cambridge University Press, 1999).
49. André Raymond, *Artisans et commerçants au Caire au XVIIIe siècle* (2 vols, Damascus: Institut français de Damas, 1973–74).
50. Published in New York by Columbia University Press in 1989.

51. Naturally, I am not claiming that empirical research has been or should be limited to urban history, but merely that it is the stark difference between the textual ideal and practice in urban history that acutely demonstrates the need for empirical research.
52. Hathaway, 'Rewriting eighteenth-century Ottoman history', p. 38.
53. For a monographic treatment of one of the most important reformers in the eighteenth century, see Bernard Haykel, *Revival and Reform: The Legacy of Muḥammad al-Shawkānī* (Cambridge: Cambridge University Press, 2003).
54. Fazlur Rahman, *Islam* (Chicago: Chicago University Press, 1979). For a critique of this concept, see R. S. O'Fahey and Bernd Radtke, 'Neo-Sufism reconsidered', *Der Islam*, 70, 1993, pp. 52–87.
55. Examples are John O. Voll, 'Linking groups in the networks of eighteenth century revivalist scholars: the Mijzāzī family of Yemen', in Nehemia Levtzion and John O. Voll (eds) *Eighteenth Century Renewal and Reform in Islam* (Syracuse: Syracuse University Press, 1987) pp. 69–92; John O. Voll, 'Muḥammad Yaḥyā al-Sirhindī and Muḥammad ibn ᶜAbd al-Wahhāb: an analysis of an intellectual community in eighteenth century Madina', *Bulletin of the School of Oriental and African Studies*, 38 (1) 1975, pp. 32–9; and John O. Voll, "ᶜAbdallah Ibn Salīm al-Baṣrī and 18th century Ḥadīth studies', *Die Welts des Islams*, 42 (3) 2002, pp. 356–72. See also Bashir Nafi, 'Taṣawwuf and reform in pre-modern Islamic culture: in search of Ibrāhīm al-Kūrānī', *Die Welts des Islams*, 42 (3) 2002, pp. 307–55.
56. Reinhard Schulze, 'Das islamische achtzehnte Jahrhundert: Versuch einer historiographischen Kritik', *Die Welt des Islams*, 30, 1990, pp. 140–59; and Reinhard Schulze, 'Was ist die islamische Aufklärung?' *Die Welt des Islams*, 36 (3) 1996, pp. 276–325. For an extensive bibliography of the debate, see Stefan Reichmuth, 'Arabic literature and Islamic scholarship in the 17th/18th century: topics and biographies', *Die Welt des Islams*, 42 (3) 2002, pp. 281 n.1. For an English summary of the debate, see Albrecht Hofheinz, 'Illumination and Enlightenment revisited, or: pietism and the roots of Islamic modernity', unpublished, available at http://195.37.93.199/hofheinz/HOFHEINZ.htm (I am grateful to the author for allowing me to cite the paper here.)
57. See Hofheinz, 'Illumination and Enlightenment revisited', pp. 6–8; Bernd Radtke *Autochthone islamische Aufklärung im 18. Jahrhundert, Theoretische und filolgische Überlegungen. Fortsetzung einer Debatte* (Utrecht: M. Th. Houtsma Stichting, 2000).
58. Reichmuth, 'Arabic literature and Islamic scholarship', p. 282.
59. In this regard Ahmad Dallal has located originality while simultaneously exercising caution by differentiating between the different reform movements. See his 'The origins and objectives of Islamic

revivalist thought, 1750–1850', *Journal of the American Oriental Society*, 113 (3) 1993, pp. 341–59.

60. Khaled El-Rouayheb, 'Opening the gate of verification: the forgotten Arab–Islamic florescence of the 17th century', *International Journal of Middle Eastern Studies*, 38 (2) 2006, pp. 263–81; Khaled El-Rouayheb, 'Was there a revival of logical studies in eighteenth-century Egypt?' *Die Welts des Islams*, 45 (1) 2005, pp. 1–19; and Khaled El-Rouayheb, 'Sunni Muslim scholars on the status of logic, 1500–1800', *Islamic Law and Society*, 11 (2) 2004, pp. 213–32.

61. One of the few exceptions is Barbara Rosenow-von Schlegell's treatment of the Damascene Sufi and scholar ʿAbd al-Ghanī al-Nābulusī. Her study reveals that much of al-Nābulusī's polemics constituted an engagement with the Kadızadeli movement. See Barbara Rosenow-von Schlegell, 'Sufism in the Ottoman Arab world: Shaykh ʿAbd al-Ghanī al-Nābulusī' (Ph.D. dissertation, University of California, Berkeley, 1997).

62. In this regard, Peter Gran's study of al-ʿAṭṭār in *Islamic Roots of Capitalism* is an exception.

63. Madeline C. Zilfi, *The Politics of Piety: The Ottoman Ulema in the Post-Classical Age (1600–1800)* (Minneapolis: Bibliotheca Islamica, 1988).

64. Fleischer, *Bureaucrat and Intellectual*.

65. Kafadar, 'The question of Ottoman decline', p. 22.

66. Ibid., p. 32.

67. Kafadar had worked on this issue in his earlier essay, 'The myth of the golden age'.

68. Kafadar, 'The question of Ottoman decline', p. 34.

69. Recently, Dror Zeʾevi has called for a return to the Napoleonic moment as the marker of modernity, as he sees in the colonial encounter the beginning of modernity for both East and West. See his 'Back to Napoleon? Thoughts on the beginning of the modern era in the Middle East', *Mediterranean Historical Review*, 19 (1) 2004, pp. 73–94.

70. Ibid., p. 56.

71. Published in London by I.B.Tauris in 2000. This is the English version of *Kultur und Alltag im Osmanischen Reich* (Munich: C. H. Beck'sche, 1995).

72. Donald Quataert (ed.) *Consumption Studies and the History of the Ottoman Empire, 1550–1922: An Introduction* (Albany: State University of New York, 2000). A year earlier, James Paul Grehan finished a dissertation entitled 'Culture and consumption in eighteenth-century Damascus' (Ph.D. dissertation, University of Texas at Austin, 1999).

73. On the attitude to disability, see Sara Scalenghe 'The deaf in Ottoman Syria, 16th–18th centuries', *Arab Studies Journal*, 12–13, 2004–2005, pp. 10–25; on public gardens, see Shirine Hamadeh, 'Public spaces and the garden culture of Istanbul in the eighteenth century', in Virginia Aksan and Dan Goffman (eds) *The Early Modern Ottomans: Remapping the*

## NOTES FOR CHAPTER 1

Empire (Cambridge: Cambridge University Press, forthcoming); on homoeroticism, see Khaled El-Rouayheb, *Before Homosexuality in the Arab-Islamic World, 1500–1800* (Chicago: Chicago University Press, 2005); and Walter G. Andrews and Mehmed Kalpaklı, *The Age of Beloveds: Love and the Beloved in Early Modern Ottoman and European Culture and Society* (Durham: Duke University Press, 2005); on popular protest, see James Grehan, 'Street violence and social imagination in late-Mamluk and Ottoman Damascus (*c.* 1500–1800)', *International Journal of Middle East Studies*, 35 (2) 2003, pp. 214–36; and for references on coffee house culture, see Alan Mikhail and Ali Çaksu's contributions in this volume.

74. İslamoğlu-İnan, 'Introduction', pp. 4 and 5.
75. Kafadar, 'The question of Ottoman decline', p. 63.
76. Cemal Kafadar, 'Self and others: the diary of a dervish in seventeenth century Istanbul and first-person narratives in Ottoman literature', *Studia Islamica*, 69 (1989), pp. 121–50.
77. Derin Terzioğlu, 'Man in the image of God in the image of the times: Sufi self-narrative and the diary of Niyāzī-i Mıṣrī (1618–94)', *Studia Islamica*, 94, 2002, pp. 139–65.
78. Dana Sajdi, 'A room of his own: the "history" of the barber of Damascus (fl. 1762)', *The MIT Electronic Journal of Middle East Studies*, 4, 2004, pp. 19–35.
79. Astrid Meier, 'Perceptions of a new era? Historical writing in early modern Ottoman Damascus', *Arabica*, 4, 2004, pp. 419–34. It is noteworthy that the journal issue is devoted to the *early modern* history of the Levant under the editorship of Thomas Philipp.
80. *In Praise of Books: A Cultural History of Cairo's Middle Class, Sixteenth to the Eighteenth Century* (Syracuse: Syracuse University Press, 2003). One of the earlier treatments of reading and book history in the Ottoman empire is the issue of *Revue du mondes musulmans et de la Méditerannée*, 87–88 (1999). The title of the collection is 'Livres et lectures dans le monde ottoman'. For book ownership in eighteenth-century Damascus, see the statistical study by Colette Establet and Jean Paul Pascual, 'Le livres des gens à Damas vers 1700', *Revue du mondes musulman et la Méditerranée*, 87–8 (1999), pp. 143–75.
81. Ariel Salzmann, 'The age of tulips: confluence and conflict in early modern consumer culture (1550–1730)', in Donald Quataert (ed.) *Consumption Studies and the History of the Ottoman Empire, 1550–1922: An Introduction* (Albany: State University of New York Press, 2000) pp. 83–106.
82. On public gardens, see Hamadeh, 'Public spaces'; on new architectural trends, see Tülay Artan, 'Architecture as a theatre of life: profile of the eighteenth century Bosphorus' (Ph.D. dissertation, Massachusetts Institute of Technology, 1989).

83. Salzmann, 'The age of tulips', p. 88.
84. Ibid., p. 83.
85. While I was writing this, a number of senior colleagues sent postings on one of the professional electronic mail lists to express their frustration at working with educational documentary film productions on the Ottoman empire. No matter how much these scholars have tried to influence content and approach, the films have invariably portrayed the Ottoman empire in the post-sixteenth century as one in decline. About a recent history channel production entitled 'The Ottoman Empire: the war machine' in which he participated, Donald Quataert commented, 'the presentation of these centuries of decline included film makers' statements about the Ottomans' lack of an economy, political order and culture, not to mention the absence of any social formation.' Message dated 27 August 2006 on H-Turk, Humanities and Social Sciences On-Line, http://h-net.msu.edu/cgi-bin/logbrowse.pl?trx=vx&list=h-turk&month=0608&week=d&msg=WnSYyUpI6e3kVX4dTgiwYw&user=&pw= There are subsequent messages on the same subject by Suraiya Faroqhi, Amy Singer and Cornell Fleischer.
86. See Aijaz Ahmad, 'Empire comes to Lebanon', *Frontline*, 23 (15) 29 July to 11 August 2006, http://www.hinduonnet.com/fline/fl2315/stories/20060811005800600.htm
87. In this regard, see Rifaʿat Abou-El-Haj, 'The social uses for the past: recent Arab historiography of Ottoman rule', *International Journal of Middle East Studies*, 14 (2) 1982, pp. 185–201. For Turkish nationalist historiography, see Halil Berktay, 'The search for the peasant in Western and Turkish historiography', in Halil Berktay and Suraiya Faroqhi (eds) *New Approaches to State and Peasant in Ottoman History* (London: Frank Cass, 1992) pp 109–84.
88. See Abou-El-Haj's afterword, 'Theorizing beyond the nation-state', to his book *Formation of the Modern State*.
89. The emerging field of world history promises new conceptualizations. For a contribution to world history by an Ottomanist, see Peter Gran, *Beyond Eurocentricism: A New View of Modern World History* (Syracuse: State University of New York Press, 1996).

## Chapter 2: The Perception of Saadabad: The 'Tulip Age' and Ottoman–Safavid Rivalry by *Can Erimtan*

1. Mehmed Efendi Râşid, *Tarih-i Râşid* (6 vols, Istanbul: Matbaa-ı Âmire, 1282/1865, second edition) vol. 5, *Hitâm-ı Binâ-yı Saadabad*, pp. 443–5. Vol. 6 of *Tarih-i Râşid* is *Tarih-i Çelebizâde* by Çelebizâde Ismail Asim Efendi.
2. During the tenth International Congress of Turkish Art in 1995, I first

suggested an intra-Ottoman interpretation of Saadabad, as well as a possible link up between the construction of Saadabad in Istanbul and Ahmed III's political and military programmes in Iran. Rather than looking for external sources for the architectural configuration of Damad İbrahim's Kâğıthane project, I suggested a parallel with the architectural and wider cultural patronage of Ahmed III's father Mehmed IV (1648–87) in Edirne. Cf. Can Erimtan, 'The case of Saadabad: Westernization or revivalism?' *Art turc/Turkish Art, 10e Congrès international d'art turc, Proceedings of the 10th International Congress of Turkish Art, Geneva, Fondation Max van Berchem, September 1995* (Geneva: Fondation Max van Berchem, 1999) pp. 287–90; Attilio Petruccioli (ed.) *Gardens in the Time of the Great Muslim Empires: Theory and Design* (Leiden: E. J. Brill, 1997).

3. Ezel Kural Shaw, 'The double veil: travellers' views of the Ottoman Empire', in Ezel Kural Shaw and C. J. Heywood (eds) *English and Continental Views of the Ottoman Empire, 1500–1800* (Los Angeles: William Andrews Clark Memorial Library, 1972) pp. 1–29.
4. Charles Perry, *A View of the Levant: Particularly of Constantinople, Syria, Egypt, and Greece: In Which their Antiquities, Government, Politics, Maxims, Manners, and Customs, (with Many Other Circumstances and Contingencies) are Attempted to be Described and Treated on. In Four Parts* (London: T. Woodward & J. Shuckburgh, 1743) pp. 24–5.
5. Mehmed Efendi Râşid, *Tarih-i Râşid*, vol. 5, pp. 213–14 ('İrsâl-i Elçi-i Cânib-i Fırânçe').
6. Göçek even claims that the *Cedvel-i Sim* was 'copied most likely from Versailles'. The eminent Eldem admits that the *Cedvel-i Sim* is somewhat reminiscent of the canal at Fontainebleau, but continues that he was unable to detect any traces of French art in the layout of the canal: 'Fontainebleau kanalını olsa olsa biçim ve uzunluğu ile andıran Cetvel-i Sîmden başka, bu kompozisyonda Fransız sanatının etkisi hatırlatan bir bölüm görmemekte olduğumu itiraf ederim'. F. M. Göçek, *East Encounters West: France and the Ottoman Empire in the Eighteenth Century* (New York: Oxford University Press, 1987) pp. 75–6; S. H. Eldem, *Sa'dabad* (Istanbul: Devlet Kitapları Müdürlüğü, 1977).
7. Literally, Eldem writes that '[b]öyle olduğu halde ... Türk geleneğine yabancılığını tanıtlamağa çalışmanın yersiz ve gereksizliği meydandadır'; [and] '[b]undan başka, Çağlayanların bütünüyle Türk mimarî tarzı ve dekoruna sadık kaldıkları ... unutmamalıdır', S. H. Eldem, *Sa'dabad*, önsöz/preface.
8. Compare S. Bozdoğan, 'In search of a national architecture', in H.-U. Khan (ed.) *Sedad Eldem* (Singapore: Concept Mediapp, 1987).
9. Heidi Walcher says that 'Shah Abbas I himself designed and planned the new city, south of the old Saljuq center ... Safavid Isfahan shows an

## NOTES FOR CHAPTERS 2

internal order, which is structured along the axial quadripartite pattern of a *chahar bagh* ... formed by the axes of the river Zayendehrud and the royal avenue *Khiaban-i Chahar Bagh*'. Heidi A. Walcher, 'Between paradise and political capital: the semiotics of Safavid Isfahan', in Jeff Albert, Magnus Bernhardsson and Roger Kenna (eds) *Transformations of the Middle Eastern Environments: Legacies and Lessons* (New Haven: Yale University Press, 1998) pp. 330–48.

10. Recently, two very different scholars have written pieces that suggest the far-reaching influence of intellectual currents active in the second constitutional era. Michael Ursinus, *Quellen zur Geschichte des Osmanischen Reiches und ihre Interpretation* (Istanbul: Isis, 1994) pp. 131–47; and Ekmeleddin İhsanoğlu, 'Osmanlı Medrese Tarihçiliğinin İlk Safhası (1916–1965) – Keşif ve Tasarlama Dönemi', *Belleten*, 164 (August) 2000, pp. 541–82.

11. The *Encümen* consisted of 12 permanent members, who either occupied posts in government departments or inside the army. Two members had been lecturers at the *Dârülfünûn*, Efdaleddin (Tekiner) Bey and Dirân Kullikân Efendi, this last one had also been a journalist attached to the daily *Sabah*. For this reason they were not to receive any wages. Tarih-i Osmanî Encümeni, 'İfâde-i Merâm', *Tarih-i Osmanî Encümeni Mecmuası* (*TOEM*), 1 (1) 1–14 April 1326/1910, pp. 1, 6 and 8.

12. Bruce McGowan, 'The age of the Ayans, 1699–1812', in Halil İnalcık and D. Quataert (eds) *An Economic and Social History of the Ottoman Empire, 1300–1914* (2 vols, Cambridge, Cambridge University Press, 1994), vol. 2 p. 640.

13. Cf. M. Gökman, *Tarihi Sevdiren Adam: Ahmet Refik Altınay – Hayatı ve Eserleri* (Istanbul: İş Bankası Yayınları, 1978).

14. Ahmed Refik, 'Lâle Devri', *İkdam*, 5763 (9 March 1913). The pieces were subsequently collectively published in book form. Ahmed Refik, *Lâle Devri (1130–1143)* (Istanbul: Kitabhâne-i İslam ve Askeriyye, 1331/1915, first edition).

15. My thesis entitled 'Ottomans looking West? The idea of a "Tulip Age (1718–30)" and its development in Turkish historiography, 1908–50' (D.Phil. dissertation, Oxford University, 2003) deals in great detail with the development of the trope of the beneficial effects of Damad İbrahim's tenure as grand vizier. For a detailed treatment of the topos of the *Lâle Devri* and its sources, see the article I wrote based on my doctoral research. C. Erimtan, 'The sources of Ahmed Refik's *Lâle Devri* and the paradigm of the "Tulip Age": a teleological agenda', in M. Kagar and Zeynep Durukal (eds) *Festschrift in Honour of Professor Ekmeleddin İhsanoğlu* (Istanbul: IRCICA, 2006) pp. 259–78. In addition, see my book entitled *Ottomans Looking West? The Idea of the 'Tulip Age' and its Development in Turkish Historiography* (London: I.B.Tauris, forthcoming).

## NOTES FOR CHAPTER 2

16. Ahmed Cevdet, *Tarih-i Cevdet* (12 vols, Istanbul, 1270–1301/1854–84).
17. 'Fazıl Ahmed Paşanın vefâtından Damad İbrahim Paşanın devrine gelince zuhûra gelen ahvâl-ı muhtelife beyânındadır', pp. 25–38; 'İbrahim Paşa devrinden Ragıb Paşanın vefâtına kadar zuhura gelen etvâr-ı muhtelife beyânındadır', pp. 38–45 (both in Cevdet, *Tarih-i Cevdet*, vol. 1).
18. Şemdânizâde Süleyman Efendi, *Şem'dâni-zâde Fındıklılı Süleyman Efendi Târihi Mûr'i't-Tevârih*, edited by M. M. Aktepe (3 vols, Istanbul: Edebiyat Fakültesi Matbaası, 1976) vol. 1, pp. 1–10.
19. H.-Â. Yücel, 'Ahmed Refik', *Akşam*, 18 October 1937. Quoted in M. Gökman, *Tarihi Sevdiren Adam*, p. 61.
20. The term 'Whiggish history', as coined by Herbert Butterfield (1900–79) in 1931, seems apt to describe Ahmed Refik's methodological practice. Peter Burke describes a 'Whig interpretation of history' as 'the use of the past to justify the present'. P. Burke, 'Origins of cultural history', in P. Burke (ed.) *Varieties of Cultural History* (Cambridge: Polity Press, 1997), p. 1.
21. Liman von Sanders pointed out that his charge had not been a politically inspired German move: 'the activity of the military mission was to be strictly military'. The German in fact did not arrive in Istanbul until 14 December 1913, but the contract detailing his responsibilities had been drawn up the previous November. He was to occupy this post until the end of the war in 1918. Otto Liman von Sanders, *Five Years in Turkey* (Annapolis, MD: United States Naval Institute, 1928, second edition) pp. 2–3; S. J. Shaw and E. K. Shaw, *History of the Ottoman Empire and Modern Turkey* (2 vols, Cambridge: Cambridge University Press, 1977), vol. 2, p. 308.
22. Refik, *Lâle Devri*, p. 93.
23. Tayyarzâde Ahmed Atâ, *Tarih-i Atâ* (5 vols, Istanbul, 1293/1876). The information on Damad İbrahim can be found in vol. 2, p. 156.
24. S. Aşgin, 'Hadikatü'l-Vüzera Üzerine Bir İnceleme', *OTAM*, 14, 2003, pp. 145–61; and Osmanzade Taib et al., *Hadikat ül-Vüzerâ* (Istanbul: Ceride-i Havadis Matbaası, 1271/1854–5, facsimile edition, Freiburg, 1969).
25. Dilaverzâde Ömer Efendi, '(Damad İbrahim Paşa)', in *Hadikat ül-Vüzerâ*, pp. 29–36.
26. İbrahim Müteferrika, *Usûl ül-Hikem fi Nizâm ül-Ümem* (Istanbul: Matbaa-ı Âmire, 1144/1732).
27. N. Berkes, *The Development of Secularism in Turkey* (Montreal: McGill University Press, 1964) pp. 42–5.
28. Müteferrika, *Usûl ül-Hikem*, p. 39.
29. Refik, *Lâle Devri*, pp. 36–7.
30. Ibid., p. 37.
31. The monograph 'Fatma Sultan' was first serialized in *İkdam* (9, 13, 15, 16, 18, 20, 22 December 1332/1916). Ahmed Refik, *Fatma Sultan*:

## NOTES FOR CHAPTERS 2

*Garyrî Matbû Vesikalara Nazaran Yazılmışdır* (Istanbul: Diken Matbaası, n.d.) p. 43.
32. A. Vandal, *Une ambassade française en Orient sous Louis XV: la mission du Marquis de Villeneuve 1728–1741* (Paris: E. Plon, Nourrit & Cie, 1887) p. 90.
33. Refik, *Fatma*, p. 43.
34. Cf. F. R. Unat, *Osmanlı Sefirleri ve Sefâretnâmeleri*, edited by B. S. Baykal (Ankara: Türk Tarih Kurumu, 1968).
35. The report of Yermisekiz Çelebi, 'Takrir-i Sefer-i Müşârünileyh' is published in Mehmed Efendi Râşid, *Tarih-i Râşid*, vol. 5, pp. 330–67.
36. This *topos* was first introduced into mainstream literature by the renowned academic and writer Ahmed Hamdi Tanpınar. A. H. Tanpınar, *Ondokuzuncu Asır Türk Edebiyatı Tarihi* (Istanbul: Istanbul Üniversitesi Edebiyat Fakültesi Yayınları, 1942), pp. 8, 62 and 190.
37. S. J. Shaw and E. K. Shaw, *History of the Ottoman Empire*, vol. 1, p. 233; *Encyclopedia of Islam*, s.v. 'Ahmad III'; ibid., s.v. 'Lâle Devri'.
38. A. Wheatcroft, *The Ottomans* (London: Viking, 1993) p. 81.
39. A. Rigney, 'Narrativity and historical representation', *Poetics Today*, 12 (3) Fall 1991, pp. 591–605.
40. Even though no one seems to take Goodwin seriously any more, his phrases are symptomatic of the teleological nature of the appreciation of the material culture of the so-called 'Tulip Age'. G. Goodwin, *A History of Ottoman Architecture* (London: Thames & Hudson, 1971) p. 373.
41. R. W. Olson, 'The esnaf and the Patrona Halil rebellion of 1730: a realignment in Ottoman politics', *Journal of the Economic and Social History of the Orient*, 17, 1974, pp. 329–30.
42. A. Salzmann, 'The age of tulips', pp. 83–106.
43. Ş. Mardin, 'Center–periphery relations: a key to Turkish politics', *Daedalus*, 102 (1) Winter 1973, p. 175.
44. Ibid.
45. The art historian Esin Atıl made the following observation in the late 1960s: 'the everlasting court parties sponsored by Ibrahim Paşa taking place in waterside pavilions on the Bosporus and Golden Horn have close resemblance to the *fêtes champêtres* of Rococo France.' Apparently unfounded and anachronistic statements such as these may have led Silay to regard Ahmed III and Damad İbrahim as secularizers *avant-la-lettre*. E. Atıl, 'Surname-i Vehbi: an eighteenth century Ottoman book of festivals' (Ph.D. dissertation, University of Michigan, 1969) p. 346; Kemal Silay, *Nedim and the Poetics of the Ottoman Court: Medieval Inheritance and the Need for Change* (Bloomington: Indiana University Press, 1994) p. 79.
46. Hayden V. White, 'The historical text as a literary artefact', *Clio*, 3 (3)

(1974); republished in Hayden V. White, *Tropics of Discourse: Essays in Cultural Criticism* (Baltimore: Johns Hopkins University Press, 1985) pp. 81–100.

47. F. R. Ankersmit, *Historical Representation* (Stanford: Stanford University Press, 2001).
48. *Encyclopedia of Islam*, s.v. 'Ahmad III'.
49. A. Y. Ocak, 'Islam in the Ottoman Empire: a sociological framework for a new interpretation', *International Journal of Turkish Studies*, 9 (1 and 2) Summer 2003, pp. 183–97.
50. R. Ettinghausen, 'Introduction', in E. B. Macdougal and R. Ettinghausen (eds) *The Islamic Garden* (Washington: Dumbarton Oaks, 1976) p. 3.
51. E. Koch, 'Diwan-i Amm and Chihil Sutun: the audience halls of Shah Jahan', *Muqarnas*, 11, 1994, pp. 143–65.
52. S. P. Blake, *Shahjahanabad: The Sovereign City in Mughal India 1639–1739* (Cambridge: Cambridge University Press, 1991).
53. Recently, Sanjay Subrahmanyam wrote an interesting article about inter-dynastic communications and exchanges, particularly paying attention to 'empires ... [that] belonged to overlapping cultural zones [such as] the [empires of the] Ottomans, Safavids and Mughals'. S. Subrahmanyam, 'Beyond incommensurability: understanding inter-imperial dynamics', 2005. http://repositories.cdlib.org/uclasoc/trcsa/32
54. Ahmed Yaşar Ocak has recently argued that the relationship between the Ottomans and the Safavids has not been fully investigated by Turkish historians of the Ottoman Empire. He claims that Western historians (*batılı tarihçiler*), by contrast, have traditionally displayed a greater interest in the interactions of these two Islamic rivals. A. Y. Ocak, 'Osmanlı Kaynaklarında ve Modern Türk Tarihçiliğinde Osmanlı-Safevî Münasebetleri (XVI–XVII Yuzyıllar)', *Belleten*, 66 (246) 2002, pp. 503–16; cf. Erimtan, 'The case of Saadabad'; Shirine Hamadeh, 'Ottoman expressions of early modernity and the "inevitable" question of Westernization', *Journal of the Society of Architectural Historians*, 61 (1) March 2004, pp. 32–51.
55. Sussan Babaie declares that 'the Chihil Sutun was the largest palace within the confines of the Daulatkhana, the palace precinct in Isfahan.' Babaie quotes her own work entitled 'Safavid palaces at Isfahan: continuity and change (1599–1666)' (Ph.D. dissertation, New York University, 1994) when talking about the Chihil Sutun. Sussan Babaie, 'Shah ᶜAbbas II, the conquest of Qandahar, the Chihil Sutun, and its wall paintings', *Muqarnas*, 11, 1994, p. 126.
56. Babaie states that they are actually 'eighteen slender wooden columns'. J. Chardin, *Voyages de Monsieur Chevalier Chardin en Perse et autres lieux d'Orient* (4 vols, Amsterdam: Chez Jean Louis de Lorme, 1711), vol. 3, pp. 56–7, 59–60; S. S. Blair and J. M. Bloom, *The Art and*

## NOTES FOR CHAPTERS 2

Architecture of Islam 1250–1800 (New Haven: Yale University Press, 1995) pp. 192–5.
57. Shirine Hamadeh, 'Ottoman expressions of early modernity', pp. 32–51.
58. Robert Hillenbrand remarks that a numerical explanation of the name Chihil Sutun 'is surely a picturesque fantasy', indicating that 'chihil' most probably denotes 'many' rather than 'forty' pillars. R. Hillenbrand, 'Safavid architecture', in P. Jackson and L. Lockhart (eds) *The Cambridge History of Iran* (7 vols, Cambridge: Cambridge University Press, 1986) vol. 6, *The Timurid and Safavid Periods*, p. 797.
59. Krautheimer obviously attempted to apply Erwin Panofsky's (1892–1968) insights on the iconography and iconology of the pictorial arts to the field of architecture (cf. his *Studies in Iconology*, originally published in 1939 by Oxford University Press). Richard Krautheimer, 'Introduction to an iconography of mediaeval architecture', *Journal of the Warburg and Courtauld Institutes*, 5, 1942, p. 10.
60. Gülru Necipoğlu, 'The suburban landscape of sixteenth-century Istanbul as a mirror of classical Ottoman garden culture', in Attilio Petruccioli (ed.) *Gardens in the Time of the Great Muslim Empires: Theory and Design* (Leiden: E. J. Brill) p. 32.
61. Ibid.
62. Mahvash Alemi, 'Chahar Bagh', *Environmental Design: Journal of the Islamic Environmental Research Centre*, 1, 1986, pp. 38–45.
63. Ibid., p. 38.
64. Gülru Necipoğlu, 'The suburban landscape', pp. 33 and 39.
65. Ibid., p. 32; *Dünden Bugüne İstanbul Ansiklopedisi*, s.v. 'Karabali Bahçesi'; Muzaffer Erdoğan, 'Osmanlı Devrinde İstanbul Bahçeleri', *Vakıflar Dergisi*, 4, 1958, p. 170.
66. Muzaffer Erdoğan mentions that the garden known as *Bagçe-i Bâli-i Siyah* in the sixteenth and seventeenth centuries received the denomination *Bagçe-i Karabâli* in documents pertaining to the late seventeenth and early eighteenth centuries. Erdoğan, 'Osmanlı Devrinde', p. 170.
67. According to the pharmacist Reinhold Lubenau (1566–1620), present in Istanbul in 1587, the layout at the *Bagçe-i Karabâli* included a panel representing Sultan Selim I's (1512–20) victorious battle at Çaldıran (23 August 1514/2 Recep 920). Necipoğlu, 'The suburban landscape', p. 33.
68. Sultan Beyazid II (1481–1512) pursued a policy of appeasement towards Shah Ismaᶜil and the Safavid threat to the Ottoman state. Once, şehzâde [prince] Selim forcibly occupied the throne on 7 Safer 918/24 April 1512, however, he immediately initiated a strict policy to suppress the threat to the central authority posed by an elaborate network of Safavid agents active inside the Ottoman dominions. In pursuing these goals Selim the

## NOTES FOR CHAPTER 2

Grim [Yavuz] transformed the Ottoman state into a vehement defender of the *Sunni* creed. Adel Allouche, *The Origins and Development of the Ottoman–Safavid Conflict (906–962/1500–1555)* (Berlin: K. Schwarz Verlag, 1983) pp. 89, 112, 167–9; and Irene Beldiceanu-Steinherr, 'Le règne de Selim Ier: tournant dans la vie politique et religieuse de l'empire ottoman', *Turcica*, 6, 1975, p. 34.

69. Heidi Walcher ('Between paradise and political capital', p. 330) declares that 'the visual image of Isfahan has been inextricably shaped both by its architecture and its royal palace gardens.'
70. Râşid, *Tarih-i Râşid*, vol. 5, pp. 163–4 ('İrsâl-ı Elçi- Bi-Cânib-i Şah-ı Acem').
71. Râsid Efendi recorded the following telling phrase in his chronicle: 've [Dürrî Efendinin] getirdiği cevâb-nâme ve takririnden hakikat-ı hale ıtlâ hâsıl oldu', *Tarih-i Râşid*, vol. 5, p. 371.
72. Ahmed Efendi Dürrî, *Relation de Dourry Effendy, ambasssadeur de la Porte othomane auprès du Roi de Perse, en 1720, présentée au Sultan Ahmed III*, edited by L.-M. Langlès (Paris: Ferra, 1810).
73. R. W. Olson, *The Siege of Mosul and Ottoman–Persian Relations 1718–1743* (Bloomington: Indiana University Press, 1975) p. 43.
74. Taking the long view, John Foran states that 'long- and medium-term structural factors combined with a series of contingent historical circumstances to bring about the fall of the [Safavid] dynasty' in 1722. John Foran, 'The long fall of the Safavid dynasty: moving beyond the standard views', *International Journal of Middle East Studies*, 24 (2) May 1992, pp. 281–304.
75. The decision to commence hostilities was presented as a religious duty because the inhabitants of the Iranian lands had been found guilty of apostasy: 'El-Cevab: Diyarlari darulharbdir ve uzerlerine ahkam-i murteddin icra olunur'. The *fetva* is quoted in Y. Halaçoğlu, *XIV–XVII: Yüzyıllarda Osmanlılarda Devlet Teşkilâtı ve Sosyal Yapı* (Ankara: Türk Tarih Kurumu Basımevi, 1995), appendix VI, p. 209; Râşid, *Tarih-i Râşid*, vol. 6, 64–5 ('Sûret-i Fetvâ-yı Şerife').
76. S. A. Arjomand, 'The Mujtahid of the age and the Mulla-bashi', in Said Amir Arjomand (ed.) *Authority and Political Culture in Shiʿism* (Albany: State University of New York Press, 1988) pp. 84–5.
77. T. J. Krusinski, *The History of the Revolution of Persia*, translated by Father J. A. du Cerceau (2 vols, London: J. Pemberton, 1728), vol. 1, p. 125.
78. S. H. Eldem, *Köşkler ve Kasırlar: A Survey of Turkish Kiosks and Pavilions* (2 vols, Istanbul: Kutulmuş Matbaasi, 1968–74), vol. 1, p. xvii.
79. R. Hillenbrand, 'Safavid architecture', pp. 760, 797.
80. Numerous examples can be found in Çelebizâde's text in Râşid, *Tarih-i Râşid*, vol. 6, *passim*.

## NOTES FOR CHAPTERS 2

81. Gel hele bir kerrecik seyr et göze olmaz yasağ Oldu Saadabad şimdi sevdiğim dağ üstü bağ Çar-bağ-ı Isfahanı eylemiştir dağ bağ Oldu Saadabad şimdi sevdiğim dağ üstü bağ. Ahmed Nedim, *Nedim Divanı*, edited by A. Gölpınarlı (Istanbul: İnkılâp ve Aka Kitapevleri, n.d. second edition) pp. 346-7 (quotation 346).
82. Gülru Necipoğlu, 'From international Timurid', p. 154.
83. Ibid., p. 155.
84. Early eighteenth-century Ottomans appear to have possessed a strong historical consciousness. İbrahim Müteferrika even proceeded to print an Ottoman translation of an Arabic biography of Timur, written by Ahmad Ibn Arabshah (791-854/1392-1450) on Gurre-i Zilkade 1142 (18 May 1730). Arabshah's book *Aja'ib al-Maqdar* received the Ottoman title *Tarih-i Timûr Gürkân* (cf. Kut and Türe, *Yazmadan Basmaya*, p. 45).
85. It seems ironic that Damad İbrahim and Ahmed III ensured that the Ottoman Saadabad contained apparently readily intelligible references to Safavid Isfahan, yet concerning the issue of the Ottoman 'decorative skin' (borrowing Necipoğlu's phrase), they seem to have been equally determined to separate the Ottoman from the Timurid idiom, still employed by the Safavids.
86. Wilhelm Heinz, 'Die Kultur der Tulpenzeit des Osmanischen Reiches', *Wiener Zeitschrift für die Kunde des Morgenlandes*, 61, 1962, pp. 62-116.
87. Franz Babinger, *Die Geschichtsschreiber der Osmanen und ihre Werke* (Leipzig: Harrassowitz, 1927) pp. 260-1; W. Heinz, 'Die Kultur der Tulpenzeit', p. 80.
88. Edward Granville Browne, *A Literary History of Persia* (Cambridge: Cambridge University Press, 1951) pp. 421, 434.
89. H. Krüger, *Fetwa und Siyar. Zur internationalrechtlichen Gutachterpraxis der osmanischen Scheich ül-Islam vom 17. bis 19 Jh. unter besonderen Berücksichtigung des 'Behcet ül-Fetwa'* (Wiesbaden: Harrassowitz, 1978), pp. 103-5, 154 ; C. Imber, 'Süleyman as caliph of the Muslims: Ebu's-Su'ûd's formulation of Ottoman dynastic ideology', in G. Veinstein (ed.) *Soliman le Magnifique et son Temps* (Paris: Documentation Française, 1992) p. 183.
90. This rhetorical scheme in fact referred to the Shafi'ite jurist Ibn Juma'a (639-733 or 1241-1333), who in his *Tahrir al-Ahkam fi Tadbir Ahl al-Islam* presents the view that the seizure of power itself gave authority. K. S. Salibi, 'The Banu Jama'a: a dynasty of Shafi'ite jurists in the Mamluk period', *Studia Islamica*, 9, 1958, pp. 99-100.
91. 'İhtirâkına rızâ-yı hümâyûnum yokdur ancak hedim ve tahribine ruhsat ve iznim olmuşdu', Mustafa Sâmî, Hüseyin Şâkir and Mehmed Subhî, *Tarih-i Sâmî ü Şâkir ü Subhî* (Istanbul: Darüttıbaat-ı Âmire, 1198/1784) p. 11.

## NOTES FOR CHAPTER 3

**Chapter 3: The First Ottoman Turkish Printing Enterprise: Success or Failure? By *Orlin Sabev (Orhan Salih)***

1. Müteferrika is the name of a corps at the Ottoman court, whose members were especially attached to the person of the sultan and played an important role in public and political missions.
2. Jale Baysal, *Cennetlik İbrahim Efendi (İbrahim Müteferrika Oyunu)* (Istanbul: Cem, 1992), p. 89 ('*Terekemden yığınla satılmamış kitap çıkacak. Bastıklarımı okumadılar.*')
3. Christine Brooke-Rose interprets Salman Rushdie's and Umberto Eco's novels in this way. See Christine Brooke-Rose, 'Histoire palimpseste', in S. Collini (ed.) *Interprétation et surinterprétation* (Paris: Presses Universitaires de France, 1992) pp. 115–27.
4. [Imre] Karácson, 'İbrahim Müteferrika', *Tarih-i Osmanî Encümeni Mecmuası*, 3, 1910, pp. 178–85; reprinted in İmre Karácson, 'Müteferrika İbrâhîm', *Müteferrika*, 4, 1994, pp. 145–55.
5. Coloman de Thály (ed.) *Lettres de Turquie (1730–1739) et Notices (1740) de César de Saussure* (Budapest: Academie hongroise des sciences, 1909) p. 195.
6. Karácson, 'İbrahim Müteferrika', pp. 184–5.
7. Niyazi Berkes, 'İlk Türk Matbaası Kurucusunun Dinî ve Fikrî Kimliği', *Belleten*, 26 (104) 1962, pp. 715–37. Reprinted under the title 'Unitarianizm ve Matbaa', in Niyazi Berkes, *Felsefe ve Toplumbilim Yazıları* (Istanbul: Adam Yayınları, 1985) pp. 85–103.
8. Thály, *Lettres de Turquie*, pp. 95, 194–5.
9. Ibid., pp. 95–6, 195.
10. See the latest controversial views on this issue, namely Kemal Beydilli, 'Müteferrika ve Osmanlı Matbaası. 18. Yüzyılda İstanbul'da Kitabiyat', *Toplumsal Tarih*, 128 (August 2004) pp. 44–52; Erhan Afyoncu, 'İbrahim Müteferrika'nın Yeni Yayınlanan Terekesi ve Ölüm Tarihi Üzerine', *Türklük Araştırmaları Dergisi*, 15, 2004, pp. 349–62.
11. Karácson, 'İbrahim Müteferrika', p. 185.
12. L. Hopp, 'İbrahim Müteferrika (1674/75?–1746): fondateur de l'imprimerie turque', *Acta Orientalia Academiae Scientiarum Hungaricae*, 29 (1) 1975, p. 112.
13. Jale Baysal, 'II. Rákóczi Ferenc'in Çevirmeni Müteferrika İbrahim ve Osmanlı Türklerinin İlk Bastıkları Kitaplar', *Türk–Macar Kültür Münasebetleri Işığı Altında II. Rákóczi Ferenc ve Macar Mültecileri Sempozyumu/Symposium on Rákóczi Ferenc II and the Hungarian Refugees in the Light of Turco–Hungarian Cultural Relations* (Istanbul: İ. Ü. Edebiyat Fakültesi, 1976) p. 221; Jale Baysal, *Kitap ve Kütüphane Tarihi'ne Giriş* (Istanbul: Türk Kütüphaneciler Derneği, 1991) p. 75; Hidayet Nuhoğlu, 'Müteferrika Matbaası ve Bazı Mülâhazalar', in G.

## NOTES FOR CHAPTER 3

Eren (ed.) *Osmanlı* (12 vols, Ankara: Yeni Türkiye, 1999), vol. 7, pp. 221–9; Hidayet Nuhoğlu, 'Müteferrika Matbaası ve Bazı Mulâhazalar', in M. Armağan (ed.) *İstanbul Armağanı 4: Lâle Devri* (4 vols, Istanbul: İstanbul Büyükşehir Belediyesi Kültür İşleri Daire Başkanlığı Yayınları, 2000) vol. 4, pp. 211–25.
14. Niyazi Berkes, *Türkiye'de Çağdaşlaşma*, edited by A. Kuyaş (Istanbul: Yapı Kredi Yayınları, 2002) pp. 61–3.
15. A. D. Jeltyakov, *Türkiye'nin Sosyo-Politik ve Kültürel Hayatında Basın (1729–1908 Yılları)* (Ankara: Basın Yayın Genel Müdürlüğü, 1979) pp. 29–31.
16. J. S. Szyliowicz, 'Functional perspectives on technology: the case of the printing press in the Ottoman empire', *Archivum Ottomanicum*, 11, 1988, pp. 249–59.
17. Hüseyin Gazi Topdemir, *İbrahim Müteferrika ve Türk Matbaacılığı* (Ankara: T. C. Kültür Bakanlığı, 2002) pp. 52–6.
18. Osman Ersoy, 'İlk Türk Basımevi'nde Basılan Kitapların Fiyatları', *Basım ve Yayıncılığımızın 250. Yılı Bilimsel Toplantısı, 10–11 Aralık 1979, Ankara. Bildiriler* (Ankara: Türk Kütüphaneciler Derneği, 1980) pp. 69–77.
19. Ibid., pp. 77–8.
20. Meropi Anastassiadou, 'Les inventaires après décès de Salonique à la fin du XIXe siècle: source pour l'étude d'une société au seuil de la modernisation', *Turcica*, 25, 1993, pp. 97–135; Tülay Artan, 'Terekeler Işığında 18. Yüzyıl Ortasında Eyüp'te Yaşam Tarzı ve Standartlarına Bir Bakış. Orta Halliliğin Aynası', in T. Artan (ed.) *18. Yüzyıl Kadı Sicilleri Işığında Eyüp'te Sosyal Yaşam* (Istanbul: Tarih Vakfı, 1998) pp 49–64; Ömer Lütfi Barkan, 'Edirne Askerî Kassamına ait Tereke Defterleri (1545–1659)', *Belgeler. Türk Tarih Belgeleri Dergisi*, 3 (5–6) 1966, pp. 1–479; Colette Establet and Jean-Paul Pascual, 'Damascene probate inventories of the 17th and 18th centuries: some preliminary approaches and results', *International Journal of Middle East Studies*, 24 (3) 1992, pp. 373–93; Colette Establet and Jean-Paul Pascual, *Ultime voyage pour la Mecque: les inventaires après deces de pèlerins morts à Damas vers 1700* (Damas: Institut français d'études arabes de Damas, 1998); Suraiya Faroqhi, 'Wealth and power in the land of olives: the economic and political activities of Müridoğlu Hacı Mehmed Ağa, notable of Edremit (died in or before 1823)', in Suraiya Faroqhi, *Making a Living in the Ottoman Lands 1480–1820* (Istanbul: ISIS, 1995) pp. 291–311; Lajos Fekete, 'XVI. Yüzyılda Taşralı Bir Türk Efendisinin Evi', *Belleten*, 29 (116) 1965, pp. 615–38; Ibolya Gerelyes, 'Inventories of Turkish estates in Hungary in the second half of the 16th century', *Acta Orientalia Academiae Scientiarum Hungaricae*, 39 (2–3) 1985, pp. 275–338; Fatma Müge Göçek, *Rise of the Bourgeoisie, Demise of Empire:*

## NOTES FOR CHAPTER 3

*Ottoman Westernization and Social Change* (Oxford: Oxford University Press, 1996); Halil İnalcık, '15. Asır Türkiye İktisadî ve İçtimaî Tarihi Kaynakları', *İstanbul Üniversitesi İktisat Fakültesi Mecmuası*, 15 (1–4) 1954, pp. 51–73; Yuzo Nagata, *Materials on the Bosnian Notables* (Tokyo: Institute for the Study of Languages and Cultures of Asia and Africa, 1979); Christoph K. Neumann, 'Arm and reich in Qaraferye', *Der Islam*, 73, 1996, pp. 259–312; Hüseyin Özdeğer, *1463–1640 Yılları Bursa Şehri Tereke Defterleri* (Istanbul: İ. Ü. İktisat Fakültesi, 1988); Said Öztürk, *Askerî Kassama ait Onyedinci Asır İstanbul Tereke Defterleri (Sosyo-Ekonomik Tahlil)* (Istanbul: Osmanlı Araştırmaları Vakfı, 1995); Abdul-Karim Rafeq, 'Registers of succession and their importance for socio-economic history: two samples from Damascus and Aleppo, 1277/1861', in J.-L. Bacqué Grammont, İ. Ortaylı and E. van Donzel (eds) *CIÉPO: Osmanlı Öncesi ve Osmanlı Araştırmaları Uluslararası Komitesi. VII. Sempozyumu Bildirileri: Peç: 7–11 Eylül 1986* (Ankara: TTK, 1994) pp. 479–91; Yvonne J. Seng, 'The Üskûdar estates (tereke) as records of daily life in an Ottoman town 1521–24' (Ph.D. dissertation, University of Chicago, 1991); Gilles Veinstein, 'Note sur les inventaires après décès ottomans', in Rémy Dor and Michel Nicolas (eds) *Quand le crible était dans la paille: hommage à Pertev Naili Boratav* (Paris: Maisonneuve & Larose, 1978) pp. 383–95; Gilles Veinstein, 'Les pèlerins de la Mecque à travers quelques inventaires après décès ottomans (XVIIe–XVIIIe siècles)', *Revue de l'occident musulman et de la Méditerranée*, 31, 1981, pp. 63–71; Gilles Veinstein, 'Les inventaires après décès des campagnes militaires: le cas de la conquête de Chypre', *Bulletin of the Turkish Studies Association*, 1992, pp. 293–305; Gilles Veinstein and Yolande Triantafyllidou-Baladic, 'Les inventaires après décès ottomans de Crète', in Ad van der Woude and Anton Schuurman (eds) *Probate Inventories: A New Source for Historical Study of Wealth, Material Culture and Agricultural Development. Papers Presented at the Leemwenborch Conference, Wageningen, 5–7 May 1980* (Utrecht: HES Publishers, 1980) pp. 191–204; and М. С. Мейер, 'К характеристике правящего класса в Османской империи XVI–XVII вв. (По данным 'тереке дефтерлери')', Средневековый Восток. История, культура, источниковедение (Москва: Наука, 1980) pp. 180–9.

21. Fekete, 'XVI. Yüzyılda Taşralı Bir Türk Efendisinin Evi'; Mihaila Stajnova, 'Ottoman libraries in Vidin', *Études balkaniques*, 2, 1979, pp. 54–69.

22. Meropi Anastassiadou, 'Livres et "bibliothèques" dans les inventaires après décès de Salonique au XIXe siècle', *Revue des mondes musulmans et de la Méditerranée*, 87–88, 1999, pp. 111–41; Meropi Anastassiadou, 'Des défunts hors du commun: les possesseurs de livres dans les inventaires après décès musulmans de Salonique', *Turcica*, 32, 2000, pp. 197–252;

## NOTES FOR CHAPTER 3

Artan, 'Terekeler Işığında 18'; Colette Establet and Jean-Paul Pascual, 'Les livres des gens à Damas vers 1700'; Ali İhsan Karataş, 'Tereke Kayıtlarına Göre XVI. Yüzyılda Bursa'da İnsan–Kitap İlişkisi', *Uludağ Üniversitesi İlâhiyat Fakültesi Dergisi*, 8 (8) 1999, pp. 317–28; Ali İhsan Karataş, 'Osmanlı Toplumunda Kitap (XIV–XVI. Yüzyıllar)', in H. C. Güzel, K. Çiçek and S. Koca (eds) *Türkler* (21 vols, Ankara: Yeni Türkiye, 2002), vol. 11, pp. 896–909; A. Turgut Kut, 'Terekelerde Çıkan Kitapların Matbu Satış Defterleri', *Müteferrika*, 2, 1994, pp. 3–24; Neumann, 'Arm and reich in Qaraferye'; Orlin Sabev, 'Private book collections in Ottoman Sofia, 1671–1833 (preliminary notes)', *Études balkaniques*, 1, 2003, pp. 34–82; Öztürk, *Askeri Kassama*, pp. 174–84; Halil Sahillioğlu, 'Ottoman book legacies', in Halil Sahillioğlu (ed.) *Studies on Ottoman Economic and Social History* (Istanbul: IRCICA, 1999) pp. 189–91; Fahri Sakal, 'Osmanlı Ailesinde Kitap', in G. Eren (ed.) *Osmanlı* (12 vols, Ankara: Yeni Türkiye, 1999) vol. 11, pp. 732–8; Lale Uluç, 'Ottoman book collectors and illustrated sixteenth century Shiraz manuscripts', *Revue des mondes musulmans et de la Méditerranée*, 1998, pp. 87–8; and Орлин Събев, 'Книгата в ежедневието на мюсюлманите в Русе (1695–1786)', Алманах за историята на Русе, 4, 2002, pp. 380–194.
23. For more details about that archive, see Yvonne J. Seng, 'The Şerʿiye Sicilleri of the Istanbul Müftülüğü as a source for the study of everyday life', *Turkish Studies Association Bulletin*, 15 (2) 1991, pp. 307–25.
24. A transcription of the source in modern Turkish and a facsimile of it are appended to my monograph, published in Bulgarian. See Орлин Събев, *Първото османско пътешествие в света на печатната книга (1726–1746). Нов поглед* (София: Авангард Прима, 2004). See the review articles of Afyoncu, 'İbrahim Müteferrika'nın', pp. 349–62; and Beydilli, 'Müteferrika ve Osmanlı', pp. 50–2.
25. *El-Cildü's-sāni min Tārīh-i Naʿīmā* (Kostantiniye, 1147/1734) p. 741.
26. Hopp, 'İbrahim Müteferrika', p. 108.
27. Franz Babinger, '18. Yüzyılda İstanbul'da Kitabiyat', in N. Kuran-Burçoğlu (ed.) *Müteferrika ve Osmanlı Matbaası* (Istanbul: Tarih Vakfı Yurt Yayınları, 2004) p. 31; Ersoy, 'İlk Türk', pp. 69, 76; Orhan Kologlu, *Basımevi ve Basının Gecikme Sebepleri ve Sonuçları* (Istanbul: İstanbul Gazeteciler Cemiyeti, 1987) p. 57; and Joseph von Hammer-Purgstall, *Geschichte des Osmanischen Reiches* (10 vols, Pest: C. A. Hartleben, 1827–35) vol. 7, p. 585.
28. Şefik Ergürbüz, *Matbaacılık Tarihi* (Izmit: Işıl Kitabevi, 1947) p. 46; and Hasan Refik Ertuğ, *Basın ve Yayın Hareketleri Tarihi* (Istanbul: Yenilik Basımevi, 1970) p. 116.
29. William J. Watson, 'İbrāhīm Müteferrika and Turkish Incunabula', *Journal of the American Oriental Society*, 88, 1968, p. 436.
30. The source mentions in fact 8200 copies. This calculation, however,

NOTES FOR CHAPTER 3

takes into consideration the total print run of each of the volumes of Vankulu's Arabic–Turkish dictionary and Naʿima's *Tārīh*, each of which are in two volumes. So, if we calculate the number of initial printed titles as opposed to printed volumes, the real total number of printed copies of the editions decreases to 7200.

31. H. Omont, 'Nouveaux documents sur l'imprimerie à Constantinople au XVIIIe siècle', *Revue des Bibliothèques*, 33, 1926, pp. 6–7.
32. İsmail Hakkı Uzunçarşılı, *Osmanlı Tarihi* (8 vols, Ankara: Türk Tarih Kurumu, 1988) vol. 4, Part 2, p. 516; Joseph von Hammer-Purgstall, *Geschichte des Osmanischen Reiches*, vol. 7, p. 413.
33. М. С. Мейер, Османская империя в XVIII веке. Черты структурного кризиса (Москва: Наука, 1991) p. 184.
34. Edvard Carleson, *İbrahim Müteferrika Basimevi ve Bastiği ilk Eserler/ İbrahim Müteferrika's Printing House and its First Printed Books*, edited by M. Akbulut (Ankara: Türk Kütüphaneciler Derneği, 1979) p. 8.
35. Taner Timur, 'Matbaa, Aydınlanma ve diplomasi: Said Mehmed Efendi', *Toplumsal Tarih*, 128, August 2004, p. 59.
36. Ersoy, 'İlk Türk'.
37. See Omont, 'Nouveaux documents', pp. 9–10.
38. See İbrahim Müteferrika, 'Osmanlı Matbaasının Kuruluşu ve Başlangıcı', in N. Kuran-Burçoğlu and M. Kiel (eds) *Müteferrika ve Osmanlı Matbaası* (Istanbul: Tarih Vakfı Yurt Yayınları, 2004) pp. 72–4.
39. See Carleson, *İbrahim Müteferrika*, pp. 9–12.
40. Details are provided in Събев, *Първото османско пътешествие в света на печатната книга (1726–1746): Нов поглед* (Sofia: Avangard Prima) pp. 251–5.
41. Ersoy, 'İlk Türk', p. 76. ('*İbrahim Müteferrika'nın bastığı bu 24 cilt kitap denizi doldurmak için atılmış bir avuç kum bile değildi. Yada susuzluktan yanan bir hastaya verilen bir çay kaşığı su kadar bile toplum üzerinde etkili olamazdı*.')
42. See Lucien Febvre and Henri-Jean Martin, *L'Apparition du livre* (Paris: A. Michel, 1958) pp. 307–12; and Brian Richardson, *Printing, Writers and Readers in Renaissance Italy* (Cambridge: Cambridge University Press, 1999) pp. 25–6.
43. The *Kısmet-i Askeriye Mahkemesi* collection, for example, includes 2144 registers of the period between 1591 and 1924. See Ahmed Akgündüz (ed.) *Şerʿiye Sicilleri: Mahiyeti, Toplu Kataloğu ve Seçme Hükümler* (Istanbul: Türk Dünyası Araştırmaları Vakfı, 1988) pp. 100–16.
44. Thály, *Lettres de Turquie*, p. 95.
45. Omont, 'Nouveaux documents', p. 6.
46. See Yavuz Selim Karakışla, 'Osmanlı Kitap Tarihinde Bir Katkı: Osmanlı Devlet Arşivi'nde Bulunan, Kitap ile İlgili Bazı Belgeler (1844–1854)', *Müteferrika*, 14 (1998) pp. 41–59.

47. Johann Strauss, 'Les livres et l'imprimerie à Istanbul (1800–1908)', in P. Dumont (ed.) *Turquie: livres d'hier, livres d'aujourd'hui* (Strasbourg–Istanbul: Centre de recherche sur la civilisation ottomane et le domaine turc contemporain, Université des Sciences Humaines – Éditions ISIS, 1992) p. 5; Johann Strauss, 'İstanbul'da Kitap Yayını ve Basımevleri', *Müteferrika*, 1, 1993, p. 5.
48. More details are provided in Събев, *Първото османско*, pp. 255–60.
49. Muḥammad Ibn Jarīr al-Ṭabarī, *The History of al-Tabari: Biographies of the Prophet's Companions and their Successors*, translated by E. Landau-Tasseron (New York: The State University of New York Press, 1998).
50. See Menderes Coşkun, 'Osmanlı Hac Seyahatnamelerinde Hac Yolculuğu', in G. Eren (ed.) *Osmanlı* (12 vols, Ankara: Yeni Yürkiye, 1999) vol. 4, pp. 506–11; and Menderes Coşkun, 'The most literary Ottoman pilgrimage narrative: Nabi's Tuhfetü'l-Haremeyn', *Turcica*, 32, 2000, pp. 363–88.
51. Watson, 'İbrāhīm Müteferrika and Turkish incunabula', p. 436.
52. See Fahri Unan, 'Taşköprülü-zâde'nin Kaleminden XVI. Yüzyılın "*İlim*" ve "*Âlim*" anlayışı', *Osmanlı Araştırmaları/Journal of Ottoman Studies*, 17, 1997, pp. 149–264; and Fahri Unan, 'Osmanlı Medrese Ulemâsı: İlim anlayışı ve İmî Verim', in H. C. Güzel, K. Çiçek and S. Koca (eds) *Türkler* (21 vols, Ankara: Yeni Türkiye, 2002) vol. 11, pp. 436–45.
53. A. Ubicini, *Lettres sur la Turquie, ou tableau statistique, religieux, politique, administratif, militaire, commercial, etc. de l'Empire ottoman, depuis le Khatti-Cherif de Gulhanè (1839). Première partie. Les Ottomans* (Paris: Librairie militaire de J. Dumaine, 1853) p. 243.
54. Sigfrid H. Steinberg, *Five Hundred Years of Printing* (Harmondsworth: Penguin Books, 1977) p. 130.
55. Thály, *Lettres de Turquie*, p. 95.
56. Elizabeth L. Eisenstein, *The Printing Press as an Agent of Change: Communications and Cultural Transformations in Early-Modern Europe* (Cambridge: Cambridge University Press, 1979) p. 44.
57. Raymond Williams, *The Long Revolution* (London: Hogarth, 1992).
58. Elizabeth Eisenstein, 'The fifteenth century book revolution, some causes and consequences of the advent of printing in Western Europe', *Le Livre dans les sociétés pré-industrielles* (Athens: Kentron Neoelleon Ereunon, 1982) pp. 57–76; Elizabeth Eisenstein, 'From scriptoria to printing shops: evolution and revolution in the early printing book trade', in Kenneth E. Carpenter (ed.) *Books and Society in History, Papers of the Association of College and Research Libraries Rare Books and Manuscripts Preconference, 24–28 June 1980, Boston, Massachusetts* (New York: Bowker, 1983) pp. 29–42.
59. Robert A. Houston, *Literacy in Early Modern Europe: Culture and Education 1500–1800* (London: Longman, 1988) pp. 160–3.

## NOTES FOR CHAPTER 3

60. Jacques le Goff, *Les Intellectuels au Moyen Âge* (Paris: Éditions du Seuil, 1985) p. 187.
61. Richardson, *Printing, Writers and Readers*, p. 9.
62. Diederick Raven, 'Elizabeth Eisenstein and the impact of printing', *European Review of History/Revue européene d'histoire*, 6 (2) 1999, pp. 223–34.
63. Asa Briggs and Peter Burke, *A Social History of the Media: From Gutenberg to the Internet* (Cambridge: Polity Press, 2003) pp. 15–73; Nicholas Hudson, 'Challenging Eisenstein: recent studies in print culture', *Eighteenth-Century Life,* 26 (2) 2002, pp. 83–95; Adrian Johns, *The Nature of the Book: Print and Knowledge in the Making* (Chicago: University of Chicago Press, 1998); and David John McKitterick, *Print, Manuscript and the Search for Order, 1450–1830* (Cambridge: Cambridge University Press, 2003).
64. See Eva Hanebutt-Benz, Dagmar Glass and Geoffrey Roper (eds) *Sprachen des Nahen Ostens und die Druckrevolution: eine interculturelle Begegnung* (Mainz: Johann Gutenberg Museum, 2002).
65. See André Demeerseman, 'Un mémoire célèbre qui préfigure l'évolution moderne en Islam', *Institut des Belles Lettres Arabes*, 18, 1955, pp. 5–32; and Wahid Gdoura, *Le Début de l'Imprimerie arabe à Istanbul et en Syrie: Evolution de l'environnement culturel (1706–1787)* (Tunis: Institut Superieur de Documentation, 1985).
66. Richardson, *Printing, Writers and Readers*, p. 77.
67. Jale Baysal, *Müteferrika'dan Birinci Meşrutiyete Kadar Osmanlı Türklerinin Bastıkları Kitaplar* (Istanbul: Edebiyat Fakültesi, 1968) p. 63.
68. Ibid., pp. 71–4.
69. See Mahmud Gündüz, 'Matbaanın Tarihçesi ve İlk Kur'anı Kerim Basmaları', *Vakıflar Dergisi*, 12, 1978, pp. 335–50; Osman Keskioğlu, 'Türkiye'de Matbaa Te'sisi ve Mushaf Basımı', *Ankara Üniversitesi İlâhiyat Fakültesi Dergisi*, 15, 1967, pp. 121–39; and Nedret Kuran-Burçoğlu, 'Matbaacı Osman Bey: Saray'dan İlk Defa Kur'an-ı Kerim Basma İznini Alan Osmanlı Hattatı', *Türklük Bilgisi Araştırmaları/ Journal of Turkish Studies*, 26, 2002, pp. 97–112.
70. Anastassiadou, 'Livres et bibliothèques', p. 120.
71. Yahya Erdem, 'Sahaflar ve Seyyahlar: Osmanlı'da Kitapçılık', in Güler Eren (ed.) *Osmanlı* (12 vols, Ankara: Yeni Yürkiye, 1999) vol. 11, p. 725.
72. Topdemir, *İbrahim Müteferrika*, pp. 30–2.
73. Server İskit, *Türkiye'de Neşriyat Hareketleri Tarihine Bir Bakış* (Istanbul: Maarif Vekaleti, 1939) p. 90.
74. İskit, *Türkiye'de Neşriyat Hareketleri*, pp. 145–6; *Türk (İnönü) Ansiklopedisi*, s.v. 'Basım'.
75. Baysal, *Cennetlik İbrahim Efendi (İbrahim Müteferrika Oyunu)*, p. 90 ('Belki sonraları ... çok çok sonraları okuyacaklar. Sen yolu açmadın mı?').

NOTES FOR CHAPTER 4

Chapter 4: Nahils, Circumcision Rituals and the Theatre State by Babak Rahimi

I gratefully acknowledge the assistance of Hassan Kayali, Dana Sajdi, Emma Swartz and an anonymous reviewer who read and criticized earlier versions of this chapter and provided me with useful suggestions.

1. Abou-El-Haj, *Formation of the Modern State*, p. 64.
2. This claim challenges Suraiya Faroqhi's argument that changes in land tenure configuration was a product of external forces, namely the expansion of world market networking on the Ottoman economy. See Faroqhi's, *Towns and Townsmen*.
3. See İnalcik, 'Military and fiscal transformations', p. 194.
4. Salzmann, 'An ancien regime revisited', p. 405. See also Ariel Salzmann, *Tocqueville in the Ottoman Empire: Rival Paths to the Modern State* (Leiden: E. J. Brill, 2004).
5. See the next section for a definition of 'theatre state'.
6. Clifford Geertz, *Negara: The Theater State in Nineteenth-Century Bali* (Princeton: Princeton University Press) p. 136.
7. As Max Weber described it, state building hinges mainly on the process by which states can monopolize the means of violence or 'the monopoly of the legitimate use of physical force within a given territory.' Max Weber, 'Politics as vocation', in *From Max Weber: Essays in Sociology*, edited and translated by H. H. Gerth and C. W. Mills (London, Routledge, 1991) p. 78.
8. As a territorial state expands, its monopolization of coercion and centralization of institutions grows and it becomes increasingly able to deprive (semi) autonomous subgroups of the right to maintain power. It is at this crucial stage that non-state forms of violence in terms of warfare are considered 'illegitimate' and 'criminal' with the growing centralization of the state. See C. Tilly, 'War making and state making as organized crime', in P. Evans, D. Rueschemeyer and T. Skocpol (eds) *Bringing the State Back In* (Cambridge: Cambridge University Press, 1985) pp. 295–315.
9. Edward Muir, *Ritual in Early Modern Europe* (Cambridge: Cambridge University Press, 1997) pp. 245–6.
10. Blaise de Vigenère, 'Les illustrations de Blaise de Vigenère Bourbonnois', in Laonicus Chalkokondyles, *Histoires de la decadence de l'Empire grec et establissement de celuy des Turcs* (Paris: C. Sonnius, 1660) p. 265. See also Mehmed Arslan, 'A great Ottoman festivity: circumcision feasts of Prince Mehmed III', in Hasan Celâl Güzel, C. Cem Oguz and Osman Karatay (eds) *The Turks* (6 vols, Ankara: Yeni Turkiye Arsalan, 2002) vol. 3, p. 982.

## NOTES FOR CHAPTER 4

11. One exception to the palace ceremonies was the 1475 circumcision of Sultan Mehmed's two sons, Beyazit and Mustafa, performed on an island near Edirne. Metin And, *A History of Theatre and Popular Entertainment in Turkey* (Ankara: Forum Yayinlari, 1963–64) p. 17.
12. This was evident mainly in the 1582 ceremonies.
13. Arslan, 'A great Ottoman festivity', p. 981.
14. Metin And, *Osmanli Şenliklerinde Türk Sanatlari* (Ankara: Kültüre ve Tuizm Bakanliği, 1982).
15. Suraiya Faroqhi, *Subjects of the Sultan*, p. 172.
16. Robert Elliott Stout, 'The Sūr-i Humāyun of Murad III: a study of Ottoman pageantry and entertainment' (Ph.D. dissertation, Ohio State University, 1966) p. 268.
17. The earliest illustrated version of a *Surnameh* appeared in the late sixteenth century for the 1582 circumcision festivals patronized by Murad III in honour of his son, Mehmed III. Esin Atil, 'The story of an eighteenth-century Ottoman festival', *Muqarnas*, 10, 1993, p. 182; and Derin Terzioğlu, 'The imperial circumcision festival of 1582: an interpretation', *Muqarnas*, 12, 1995, p. 97 n.4 for information with regard to the location of the 1582 *Surnameh*.
18. See also Le Vigne de Pera (1909) 'Letter from Constantinople ... to the English court', in Arthur John Butler (ed.) *Calendar of State Papers, Foreign Series of the Reign of Elizabeth* (London: HM Stationery Office, May–December 1582) vol. 16, pp. 177–8.
19. Gülru Necipoğlu, 'Plans and models in 15th- and 16th-century Ottoman architectural practice', *Journal of the Society of Architectural Historians*, 45 (3) 1986, pp. 224–43.
20. George Lebelski, 'A true description of the magnificall tryumphes and pastimes', in M. And, *A History of Theater and Popular Entertainment in Turkey* (Ankara: Forum, 1963–64) p. 120.
21. The *Sūrname-i Humāyūn* lists 148 guilds participating in the 1582 ceremonies, while von Haunolth mentions 179 (non-entertaining) guilds. See R. E. Stout, 'The Sūr-i Humāyun of Murad III', p. 248.
22. Arslan, 'A great Ottoman festivity', p. 980.
23. For a Bakhtinian interpretation of the ceremonies, see D. Terzioğlu, 'The imperial circumcision festivals of 1582'.
24. See Evliya Çelebi, *Narrative of Travels in Europe, Asia, and Africa in the Seventeenth Century*, translated by Ritter Joseph von Hammer (2 vols, New York: Johnson Reprint Corp, 1896) vol 1, p. 119.
25. D. Terzioğlu, 'The imperial circumcision festival of 1582', p. 89. For 1720 guild processions, see Esin Atil, *Levni and the Surname: The Story of an Eighteenth-Century Ottoman Festival* (Istanbul, Koçbank, 1999), p. 144.
26. And, *Osmali Şenliklerinde*, p. 111 n.26.
27. Atil, *Levni and the Surname*, pp. 148–9.

## NOTES FOR CHAPTER 4

28. See D. Terzioğlu, 'The imperial circumcision festival of 1582', p. 91.
29. This was most ostensible in the seventeenth-century cities of Cairo and Istanbul, where guild associations practised the same business irrespective of religious affiliation in the same market place. Halil İnalcik and Donald Quataert (eds) *An Economic and Social History of the Ottoman Empire: 1300–1914* (2 vols, Cambridge: Cambridge University Press, 1994) vol. 2, p. 590.
30. Faroqhi, *Subjects of the Sultan*, pp. 166–7.
31. Arslan, 'A great Ottoman festivity', p. 980.
32. For a study of *nakhil*, see Frank J. Korom, *Hosay Trinidad: Muharram Performances in an Indo-Caribbean Diaspora* (Philadelphia: Pennsylvania University Press, 2003) pp. 46–7.
33. Stout, 'The Sūr-i Humāyun of Murad III', p. 83.
34. Ibid., p. 99.
35. Arslan, 'A great Ottoman festivity', p. 980.
36. Shown in *Surnameh* of Vehbi. See Figure 2 in Esin Atil, 'The story of an eighteenth-century Ottoman festival', p. 186.
37. Atil, *Levni and the Surname*, pp. 134–5.
38. Ibid., p. 136.
39. Faroqhi, *Subjects of the Sultan*, p. 172.
40. As in the 1582 processions, the five large *nahils* are carried through the city for a week before they are returned to the palace.
41. Ibid., p. 165.
42. Mary Douglas, *Purity and Danger: An Analysis of Concepts of Pollution and Taboo* (London: Routledge & Kegan Paul, 1966).
43. Quoted in Peirce, *The Imperial Harem*, p. 193. See Joseph von Hammer-Purgstall, *Histoire de l'Empire ottoman depuis son origine jusqu'à nos jours* (18 vols, Paris: Bellizard, Barthès, Dufour et Lowell, 1835–37) vol. 7, p. 157.
44. As Peirce notes, this dramatic representation 'is reminiscent of episodes in the central Asian Turkish epic tales of Dede Korkut, familiar to the Ottomans, where women, especially mothers, take up arms to save young men unable to defend themselves (Peirce, *The Imperial Harem*, p. 193).
45. Ibid., p. 193.
46. See Victor Turner, *The Ritual Process: Structure and Anti-structure* (New York: Aldine, 1995).
47. See *Encyclopedia of Islam*, s.v. 'Khitan'.
48. The circumcision ceremonies in honour of princes Bayezid and Cihangir were celebrated on 11 November 1539 alongside those of the marriage of Süleyman's daughter Mihrimah to Rüstem Pasha, the grand vizir of the sultan. See Esin Atil, *Süleymanname: The Illustrated History of Süleyman the Magnificent* (Washington: National Art Gallery and H. N. Abrams, 1986) p. 179.

49. Stout, 'The Sūr-i Humāyun of Murad III', p. 70.
50. Ibid., p. 46.
51. John. R. Perry, 'Toward a theory of Iranian urban moieties: the Haydariyyah and Niʿmatiyyah revisited', *Iranian Studies*, 32, 1999, p. 70.
52. This 'radical change' actually took place in the course of two centuries under Safavid rule. The processional dimension echoes Calmard and Chelkowski's point that the Safavid Muharram ceremonies were a form of political patriotic events. It was in the political pomp and the official glamour of the ceremonies that the rituals transcended the quality of mere religious 'devotionalism'. See Peter J. Chelkowski, 'Taʿziyeh: indigenous avant-garde theatre of Iran', in Peter J. Chelkowski (ed.) *Taʿziyeh: Ritual and Drama in Iran* (New York: New York University Press, 1979) p. 2.
53. See Babak Rahimi, 'The Safavid camel sacrifice rituals', *Iranian Studies*, 37 (3) 2004, pp. 451–78.

### Chapter 5: Janissary Coffee Houses in Late Eighteenth-Century Istanbul by Ali Çaksu

I would like to thank Dr Dana Sajdi for her kind help and valuable suggestions regarding the revision of the text before publication.

1. For works on coffee shops see, Hélène Desmet-Grégoire and François Georgeon (eds) *Cafés d'Orient revisités* (Paris: Centre National de la Recherche Scientifique Editions, 1997); Burçak Evren, *Eski İstanbul'da Kahvehaneler* (Istanbul: Milliyet Yayınları, 1996); Ralph S. Hattox, *Coffee and Coffeehouses: The Origins of a Social Beverage in the Medieval Near East* (Seattle: University of Washington Press, 1985); Ekrem Işın, 'Bir içecekten daha fazla: kahve ve kahvehanelerin toplumsal tarihi' ('More than a beverage: a social history of coffee and coffeehouses') in Selahattin Özpalabıyıklar (ed.) *Tanede Sakli Keyif, Kahve* (*Coffee, Pleasures Hidden in a Bean*) (Istanbul: Yapı Kredi Kültür Sanat Yayıncılık, 2001) pp. 10–43; Cengiz Kırlı, 'The struggle over space: coffeehouses of Ottoman Istanbul, 1780–1845' (Ph.D. dissertation, State University of New York, Binghamton, 2000); Cengiz Kırlı, 'Kahvehaneler ve Hafiyeler: 19. Yüzyıl Ortalarında Osmanlı'da Sosyal Kontrol', *Toplum ve Bilim*, 83, 2000, pp. 58–79; Cengiz Kırlı, 'İstanbul: Bir Büyük Kahvehane', *İstanbul Dergisi*, 47, 2003, pp. 75–8; and Ahmed Yaşar, 'The coffeehouses in early modern Istanbul: public space, sociability and surveillance' (MA thesis, Boğaziçi University, 2003). For some studies on Janissaries see, *Encyclopedia of Islam*, s.v. 'Yeni Çeri'; Godfrey Goodwin, *The Janissaries* (London: Saqi Books 1997); Cemal Kafadar, 'Yeniçeri–Esnaf relations: solidarity and conflict' (MA thesis, McGill University, 1981); Cemal Kafadar, 'On the purity and corruption of the Janissaries', *Turkish Studies Association Bulletin*, 15, 1991, pp. 273–9; and A. Raymond, *Le Caire des Janissaires*:

## NOTES FOR CHAPTER 5

l'apogée de la ville ottomane sous Abd al-Rahman Kathuda (Paris: Centre National de la Recherche Scientifique Editions, 1995). Works that briefly mention Janissary coffee houses are, Işın, 'More than a beverage', pp. 33–5; Kırlı, 'The struggle over space', pp. 112–30, Kırlı, 'İstanbul', p. 76; Kırlı, 'Kahvehaneler ve Hafiyeler', pp. 67–8; Reşad Ekrem Koçu, Yeniçeriler (Istanbul: Koçu Yayınları, 1964) pp. 296–9; and Yaşar, 'The coffeehouses in early modern Istanbul', pp. 61–7.

2. Based on statistics provided by Kırlı in his work on early nineteenth-century coffee shops, we know that one out of every seven or eight shops in Istanbul was a coffee house. The great majority of the coffee houses, most of which were small enterprises, were run by Muslims. One Muslim trader out of four ran a coffee house, and a significant number of the Muslims who ran coffee houses were related to the Janissary corps. See Kırlı, 'İstanbul', pp. 75–6. For this 'overwhelming presence of the janissaries in coffee house business', see also Kırlı's 'The struggle over space', 112ff.

3. For instance, during the reigns of Mehmed II and Süleyman the Magnificient the number of Janissaries are estimated to have been between 12,000 and 14,000 (Encyclopedia of Islam, s.v. 'Yeni Çeri').

4. See for example Gerhard Schwartz, Die Janitscharen: geheime Macht des Türkenreichs (Vienna: Amelthea, 1990).

5. The formation of 196 ortas goes back to the late fifteenth century. Encyclopedia of Islam, s.v. 'Yeni Çeri'.

6. Câbî Ömer Efendi, Câbî Târihi (Târîh-i Sultân Selîm-i Sâlis ve Mahmûd-ı Sânî), 2 vols with consecutive pagination edited by Mehmed Ali Beyhan (Ankara: Türk Tarih Kurumu, 2003) vol. 1, pp. 197, 239.

7. The term 'esnafization' of the Janissary appears in Kafadar, 'Yeniçeri-esnaf relations', p. 82. On Janissary-esnaf connections, see also Olson, 'The esnaf and the Patrona Halil rebellion', pp. 329–44; and Olson, 'Jews, Janissaries, esnaf and the revolt of 1740 in Istanbul: social upheaval and political realignment in the Ottoman Empire', Journal of the Economic and Social History of the Orient, 20, 1977, pp. 185–207.

8. Originally one orta consisted of 60–70 soldiers. Later, in the middle of the eighteenth century the number of Janissaries in an orta began to inflate up to 200 and even 300 people. The total number of Janissaries rose to 45,000 in the reign of Mehmed III, 110,000 during Selim III, and 140,000 during Mahmud II. These figures are for the Janissaries who received salaries from the treasury and wielded arms. As well as the main salary books for the current members of the Janissary, there were also salary books for those retired, who received pensions according to their seniority and service at the corps. So when we include the retired, the number of Janissaries at the last period is around 200,000. After the devşirme law was abolished and the corps

was opened to the public, a new registry for Janissary aspirants was established. However, the latter received a salary only when they entered the corps to fill the recently vacant positions. In addition, many people were registered unlawfully or improperly but received salaries. See Abdi Efendi, *1730 Patrona İhtilâli Hakkında Bir Eser: Abdi Tarihi*, edited by Faik Reşit Unat (Ankara: Türk Tarih Kurumu, 1943), p. 43 (henceforth Abdi Efendi, *Abdi Tarihi*).

9. *Dünden Bugüne İstanbul Ansiklopedisi*, s.v. 'Kahvehaneler'; and Kırlı, 'İstanbul', p. 76. According to Işın, 'at the outset, these establishments were similar to guild coffeehouses with the exception that their clientele were drawn from the members of a particular Janissary regiment. ... Eventually, however, they turned into dives run under the supervision of the Janissaries who policed Istanbul's streets.' Işın, 'More than a beverage', p. 33.

10. Kafadar, 'Yeniçeri-esnaf relations', p. 70.

11. Namık Kemal, 'Usûl-u Meşveret Hakkında Mektuplar', *Hürriyet*, 14 September 1868, p. 6, quoted in Şerif Mardin, 'Freedom in an Ottoman perspective', in Metin Heper and Ahmed Evin (eds) *State, Democracy and the Military: Turkey in the 1980s* (Berlin: Walter de Gruyter, 1988) p. 32. The following striking example too seems to justify this view. 'The register reveals that guilds in early nineteenth century Istanbul tended to elect their stewards from among Muslims, and particularly Janissaries, to have a better voice in their dealings with the state. For example, the steward of gardeners, Ömer beşe was apparently a Janissary, although 95 per cent of the gardeners were Orthodox Christians' (Kırlı, 'The struggle over space', pp. 117–18).

12. Material and moral degeneration of the corps and unruly and inefficient Janissaries in a way brought the end to the corps. The historian, Şanizade writes that some corrupt so-called Janissaries in the city were so involved in criminal activities and intimidation that even the *esnaf*, who had formerly supported some Janissary uprisings, began to turn against them. Those activities included usurpation, kidnapping, receiving ransom, rape and sexual harassment. See Ataullah Şânîzâde, *Târîh-i Şânîzâde* (4 vols, Istanbul: various publishers, 1284–99/1867–75) vol. 1, p. 217 ff.

13. Military reforms, which were crucial for the empire, were rejected and prevented by the Janissaries who not only refused any suggestion of reform even to adapt to modern military technologies and education, but also hindered the formation of forces meeting modern needs. Thus, Selim III's Nizâm-ı Cedîd and Alemdar Mustafa Paşa's Sekbân-ı Cedîd were abolished by two bloody Janissary uprisings in 1807 and 1808 respectively. The Janissaries resisted, since their very positions in Ottoman society as well as that of their supporters among the ruling

## NOTES FOR CHAPTER 5

classes and segments of society in Istanbul depended on old monopolies that such reforms would have broken. For a narration and evaluation of the Nizâm-ı Cedîd experience, see for instance, Stanford S. Shaw, 'The origins of Ottoman military reform: the Nizam-ı Cedid army of Sultan Selim III', *The Journal of Modern History*, 37 (3) 1965, pp. 291–306.

14. Before proceeding, a word on a problem with our sources is necessary: a lot of information on Janissaries and their coffee houses in the late period is found in chronicles written by the official historians. These works clearly display the distortions that one may expect from the official viewpoint and deserve our caution and scepticism. Even the language used by most of the chroniclers in characterizing the Janissaries show them to be enemies of both the state and the people. For instance, Mehmed Es'ad Efendi's work *Üss-i Zafer* (Istanbul: Matbaa-i Süleyman Efendi, 1293/1876–77), which treats the abolition of the Janissary corps, celebrates the event and describes the Janissaries as 'traitors' and 'infidels'. (There is also a recent edition of this work, *Üss-i Zafer: Yeniçeriliğin Kaldırılmasına Dair* edited and transcribed into modern Turkish by Mehmed Arslan (Istanbul: Kitabevi, 2005), vol. 58, 230 pp.) Clearly, Es'ad Efendi's ambition to become Şeyhülislam, and his rapid rise in the bureaucracy following the dismantling of the corps, which he actively supported, is connected to his bias against the institution. See the editor's introductory notes in 'Sahhâflar Şeyhi-zâde Seyyid Mehmed Es'ad Efendi', *Vak'anüvîs Es'ad Efendi Tarihi*, edited by Ziya Yılmazer (Istanbul: Osmanu Araştırmaları Vakfi, 2000), pp. 85–6 and 89 (henceforth, Es'ad Efendi', *Es'ad Efendi Tarihi*). However, we are fortunate to have two accounts that are relatively less hostile to the Janissaries. Şanizade's *Târîh-i Şânîzâde* is overall more balanced in content and language. It is notable, however, that the author himself became a victim of the events he was narrating: during the incident of the corps he was charged with being a Bektashi, removed from his post and sent into exile. See, Mehmed Dâniş Bey's *Netîcetü'l-Vekayi'*, published under the title *Yeniçeri Ocağının Kaldırılışı ve II. Mahmud'un Edirne Seyahati: Mehmet Dâniş Bey ve Eserleri*, edited by Şamil Mutlu (Istanbul: Edebiyat Fakültesi Basımevi, 1994) p. 74 (henceforth Dâniş Bey, *Netîcetü'l-Vekayi'*). The second less hostile account is that of Câbî Ömer Efendi, who was a tax collector (*câbî*) for a public endowment in Istanbul. Unlike the official histories of his era, Câbî provides vast materials absent elsewhere. Although the author had friends in the bureaucracy from whom he obtained copies of some official documents for his history, he is hardly worried about presenting the official viewpoint. Actually, the concern with Câbî's history is the opposite: he includes oral narratives from ordinary people in coffee houses and in the marketplace, which may reflect rumors and popular conceptions

## NOTES FOR CHAPTER 5

and views; however, I have made extensive use of this source, not only to counterbalance the sources mentioned above, but for *Câbî Târihi*'s intrinsic value, which provides rich material on life in the city as well as physical descriptions of dwellings.

15. Kırlı ('İstanbul', p. 75) mentions that many Janissary cafés were small, yet we know from other sources that some were rather big enterprises and brought high incomes to their owners. Here perhaps one should differentiate two types of Janissary coffee houses: the larger ones owned or run by active Janissaries from the corps with high ranks, and the other, smaller types, run by traders who were affiliated with the Janissary corps. Here, I shall focus on the former because there is more substantial information on them and their activities.
16. Câbî Ömer Efendi, *Câbî Târihi*, vol. 1, p. 182; Dâniş Bey, *Netîcetü'l-Vekayi*<sup>c</sup>, p. 74.
17. Their architecture and decoration reflected the aesthetic taste of the Janissaries. From accounts of the condition of Janissary barracks, coffee houses and even tents during military expeditions, one gets the impression that Janissaries placed much importance on cleanliness, beauty and decoration, even in their most 'corrupt' times. Janissary art and aesthetics seem to have been neglected in Ottoman history. After all, the world famous and much studied architect, Sinan, came out of the corps and took part in military expeditions for many years before he became Süleyman the Magnificent's chief architect in his fifties.
18. Koçu, *Yeniçeriler*, p. 286.
19. Câbî Ömer Efendi, *Câbî Târihi*, vol. 1, p. 249, vol. 2, pp. 729, 1054–5.
20. Dâniş Bey, *Netîcetü'l-Vekayi*<sup>c</sup>, p. 75.
21. Câbî Ömer Efendi, *Câbî Târihi*, vol. 1, p. 182; Şânîzâde, *Târîh-i Şânîzâde*, vol. 2, pp. 41–2.
22. Koçu, *Yeniçeriler*, p. 286; *İstanbul Ansiklopedisi*, s.v. 'Çardak İskelesi Yeniçeri Kahvehanesi'.
23. For literary, musical and entertainment activities in Janissary coffee houses, see for instance Koçu, *Yeniçeriler*, p. 297; and *Dünden Bugüne İstanbul Ansiklopedisi*, s.v. 'Kahvehaneler'.
24. The state showed very little tolerance of *devlet sohbeti*. Those who were involved, of whom a great number were Janissaries, were exiled. There was even a case of women being imprisoned for engaging in political discussion in the public bath. The authorities did not even spare the places where such discussion took place, and thus a number of barber shops and coffee houses were closed down. See, Câbî Ömer Efendi, *Câbî Târihi*, vol. 1, p. 392.
25. Mustafa Efendi Na<sup>c</sup>îmâ, *Târîh-i Na<sup>c</sup>îmâ: Ravdat-ül Hüseyn fî Hülâsat-i Ahbâr-il Hâfikeyn* (6 vols, Istanbul: Matbaa-i Âmire, 1281–83/1864–66) vol. 3, p. 171.

## NOTES FOR CHAPTER 5

26. *Türkiye Diyanet Vakfı İslâm Ansiklopedisi*, s.v. 'Kahve'.
27. Dâniş Bey, *Netîcetü'l-Vekayi<sup>c</sup>*, p. 74.
28. The corps became a major actor in politics and in emergency situations entered into pragmatic and short-lived alliances with other actors such as the *ulema* and *esnaf* as times and conditions allowed. When a sultan died, the support of the Janissaries during the temporary vacuum of political power was considered vital by the rival princes aspiring to the throne. Kafadar, 'Yeniçeri-esnaf relations', pp. 68–9.
29. Câbî Ömer Efendi, *Câbî Târihi*, vol. 1, p. 72.
30. Ibid., vol. 1, p. 130.
31. In *Câbî Târihi*, Câbî Ömer Efendi relays to us the arguments advanced by the Janissaries. According to them, the elite (*'paşalılar'*) were always after their self-interest (vol. 1, p. 131), got rich through unlawful means (vol. 1, p. 487), and while sitting in their mansions blamed the Janissaries for all the troubles and even accused them of treason (vol. 1, pp. 377, 487). Their argument continues that the elite alleged that Janissaries did not do their duties, wasted state money, prepared their plots and conspiracies at both coffee house and barrack, and even in the battlefield, as it was claimed by the elite that the Janissaries 'fought for money, not for religion' (vol. 1, p. 116 and vol. 2, p. 814). In their argument, the Janissaries go so far as to suggest that by being sent to battle, the authorities were 'conspiring' to get the Janissaries annihilated by enemy armies (vol. 1, pp. 118, 416, 455, 528, 659). Thus, the Janissary reach a 'seditious' end to the argument: if jihad were obligatory on all Muslims, then statesmen and *ulema* must also go on military expeditions (vol. 1, pp. 416, 441, 445, 446).
32. Câbî Ömer Efendi, *Câbî Târihi*, vol. 1, p. 287 and vol. 2, p. 992. Câbî Ömer Efendi gives us an idea of the scale and nature of the immigration from the countryside. Although 'most of the members of the Janissary corps are from Anatolia', the 25th *orta* was mostly composed of Kurds, and those from Erzurum and Van, while most of the members of the 56th *orta* were from Gerede and some were Kurdish, *Câbî Târihi*, vol. 1, pp. 417, 440, 502.
33. Kırlı, 'The struggle over space', p. 128.
34. Yaşar, 'The coffeehouses in early modern Istanbul', p. 64.
35. Even today this trait is alive in some districts of Istanbul where one finds cafés frequented by people coming from the same small town or village.
36. Janissary involvement in criminal and illegal activities will be treated below, but for examples see note 13 above.
37. Şânîzâde, *Târîh-i Şânîzâde*, vol. 1, p. 106.
38. Abdi Efendi, *Abdi Tarihi*, p. 26; and for a study of the social and political factors that contributed to the uprising, see M. Münir Aktepe,

## NOTES FOR CHAPTER 5

       *Patrona İsyanı, 1730* (Istanbul: İstanbul Edebiyat Fakültesi Basımevi, 1958).
39. Kırlı, 'İstanbul', p. 76.
40. Abdi Efendi, *Abdi Tarihi*, p. 37.
41. *İstanbul Ansiklopedisi*, s.v. 'Çardak İskelesi Yeniçeri Kahvehanesi'.
42. A few of them are listed in the index provided at the end of the article.
43. Mehmed Es<sup>c</sup>ad, *Es<sup>c</sup>ad Efendi Tarihi*, pp. 611–12.
44. It seems to me that the Janissaries' *devlet sohbeti* began to take on a different form in the nineteenth century. It started to move beyond criticizing corrupt officials or behaviour to questioning the legitimacy of the political system, especially hitherto accepted principles like the Ottoman dynasty's unquestioned right to rule and the concept of martyrdom at war. The authorities must surely have felt threatened by such discussions.
45. Dâniş Bey, *Netîcetü'l-Vekayi<sup>c</sup>*, p. 75.
46. Kırlı, 'Kahvehaneler ve Hafiyeler', p. 67.
47. Dâniş Bey, *Netîcetü'l-Vekayi<sup>c</sup>*, p. 75.
48. According to Âşıkpaşazâde, the process was the other way around: it was the Bektashis who received their headdress from the Janissaries. See Ahmed Âşıkpaşazâde, *Âşıkpaşazâde Tarihi* (Istanbul: Matbaa-i Amire, 1332/1914) p. 205.
49. A couplet from the famous Janissary *gülbank* (ceremonial prayer) mentions Hacı Bektaş as the patron-saint and (spiritual) sultan of the corps: *Gülbank-ı Muhammedî, nûr-ı Nebî, kerem-i Alî/Pîrimiz, hünkârımız Hacı Bektâş-ı Velî*. The Muhammedan *gülbank*, the Prophet's light, and Ali's magnanimity/Our patron-saint and sultan Hacı Bektaş.
50. According to the official view, contemporary Bektashis became extremely 'corrupt'. Several documents, all Hatt-ı Hümayun, from the Başbakanlık Osmanlı Arşivi (Prime Ministerial Ottoman Archives) in Istanbul, henceforth BOA, mention the corruption issue: 'the Bektashis who have opened *tekke*s in Eyüp, Üsküdar and Bosporus seduce and mislead the people', 17351 (dated 1242/1826–7); 'Bektashi sedition', 17383 (1241/1825–6); 'cleansing of the Bektashi sedition', 17322 (1241/1825–6); 'Bektashis who corrupt and spoil the people', 19426 (dated 1243/1827–8). 'Spoiling of the people' by the Bektashis is also mentioned in two contemporary sources: Dâniş Bey, *Netîcetü'l-Vekayi<sup>c</sup>*, pp. 72–3; and Mehmed Es<sup>c</sup>ad, *Üss-i Zafer*, p. 214.
51. John Kingsley Birge, *The Bektashi Order of Dervishes* (London and Connecticut: Luzac & Co. and Hartford Seminary Press, 1937) p. 74.
52. For a dissenting voice that challenges the existence of the Bektashi–Janissary connection, see Reha Çamuroğlu, *Yeniçerilerin Bektaşiliği ve Vaka-i Şerriye* (Istanbul: Ant Yayınları, 1991). Yet his argument is somewhat emotional, and based on reasoning rather than concrete evidence.

## NOTES FOR CHAPTER 5

53. Dünden Bugüne İstanbul Ansiklopedisi, s.v. 'Bektaşîlik' and 'Kahvehaneler'; Işın, 'More than a beverage', pp. 33–4; and Koçu, Yeniçeriler, p. 297.
54. Mehmed Es'ad, Üss-i Zafer, pp. 140–1. For details see, Koçu, Yeniçeriler, pp. 298–9.
55. İstanbul Ansiklopedisi, s.v. 'Ellialtıncı Yeniçeri Ortası, Ellialtılılar'.
56. A regulation on *ihtisâb* institution (İhtisâb Ağalığı Nizamnâmesi), made following the abolition of the Janissary corps in 1826, mentions the coffee house functioning as an *ihtisab* office too. Osman Nuri Ergin, *Mecelle-i Umûr-ı Belediyye* (Istanbul: İstanbul Büyükşehir Belediyesi, 1995) p. 328.
57. Arthur Leon Horniker, 'The corps of the Janizaries', *Military Affairs*, 8 (3) Autumn 1944, p. 199.
58. Câbî Ömer Efendi, *Câbî Târihi*, vol. 1, pp. 363–4.
59. Ibid., vol. 1, pp. 247–9, 253.
60. This is supported by Kırlı, who states that coffee houses 'served as commercial venues where merchants struck deals, ship captains arranged their next load and brokers looked for potential customers'. Cengiz Kırlı, 'Coffeehouses: public opinion in the nineteenth-century Ottoman Empire', in Armando Salvatore and Dale F. Eickelman (eds) *Public Islam and the Common Good* (Leiden: E. J. Brill, 2004) p. 76.
61. In this chapter, I employ the term 'mafia' in the sense of 'a group of people of similar interests or backgrounds prominent in a particular field or enterprise'. *Merriam-Webster's Collegiate Dictionary*, s.v. 'mafia'. And by 'mafia activities', I mean illegal activities focusing especially on some business and financial transactions in the city, such as arbitrary or forced determination of the prices of some services or goods, claiming a share of someone else's business, racketeering and coerced debt-collection.
62. Also, the wages of the craftsmen and artisans who worked on these constructions were very high. Dâniş Bey, *Netîcetü'l-Vekayi'*, p. 74.
63. Câbî Ömer Efendi, *Câbî Târihi*, vol. 1, p. 182.
64. Mehmed Es'ad, *Üss-i Zafer*, p. 140.
65. See for instance, Câbî Ömer Efendi, *Câbî Târihi*, vol. 1, p. 439 and vol. 2, p. 755; Mehmed Es'ad, *Üss-i Zafer*, p. 141.
66. Mehmed Es'ad, *Üss-i Zafer*, p. 140; Koçu, *Yeniçeriler*, p. 292.
67. Sometimes the *zorba* would want to establish or continue to hold a monopoly on the construction business, and would insist that all construction materials and work be provided through him at his own inflated prices.
68. Mehmed Es'ad, *Üss-i Zafer*, p. 140.
69. Ibid., p. 138. Sometimes leading members of different *orta*s would conduct duels with swords at Hendekbaşı, Galata, to establish rights of axe-hanging.
70. Câbî Ömer Efendi, *Câbî Târihi*, vol. 1, pp. 245, 246 ff., 329 and vol. 2, p. 963.

71. Ibid., vol. 2, pp. 766–7.
72. Ibid., vol. 1, pp. 385, 386, 624, 677 and vol. 2, p. 730.
73. Koçu, Yeniçeriler, p. 293.
74. For a clash that broke out in Galata among several ortas see BOA, Hatt-ı Hümayun, 19314/A, 19378, 19385 (dated 1234/1818–9).
75. Mehmed Es'ad, Üss-i Zafer, p. 138.
76. Ibid., p. 470.
77. Kahvecioğlu or Kalyoncu Burunsuz Mustafa was executed during the time of Alemdar Mustafa Pasha in front of his own coffee house at Galata. Câbî Ömer Efendi, Câbî Târihi, vol. 1, p. 249; Şânîzâde, Târîh-i Şânîzâde, vol. 1, p. 90.
78. He was a chief pursuivant (başçavuş) at the navy. Due to his corruption and oppression, he was later dismissed from the office of Başağa and exiled to Anatolia in 1813. Câbî Ömer Efendi, Câbî Târihi, vol. 2, pp. 1054–5.
79. İstanbul Ansiklopedisi, s.v. 'Çardak İskelesi Yeniçeri Kahvehanesi'.
80. Koçu, Yeniçeriler, p. 299.
81. İstanbul Ansiklopedisi, s.v. 'Balaban İskelesi Kahvehaneleri'.
82. He was executed following the events of 1826. Mehmed Es'ad, Es'ad Efendi Tarihi, p. 645; Mehmed Es'ad, Üss-i Zafer, p. 163.
83. He was active in the events of 1826 and was then executed in front of Hasan Paşa Hanı, most probably in front of his coffee house. Mehmed Es'ad, Es'ad Efendi Tarihi, p. 645; Mehmed Es'ad, Üss-i Zafer, p. 163.
84. He was executed following the events of 1826. Mehmed Es'ad, Es'ad Efendi Tarihi, p. 645; Mehmed Es'ad, Üss-i Zafer, p. 164.
85. Nahılcı, or Nakılcı, Mustafa was one of the leading figures in the events of 1826 and was executed during the event. Mehmed Es'ad, Es'ad Efendi Tarihi, pp. 609, 645. He was caught while hiding in the house of his mistress in Aksaray and brought in front of his coffee house in Kumkapı where he was executed. Mehmed Es'ad, Üss-i Zafer, pp. 162–3; Dâniş Bey, Netîcetü'l-Vekayi', p. 70.
86. Câbî Ömer Efendi, Câbî Târihi, vol. 1, pp. 129, 154.

**Chapter 6: The Heart's Desire: Gender, Urban Space and the Ottoman Coffee House by *Alan Mikhail***

Versions of this chapter were presented at conferences in Princeton, Berkeley and Washington, DC. I would especially like to thank Dana Sajdi for including me in her conference 'Rethinking Culture in the Ottoman Eighteenth Century' at Princeton University in January 2005 and for her extremely pertinent, patient and informed comments on earlier drafts of this article. For their help with the writing, conceptualization and research of this piece, I wish to thank the

## NOTES FOR CHAPTER 6

following individuals: Walter Andrews, Carel Bertram, Douglas Brookes, Julia Cohen, Murat Dağlı, Beshara Doumani, Khaled Fahmy, Cengiz Kırlı, Selim S. Kuru, Selma Akyazıcı Özkoçak, Malissa Taylor, Başak Tuğ, and Zeynep Türkyılmaz. Most of all, I want to express my gratitude to Leslie Peirce for reading multiple versions of this article over the span of a few years, for offering her keen analytical critiques, and for always giving of her time and expertise.

1. This Ḥadīth is recorded in the following study of the Qur'ān and Ḥadīth: Yusuf al-Qaradawi, *The Lawful and the Prohibited in Islam*, translated by Kamal El-Helbawy, M. Moinuddin Siddiqui and Syed Shukry (London: Shorouk International, 1985) p. 96.
2. For a discussion of Ottoman cafés as spaces of political subversion, for accounts of the multiple closures of these businesses, and for a general history of Ottoman coffee houses, see Desmet-Grégoire and Georgeon, *Cafés d'Orient revisités*; *Encyclopedia of Islam*, s.v. 'kahwa;' Hattox, *Coffee and Coffeehouses*; Işın, 'More than a beverage', pp. 10–43; Kırlı, 'The struggle over space'; and Michel Tuchscherer (ed.) *Le Commerce du café avant l'ère des plantations coloniales: espaces, réseaux, sociétés (XVe–XIXe siècle)* (Cairo: Institut français d'archéologie orientale, 2001).
3. Consider the following rather straightforward and somewhat romantic definition of Ottoman neighbourhood coffee houses: 'The most common type of coffeehouse in Istanbul. Nurtured by the local culture, they were therefore places of conversation whose custom was supplied by the neighborhood residents. At the same time, these venues acquired a function as hubs of social communication. The typical Ottoman whiled away the hours in the triangle formed by home, mosque and coffee house. With the opening of the neighbourhood coffeehouses at the end of the sixteenth century, everyday life embarked upon a new process of formation around a previously unknown type of space.' Quotation from İ. Gündağ Kayaoğlu, 'Kahve Sözlüğü' (The coffee glossary), in Selahattin Özpalabıyıklar Yayıncı (ed.) *Tanede Saklı Keyif (Coffee, Pleasures Hidden in a Bean)* (Istanbul: Yapı Kredi Kültür Sanat Yayıncılık) pp. 165–6.
4. Ehud Toledano likens these coffee houses to the 'local pub'. See Ehud R. Toledano, *State and Society in Mid-Nineteenth-Century Egypt* (Cambridge: Cambridge University Press, 1990) p. 242.
5. Cem Behar, *A Neighborhood in Ottoman Istanbul: Fruit Vendors and Civil Servants in the Kasap İlyas Mahalle* (Albany: State University of New York Press, 2003) p. 49.
6. Peirce, *The Imperial Harem*, p. 7. See Peirce's larger discussion of the relevant issues in her sections entitled 'The spatial dimensions of gender and power' and 'The inner as the source of power' (ibid., pp. 6–12).
7. Ibid., p. 9.

8. Gabriel Piterberg, *An Ottoman Tragedy: History and Historiography at Play* (Berkeley: University of California Press, 2003) pp. 196–8. See also Gabriel Piterberg, 'The variety of territorial sites in the poetic and historical imagination of the Ottomans' (paper presented at conference entitled 'The Meanings of Land: Law, Ideology, and Identity in the Ottoman Period', Berkeley, California, 20 October 2001).
9. Walter G. Andrews, 'Singing the alienated "I": Guattari, Deleuze and lyrical decodings of *the subject* in Ottoman *divan* poetry', *Yale Journal of Criticism*, 6 (2) 1993, p. 199. Andrews's discussion derives from Gilles Deleuze and Félix Guattari, *A Thousand Plateaus: Capitalism and Schizophrenia*, translated by Brian Massumi (Minneapolis: University of Minnesota Press, 1987).
10. See Jürgen Habermas's now classic, *The Structural Transformation of the Public Sphere: An Inquiry into a Category of Bourgeois Society*, translated by Thomas Burger (Cambridge: Massachussetts Institute of Technology Press, 1989).
11. For the most recent examples of this, see Kırlı, 'The struggle over space', pp. 1–22 and 245–85; and Uğur Kömeçoğlu, 'Historical and sociological approach to public space: the case of Islamic coffeehouses in Turkey' (Ph.D. dissertation, Boğaziçi University, 2001).
12. For a discussion of Habermas's notions of the public sphere and their many repercussions, see Craig Calhoun (ed.) *Habermas and the Public Sphere* (Cambridge: Massachussetts Institute of Technology Press, 1992). Especially instructive is the editor's introductory chapter.
13. Habermas, *Structural Transformation*, p. 45.
14. Ibid., pp. 175–6.
15. Randi Deguilhem, in 'Le café à Damas et le traité du Šayḥᶜ Ǧamāl al-Dīn al-Qāsamī al-Dimašqī', *Bulletin d'études orientales*, 45, 1993, p. 22, for instance, calls the Ottoman coffeehouse 'un lieu intermédiaire'.
16. Habermas, *Structural Transformation*, p. 33.
17. E. J. Clery, 'Women, publicity and the coffee-house myth', *Women: A Cultural Review*, 2 (2) Summer 1991, p. 169.
18. Andrews and Kalpaklı, *The Age of Beloveds*, p. 57. In a seeming contradiction, the authors later write that 'although, we have no evidence of the actual numbers of women in these (publicly visible, uncovered) categories, it is certain that there was a regular circulation of women through Ottoman public space' (ibid., p. 189).
19. Michel Foucault, 'Of other spaces', translated by Jay Miskowiec, *Diacritics*, 16 (1) Spring 1986, p. 25. Elsewhere Foucault writes that 'a whole history remains to be written of *spaces* – which would at the same time be the history of *powers* (both these terms in the plural) – from the great strategies of geo-politics to the little tactics of the habit'. Michel Foucault, 'The eye of power', in Colin Gordon (ed.) *Power/*

NOTES FOR CHAPTER 6

*Knowledge: Selected Interviews and Other Writings, 1972–1977* (New York: Pantheon Books, 1980) p. 149. For a general discussion of critical theory and the coffee house, see Kömeçoğlu, 'Historical and sociological approach to public space'.
20. Foucault, 'Of other spaces', p. 24.
21. Hattox, *Coffee and Coffeehouses*, p. 11.
22. *Encyclopedia of Islam*, s.v. 'kahwa'. Yet even in this source, coffee is acknowledged to have been in the Arabian Peninsula before the sixteenth century.
23. İbrahim Peçevi, *Tarih-i Peçevi* (2 vols, Istanbul: Matbaa-i Âmire, 1864–1867), vol. 1, pp. 363–4.
24. Katip Chelebi, *The Balance of Truth*, translated by G. L. Lewis (London: George Allen & Unwin, 1957) p. 60.
25. Mustafa Âli, *The Ottoman Gentleman of the Sixteenth Century: Mustafa Âli's Mevā'idü' n-Nefā'is fī Kavā'idi'l-Mecālis* (Tables of delicacies concerning the rules of social gatherings), translated by Douglas Brookes (Cambridge: Harvard University Department of Near Eastern Languages and Civilizations, 2003) p. 129.
26. Hattox, *Coffee and Coffeehouses*, p. 73.
27. Andreas Tietze, *Muṣṭafā ʿĀlī's Description of Cairo of 1599: text, transliteration, translation, notes* (Wien: Verlag der Österreichischen Akademie der Wissenschaften, 1975) p. 34.
28. Ibid., p. 37.
29. Alexander Russell, *The Natural History of Aleppo* (2 vols, London: G. G. and J. Robinson, 1794) vol. 1, p. 23.
30. Chelebi, *The Balance of Truth*, pp. 60–1.
31. Peçevi, *Tarih-i Peçevi*, vol. 1, p. 364.
32. Kırlı, 'İstanbul', pp. 75–6.
33. Charles White, *Three years in Constantinople; or, Domestic Manners of the Turks in 1844* (3 vols, London: Henry Colburn, 1845) vol. 1, p. 282.
34. ʿAbd al-Raḥmān al-Jabartī, *ʿAjāʾib al-Āthār fī al-Tarājim wa al-Akhbār* (4 vols, Cairo: Maṭbʿat Dār al-Kutub al-Miṣriyya, 1998) vol. 1, p. 600.
35. Ibid., vol. 3, p. 378.
36. Ibid., vol. 2, p. 232.
37. Ibid., vol. 3, p. 18.
38. Ibid., vol. 3, pp. 346–7.
39. On the cultural importance of food and social gatherings in the Ottoman world, see Hattox, *Coffee and Coffeehouses*, p. 89; and Marcus, *The Middle East on the Eve of Modernity*, p. 228. For a discussion of the role of food in Ottoman military and administrative ritual, see Peirce, *The Imperial Harem*, pp. 174–5.
40. Though Marcus asserts that 'going out to eat was an unfamiliar practice', Edward William Lane seems to suggest that eating out was

## NOTES FOR CHAPTER 6

not uncommon for nineteenth-century Egyptians (Marcus, *The Middle East on the eve of modernity*, p. 228). He writes of breakfasts of 'fool mudemmes ... sold in the morning sooks (or markets) of Cairo and other towns'. It is unclear whether the difference is between Egypt and Aleppo, between the nineteenth and eighteenth centuries, or between Marcus and Lane (Edward William Lane, Description of Egypt, edited by Jason Thompson, Cairo: The American University in Cairo Press, 2000, p. 134).

41. Nelly Hanna, *Habiter au Caire: la maison moyenne et ses habitants aux XVIIe et XVIIIe siècles* (Cairo: Institut français d'archéologie orientale, 1991) p. 142.
42. Ibid., p. 154.
43. Abraham Marcus, 'Privacy in eighteenth-century Aleppo: the limits of cultural ideals', *International Journal of Middle East Studies*, 18 (2) 1986, p. 170.
44. Antoine Abdel-Nour, *Introduction à l'histoire urbaine de la Syrie ottomane: XVIe–XVIIIe siècle* (Beirut: Librairie orientale, 1982) p. 100.
45. Dror Zeʾevi, *An Ottoman Century: The District of Jerusalem in the 1600s* (Albany: State University of New York Press, 1996) pp. 31–2.
46. On the importance of the institution of the Ottoman dinner party, see Kafadar, 'Self and others', pp. 141–4. For an Orientalist description of a nineteenth-century dinner party, see Lane, *Description of Egypt*, pp. 141–9.
47. Hattox, *Coffee and Coffeehouses*, p. 128. On the role of light and lighting in the Ottoman city, see Maurice Cerasi, 'The formation of Ottoman house types: a comparative study in interaction with neighboring cultures', *Muqarnas*, 15, 1998, pp. 133–4 and 137.
48. John Fryer, *A New Account of East India and Persia in Eight Letters* (London: R. Chiswell, 1698) p. 345.
49. In the novel *The Qadi and the Fortune Teller*, for example, the main character Abu Khalid expresses his dismay when he hears a nighttime knock on his door for 'no unannounced visitor would ever come to me or to any decent house after sunset'. See Nabil Saleh, *The Qadi and the Fortune Teller: Diary of a Judge in Ottoman Beirut (1843)* (London: Quartet Books, 1996) p. 13. Chastising visitation without proper warning or prior notice, the Ottoman historian Mustafa Âli writes in a similar vein that 'paying an untimely call inflicts torment upon that [visited] gentleman and demonstrates the low character of the caller' (Mustafa Âli, *The Ottoman Gentleman*, 167).
50. Al-Jabartī, *ʿAjāʾib al-Āthār*, vol. 3, p. 81.
51. I borrow the phrase 'conquering the night' from Cemal Kafadar's 'Coffee and the conquest of the night in the early modern era' (eleventh annual Eugene Lunn Memorial Lecture, Davis, California, 15 May 2003). See also Cemal Kafadar, 'A history of coffee' (paper presented at the

## NOTES FOR CHAPTER 6

thirteenth Economic History Congress, Buenos Aires, Argentina, July 2002). Although coffee and coffee houses did usher in a new kind of relationship between residents of early modern cities and the night, there were precedents to this phenomenon. Taverns, for instance, were places where men went after dark before and after the introduction of coffee to the Middle East. The associations between wine and taverns on the one hand and coffee and coffee houses on the other is a common theme in both the primary and secondary literature on coffee, and it is one to which we shall return below. Another connection between coffee and the night was the use of the drink by Sufis as a stimulant to stay awake during their lengthy nocturnal sessions of prayer.

52. Al-Jabartī, ʿAjāʾib al-Āthār, vol. 3, p. 4.
53. Ibid., vol. 3, p. 336.
54. White, *Three Years in Constantinople*, vol. 1, p. 280.
55. Peçevi, *Tarih-i Peçevi*, vol. 1, p. 364.
56. Tietze, *Muṣṭafā ʿĀlī's Description of Cairo*, p. 33.
57. Ibid., p. 37.
58. Al-Jabartī, ʿAjāʾib al-Āthār, vol. 3, p. 74.
59. In a decree from Istanbul to the *qāḍī* of Jerusalem on 10 Cumada I 973 (3 December 1565), we read, 'They [coffee houses] are the meeting-place of rascals (*levendat*) and ungodly people [who] day and night do not cease to act wickedly and mischievously, perniciously and refractorily'. See Uriel Heyd, *Ottoman Documents on Palestine, 1552–1615: A Study of the Firman According to the Mühimme Defteri* (Oxford: Clarendon Press, 1960) p. 161.
60. On the price of coffee in nineteenth-century Cairo, see Lane, *Description of Egypt*, p. 333. On prices in nineteenth-century Damascus, see Deguilhem, 'Le café à Damas', p. 23.
61. The literature on the Ottoman city, urban social life and related matters is by now quite large. Notable works include, but are by no means limited to, Behar, *A Neighborhood in Ottoman Istanbul*; Edhem Eldem, Daniel Goffman and Bruce Masters, *The Ottoman City between East and West: Aleppo, Izmir and Istanbul* (Cambridge: Cambridge University Press, 1999); Marcus, *The Middle East on the Eve of Modernity*; Raymond, *Artisans et commerçants*; André Raymond, *Arab Cities in the Ottoman Period: Cairo, Syria and the Maghreb* (Aldershot: Ashgate, 2002); and Heghnar Zeitlian Watenpaugh, *The Image of an Ottoman City: Imperial Architecture and Urban Experience in Aleppo in the 16th and 17th Centuries* (Leiden: E. J. Brill, 2004).
62. Evliya Çelebi, *Mısır, Sudan, Habeş (1672–1680)*, vol. 10 of *Evliya Çelebi Seyahatnamesi* (10 vols, Istanbul: Devlet Matbaası, 1896–1938) pp. 716–30. As suggested by the associated term *fellāhīn kahvehaneleri* (peasant coffee houses), *Arab kahvehaneleri* most likely refers to cafés

## NOTES FOR CHAPTER 6

frequented by Egyptian Bedouins or members of other peasant classes.
63. Mustafa Âli, *The Ottoman Gentleman*, p. 116 and p. 116 n.695. This discussion comes in a section entitled 'Abominations which are not permissible in the presence of great personages'.
64. Andreas Tietze, *Muṣṭafā ʿĀlī's Counsel of Sultans of 1581: Edition, Translation, Notes* (2 vols, Wien: Verlag der Österreichischen Akademie der Wissenschaften, 1979–1982) vol. 1, p. 38.
65. Peirce, *The Imperial Harem*, p. 271. On this point about the harem and the Topkapi Palace more generally, see Gülru Necipoğlu, *Architecture, Ceremonial, and Power: The Topkapi Palace in the Fifteenth and Sixteenth Centuries* (Cambridge: Massachussetts Institute of Technology Press, 1991); and Gülru Necipoğlu, 'Framing the gaze in Ottoman, Safavid and Mughal palaces', *Ars Orientalis*, 23, 1993, pp. 303–42.
66. Andrews and Kalpaklı, *The Age of Beloveds*, p. 275.
67. On this subject, Albert Hourani, *A History of the Arab Peoples* (New York: Warner Books, 1991) p. 123 writes that 'the quarter belonged to its inhabitants, and in a sense was an extension of the houses.'
68. Marcus, *The Middle East on the Eve of Modernity*, pp. 322–8.
69. Ibid., pp. 296–304.
70. Instructive on this point is Abraham Marcus's distinction between 'physical privacy' and the 'privacy of information'. See Marcus, 'Privacy in eighteenth-century Aleppo', pp. 165–83.
71. Behar, *A Neighborhood in Ottoman Istanbul*, pp. 44–6.
72. Janet Abu-Lughod terms this space 'semi-private space, a third category – between public and private'. See Janet L. Abu-Lughod, 'The Islamic city – historic myth, Islamic essence and contemporary relevance', *International Journal of Middle East Studies*, 19 (2) 1987, pp. 168–71.
73. Behar, *A Neighborhood in Ottoman Istanbul*, pp. 23–4.
74. The twentieth-century geographer Brian Beeley makes a similar argument with regards to the phenomenon of rural coffee houses replacing the guest rooms of private households (*misafir odası* or *misafirhane*) as spaces of male socialization. Beeley argues that newly constructed coffee houses in rural Anatolian villages between 1945 and 1960 served the needs of male villagers better than the previously preferred guest rooms of various families because coffee houses were larger and less hierarchical. Importantly, Beeley also notes that many men wanted coffee houses in their villages because they were symbols of urbanity and sophistication. Thus, Beeley shows that the village coffee house – what he terms 'a modernized version of the traditional guest room' – replaced a domestic space by better fulfilling its social role in the same way that I believe coffee houses served as domestic *selamlıks* for the poorer male residents of eighteenth and nineteenth-century Ottoman

## NOTES FOR CHAPTER 6

cities. See Brian W. Beeley, 'The Turkish village coffeehouse as a social institution', *Geographical Review*, 60 (4) October 1970, pp. 475-93.

75. There is a historic precedent in Islam for the serving and greeting of members of the opposite sex. The scholar of Islam Yūsuf al-Qaraḍāwī cites the following *Ḥadīth* from Ṣaḥīḥ Ibn Saʿd al-Anṣārī to make the point. 'Abū Usayd al-Saʿdī invited the Prophet (peace be on him) and his Companions to his wedding. The food was prepared and served by none other than his wife, Umm Usayd. She had soaked some dates in milk in a stone pot overnight. When the Prophet (peace be on him) had finished his meal, she mashed the dates and brought the drink to him.' Commenting on this *Ḥadīth*, Shaykh al-Islām Ibn Ḥajar claims that a wife is allowed to serve her husband and his male guests just as he may serve her. He qualifies his statement, however, by saying that 'it is evident that her serving the visitors is allowed only if there is no fear of temptation and if she is properly dressed; if the wife is not properly dressed (as is the case with a majority of women in our time) her appearing in front of men is *ḥarām*' (al-Qaradawi, *The Lawful and the Prohibited*, pp. 168–9). Despite these statements, Ottoman women and men still usually entertained guests in separate quarters of the home.

76. Dina Rizk Khouri, 'Drawing boundaries and defining spaces: women and space in Ottoman Iraq', in Amira El Azhary Sonbol (ed.) *Women, the Family and Divorce Laws in Islamic History* (Syracuse: Syracuse University Press, 1996) p. 185. See also Abraham Marcus, 'Men, women and property: dealers in real estate in 18th century Aleppo', *Journal of the Economic and Social History of the Orient*, 26, 1983, pp. 137–63.

77. Mustafa Âli, *The Ottoman Gentleman*, pp. 141–2. Later on Âli adds that 'the spaciousness of one's dwelling demonstrates worldly affluence.' Furthermore, he emphasizes the importance of the home as the space in which one will live for 'the rest of one's life', by stating the following: 'some learned men have said, when describing house and home, "It is the first thing that is bought".' Indeed, they have added, by way of supplementing the expression, 'And the last thing to be sold and come to an end' (Mustafa Âli, *The Ottoman Gentleman*, p. 143).

78. Ibid., p. 129.

79. Khouri, 'Drawing boundaries and defining spaces', p. 185. In his study of seventeenth-century Jerusalem, Dror Zeʾevi notes that a small house is usually termed *bayt* in the records of the Jerusalem court. This distinguishes it from the larger house known as the *dār*. Often a *dār* included within it several *buyūt* (plural of *bayt*) of various sizes (Zeʾevi, *An Ottoman Century*, p. 29).

80. We should also remember though that many women owned property and were major participants in the economic and social lives of their

cities. Afaf Lutfi al-Sayyid Marsot, for example, documents the significant property holdings of more than 40 Cairene women, a fraction of the city's wealthy female property-holding population. See Afaf Lutfi al-Sayyid Marsot, *Women and Men in Late Eighteenth-Century Egypt* (Austin: University of Texas Press, 1995) pp. 155–69. For other discussions of women and property, see Mary Ann Fay, 'The ties that bound: women and households in eighteenth-century Egypt', in Amira El Azhary Sonbol (ed.) *Women, the Family and Divorce Laws in Islamic History* (Syracuse, NY: Syracuse University Press, 1996) pp. 155–72; Mary Ann Fay, 'Women and *waqf*: property, power and the domain of gender in eighteenth-century Egypt', in Madeline C. Zilfi (ed.) *Women in the Ottoman Empire: Middle Eastern Women in the Early Modern Era* (Leiden: E. J. Brill, 1997) pp. 28–47; Khouri, 'Drawing boundaries and defining spaces', pp. 182–3; Margaret L. Meriwether, 'Women and *waqf* revisited: the case of Aleppo, 1770–1840', in Madeline C. Zilfi (ed.) *Women in the Ottoman Empire: Middle Eastern Women in the Early Modern Era* (Leiden: E. J. Brill) pp. 128–52; and Leslie Peirce, *Morality Tales: Law and Gender in the Ottoman Court of Aintab* (Berkeley: University of California Press, 2003) pp. 209–48.
81. Mustafa Âli, *The Ottoman Gentleman*, p. 129.
82. Toledano, *State and Society*, p. 243.
83. Hattox, *Coffee and Coffeehouses*, p. 125.
84. Işın, 'More than a beverage', pp. 32 and 35. The removal of one's shoes while consuming coffee in a coffee house is a practice also noticed in numerous paintings of Ottoman cafés. See, for example, ibid., pp. 23 and 29–31.
85. How was coffee made and what did it taste like in an eighteenth-century *mahalle* coffeehouse? We have few descriptions from the period that might tell us something about the taste of coffee. Edward William Lane's account of coffee from the late 1820s and early 1830s does, however, offer us a sense of coffee at that time. 'In preparing the coffee, the water is first made to boil: the coffee (freshly roasted and pounded) is then put in, and stirred, after which the pot is again placed on the fire, once or twice, until the coffee begins to simmer; when it is taken off, its contents are poured out into the cups while the surface is yet creamy. The Egyptians are excessively fond of pure and strong coffee, thus prepared; and very seldom add sugar to it (though some do so when they are unwell), and never milk or cream; but a little cardamom-seed is often added to it' (Lane, *Description of Egypt*, p. 138). Katip Çelebi notes that 'if drunk at all, it should be drunk with sugar' (Chelebi, *The Balance of Truth*, p. 62). Many sources mention mixing coffee with ginger, cloves, cardamom and the expensive ambergris. See *Encyclopaedia Iranica*, s.v. 'coffee'; *Encyclopedia of Islam*, s.v. 'kahwa';

NOTES FOR CHAPTER 6

Hattox, *Coffee and Coffeehouses*, pp. 83–7; and White, *Three Years in Constantinople*, vol. 1, pp. 277–86.
86. For a discussion of coffee house interiors, see Işın, 'More than a beverage', pp. 32–3; and A. Süheyl Ünver, *Ressam Ali Rıza Beye göre Yarım Asır Önce Kahvehanelerimiz ve Eşyası* (Ankara: Ankara Sanat Yayınları, 1967).
87. Evliya Çelebi, *Anadolu, Suriye, Hicaz (1671–1672)*, vol. 9 of *Evliya Çelebi Seyahatnamesi* (10 vols, Istanbul: Devlet Matbaası, 1896–1938) p. 377.
88. On the *waqf* complex of İpshīr Pasha, see Jean-Claude David, *Le Waqf d'Ipšīr Pāšā à Alep (1063/1653): Étude d'urbanisme historique* (Damascus: Institut français de Damas, 1982); and Watenpaugh, *The Image of an Ottoman City*, pp. 155–74.
89. David, *Le Waqf d'Ipšīr Pāšā*, p. 39; and Watenpaugh, *The Image of an Ottoman City*, pp. 162–3.
90. David, *Le waqf d'Ipšīr Pāšā*, p. 39.
91. Clery, 'Women, publicity and the coffee-house myth', p. 175. Of course the Turkish word for coffee house *kahvehane* is basically equivalent to the English version. Whereas *kahve* does indeed mean coffee, *hane*, however, does not directly translate to house. We should also note that the word *kahve* alone is often used to refer to a coffee house. While *hane* can refer simply to the physical structure of the house, it is usually used more figuratively in the sense of the home, household, or family. *Ev* is the preferred word for the physical structure of the home in Turkish, though it too can be used to refer to the family or household. Interestingly, the word for one who is married is *evli* (literally 'with house'). Thus the spatial character of the association between the home, marriage, and family is a very strong one in Turkish. Similarly, the word *evlilikdışı* (literally 'outside of the state of being with house'), which means illegitimate or unlawful, again highlights the spatial element of the moral character of the home as a place of the proper. For a thorough discussion of related topics of vocabulary, see Leslie P. Peirce, 'Seniority, sexuality and social order: the vocabulary of gender in early modern Ottoman society', in Madeline C. Zilfi (ed.) *Women in the Ottoman Empire: Middle Eastern Women in the Early Modern Era* (Leiden: E. J. Brill, 1997) pp. 169–96.
92. Lane, *Description of Egypt*, p. 333.
93. Peçevi, *Tarih-i Peçevi*, vol. 1, p. 364.
94. Watenpaugh, *The Image of an Ottoman City*, p. 163.
95. On the notion of transparency in Ottoman urban design, see Cerasi, 'The formation of Ottoman house types', pp. 133 and 137.
96. For a general discussion of Islamic cities and urban building practices, see Abu-Lughod, 'The Islamic city'; Juan Eduardo Campo, *The Other Sides of*

## NOTES FOR CHAPTER 6

*Paradise: Explorations into the Religious Meanings of Domestic Space in Islam* (Columbia: University of South Carolina Press, 1991); Besim Selim Hakim, *Arabic-Islamic Cities: Building and Planning Principles* (London: KPI, 1986); and Hisham Mortada, *Traditional Islamic Principles of Built Environment* (London: RoutledgeCurzon, 2003).

97. Hakim, *Arabic-Islamic Cities*, p. 151; Mortada, *Traditional Islamic Principles*, p. 97; and al-Qaradawi, *The Lawful and the Prohibited*, p. 316.
98. Qur'ān, 24: 37–30.
99. al-Qaradawi, *The Lawful and the Prohibited*, p. 63. Later he states, 'Prying into other peoples' private affairs and spying on their secrets is not permitted, even if they are engaged in sin, as long as they do it privately and not openly' (al-Qaradawi, *The Lawful and the Prohibited*, p. 314).
100. Muslim Ibn al-Ḥajjāj al-Qushayrī al-Nīsābūrī, *Ṣaḥīḥ Muslim* (5 vols, Beirut: Dār Ibn Ḥazm, 1995) vol. 3, pp. 1353–5.
101. This work exists in manuscript form printed lithographically in Fez in 1913. For a detailed study of the manuscript, see Hakim, *Arabic-Islamic Cities*, pp. 15–54.
102. Hakim, *Arabic-Islamic Cities*, p. 38; Mortada, *Traditional Islamic Principles*, p. 97.
103. Hakim, *Arabic-Islamic Cities*, pp. 38–9.
104. Jamel Akbar, *Crisis in the Built Environment: The Case of the Muslim City* (Singapore: Concept Media, 1988) p. 95.
105. Hakim, *Arabic-Islamic Cities*, p. 36; and Mortada, *Traditional Islamic Principles*, p. 99.
106. Hakim, *Arabic-Islamic Cities*, p. 37.
107. Âli, *The Ottoman Gentleman*, p. 116.
108. Gayatri Chakravorty Spivak, 'Can the subaltern speak?' in Cary Nelson and Lawrence Grossberg (eds) *Marxism and the Interpretation of Culture* (Urbana: University of Illinois Press, 1988) p. 287.
109. Gail Hershatter, *Dangerous Pleasures: Prostitution and Modernity in Twentieth-Century Shanghai* (Berkeley: University of California Press, 1997) p. 26. I borrow my analysis here from Joel Beinin, *Workers and Peasants in the Modern Middle East* (Cambridge: Cambridge University Press, 2001) pp. 102 and 172 n.3.
110. Ottoman spies were seemingly either unaware of or unconcerned about the following Ḥadīth from al-Bukhārī: 'he who listens clandestinely to people's conversation against their wishes will have molten lead poured into his ears on the Day of Resurrection' (al-Qaradawi, *The Lawful and the Prohibited*, pp. 315–16).
111. Kırlı, 'The struggle over space', p. 200.
112. For an additional treatment of discussion topics covered by these *jurnals*, see Kırlı, 'Coffeehouses', pp. 75–97.

## NOTES FOR CHAPTER 6

113. The *jurnal* as a class of document in the Ottoman administrative system was simply a type of report commissioned by the government that only seems to have emerged during the middle of the nineteenth century. The *jurnals* Kırlı studies are news *jurnals* (*havadis jurnalleri*), but other types of *jurnals* included censuses, statistical reports and quarantine records. See Kırlı, 'The struggle over space', p. 184 n.3.
114. An instructive comparative analysis of similar issues of speech and hearing is Dipesh Chakrabarty's discussion of the Bengali social practice of *adda*, which he loosely translates as 'the practice of friends getting together for long, informal and unrigorous conversations' (p. 181). Most useful for our present enquiries are Chakrabarty's comments on issues of place and talk, of coffee houses and tea shops, and of gender and sociability. See his chapter entitled '*Adda*: a history of sociality', in Dipesh Chakrabarty, *Provincializing Europe: Postcolonial Thought and Historical Difference* (Princeton: Princeton University Press, 2000) pp. 180–213.
115. On rumour, see Hans-Joachim Neubauer, *The Rumour: A Cultural History*, translated by Christian Braun (London: Free Association Books, 1999).
116. Al-Jabartī, *ʿAjāʾib al-Āthār*, vol. 3, p. 87.
117. For a discussion on the meanings of *sohbet* in the Ottoman world, see Andrews and Kalpaklı, *The Age of Beloveds*, pp. 106–12; and Kafadar, 'Self and others', pp. 121–50. On the differing meanings of the term *sohbet* vis-à-vis the coffee house in modern Turkey, see Kömeçoğlu, 'Historical and sociological approach to public space', pp. 172 and 199.
118. On gossip, see Patricia Ann Meyer Spacks, *Gossip* (New York: Knopf, 1985).
119. Al-Qaraḍāwī reports a *Ḥadīth* from al-Bukhārī warning that 'the one who spreads gossip which he has overheard will not enter the Garden' (al-Qaradawi, *The Lawful and the Prohibited*, p. 320).
120. Mustafa Âli, *The Ottoman Gentleman*, p. 96. Note here that this speech is described as a specifically urban phenomenon. Elsewhere Âli further differentiates between several kinds of gossipers: tell-tales, hypocrites, mischief-makers, busybodies, and backbiters (Mustafa Âli, *The Ottoman Gentleman*, pp. 55–6). For a further explanation of these categories of speech, see al-Qaradawi, *The Lawful and the Prohibited*, pp. 314–21.
121. Before the nineteenth century, the state of course was involved in the personal and political lives of its urban subjects through the institution of the court, but it is important to note that disputes among individuals were often resolved through extrajudicial means. Cases that came to court did so because one or more parties in the case brought it to the court. In other words, the state did not go out into society seeking to mediate disputes between parties. This situation changed in the

## NOTES FOR CHAPTER 6

nineteenth century when the police became a more seriously invasive social force. Interestingly, Foucault in his discussion of heterotopias eloquently associates the advent of police with the absence of a heterotopic understanding of space. 'The ship is the heterotopia *par excellence*. In civilizations without boats, dreams dry up, espionage takes the place of adventure, and the police take the place of pirates' (Foucault, 'Of other spaces', p. 27). Thus it seems that nineteenth-century Ottoman coffee houses were not the heterotopias of their seventeenth and eighteenth-century counterparts.

122. Tietze, *Muṣṭafā ʿĀlī's Counsel of Sultans*, vol. 1, p. 47.
123. *Lexicon Arabico–Persico–Turcicum*, s.v. 'namīme'.
124. *A Turkish and English Lexicon*, s.v. 'lāf'.
125. *Kâmûs-ı Türkî*, s.v. 'lāf'.
126. *A Turkish and English Lexicon*, s.v. 'qāl'.
127. *Lexicon Arabico–Persico–Turcicum*, s.v. 'qāl'.
128. Ibid., s.v. 'qīl'.
129. *Kâmûs-ı Türkî*, s.v. 'dedikodu'. In Ottoman Turkish this word literally means 'he said and he put'. See *A Turkish and English Lexicon*, s.v. 'dedi'.
130. Kırlı, 'The struggle over space', p. 182.
131. Ibid., pp. 53–4.
132. For an example of this type of conversation, see Lane, *Description of Egypt*, pp. 179–80. In this passage, Lane describes the coffee-house conversation of a group of men about the irritations caused to one of them by his wife. After discussions with his companions in the coffee house, the aggrieved man summoned his wife and divorced her on the spot in the café.
133. For an interesting discussion of differing interpretations of gossip, see Tuulikki Pietilä, *Gossip, Markets and Gender: The Dialogical Construction of Morality in Kilimanjaro* (Department of Sociology Research Report no. 233, Helsinki: University of Helsinki, 1999) pp. 9–22.
134. Julia Pardoe, *The Beauties of the Bosphorus* (London: George Virtue, 1839) p. 147.
135. Tietze, *Muṣṭafā ʿĀlī's Description of Cairo*, p. 37.
136. Âli, *The Ottoman Gentleman*, p. 129.
137. Erika Friedl, 'The dynamics of women's spheres of action in rural Iran', in Nikki R. Keddie and Beth Baron (eds) *Women in Middle Eastern History: Shifting Boundaries in Sex and Gender* (New Haven: Yale University Press, 1991) p. 196. The decision to use the terms 'public' and 'private' is Friedl's, not my own.
138. Thomas, *A Study of Naima*, p. 95.
139. Richard Sennet, *The Fall of Public Man* (New York: Alfred A. Knopf, 1977) p. 62.

## NOTES FOR CHAPTER 6

140. ᶜAbd al-Khāliq al-Dabbāgh, *Muᶜjam al-Amthāl al-ᶜĀmiyya fī al-Mūṣul* (2 vols, Baghdad: al-Hadaf Press, n.d.) vol. 2, p. 527, cited in Dina Rizk Khoury, 'Slippers at the entrance or behind closed doors: domestic and public spaces for Mosuli women', in Madeline C. Zilfi (ed.) *Women in the Ottoman Empire: Middle Eastern Women in the Early Modern Era* (Leiden: E. J. Brill) p. 115.
141. White, *Three Years in Constantinople*, vol. 1, p. 282.
142. Markman Ellis, 'Coffee-women, "The Spectator" and the public sphere in the early eighteenth century', in Elizabeth Eger, Charlotte Grant, Clíona Ó Gallchoir and Penny Warburton (eds) *Women, Writing and the Public Sphere, 1700–1830* (Cambridge: Cambridge University Press, 2001) p. 30. Emphasis added.
143. Clery, 'Women, publicity and the coffee-house myth', p. 175.
144. Alan Kaye, 'The etymology of "coffee": the dark brew', *Journal of the American Oriental Society*, 106 (3) July–September 1986, p. 558.
145. Indeed, the first definition of *qahwa* in the Arabic dictionary *Lisān al-ᶜArab* is *khamr*. The entry explains that coffee 'was so named because drinking it suppresses the appetite for food, or in other words removes one's appetite' (*Lisān al-ᶜArab*, s.v. 'qahwa'). We will have cause below to return to the literary and cultural connections between wine and coffee.
146. Chelebi, *The Balance of Truth*, p. 62. On the general medicinal properties of coffee and on the relative benefits of its consumption there was little agreement among Muslim physicians and scientists. Some claimed that coffee was beneficial for the stomach, lowered blood pressure and relieved most headaches. It could be used to treat smallpox, measles and haemorrhoids, and could heal wounds. Other physicians, however, blamed coffee for pallor, headaches, loss of libido, heat palpitations, nightmares, melancholy, haemorrhoids, dryness of the respiratory passages and insomnia. Some went so far as to say that coffee if consumed in excess could lead to brain disorders. While the Egyptian physician Dā'ūd al-Anṭākī asserted that drinking coffee with milk could cause leprosy, the Persian physician Ebn Kashef al-Din recommended washing down a lentil-sized pill of opium with coffee for the relief of hangovers from drinking wine. It was also recommended that coffee only be drunk after a light breakfast known in Persian as *takht al-qahva* (literally, 'the foundation of coffee'). In Turkish also, the word for breakfast (*kahvaltı*) derives from the fusion of the words *kahve* (coffee) and *altı* (beneath or lower). Literally, then, *kahvaltı* means coffee's foundation or coffee's underneath. The humoral qualities of coffee were also in question. Some physicians thought coffee was cold and dry and therefore associated with black bile and melancholy. Others ascribed to coffee the qualities of being hot and dry, which

meant that coffee was associated with yellow bile and the choleric. See Chelebi, *The Balance of Truth*, pp. 61–2; Michael W. Dols, *Majnūn: The Madman in Medieval Islamic Society* edited by Diana E. Immisch (Oxford: Clarendon Press, 1992) pp. 108–10; *Encyclopedia Iranica*, s.v. 'coffee'; Hattox, *Coffee and Coffeehouses*, pp. 61–71; and Bennett Alan Weinberg and Bonnie K. Bealer, *The World of Caffeine: The Science and Culture of the World's Most Popular Drug* (New York: Routledge, 2002) pp. 269–315.

147. Clara Erskine Clement Waters, *Constantinople: The City of the Sultans* (Boston: Estes and Lauriat, 1895) pp. 250–4, 277–8. The coffee a young girl served to her prospective husband and his family was termed *görücü kahvesi* (matchmaker coffee). See Kayaoğlu, 'Kahve Sözlüğü', 163, 165.

148. For a compendium of Ottoman poetry about coffee, see Nâmık Açıkgöz, *Kahvenâme: klâsik Türk Edebiyatında Kahve* (Ankara: Akçağ Basım Yayım Pazarlama, 1999). For similar compendia of Arabic poetry, see ᶜAbd al-ᶜAziz ibn Nāṣir ibn Saᶜūd al-ᶜAbd Allah, *al-Qahwa wa al-Kayf bayna al-Māḍī wa al-Ḥāḍir* (Riyadh: Maṭābiᶜ al-Ḥamīdī, 2000); and Maḥmūd Mufliḥ al-Bakr, *al-Qahwa al-ᶜArabiyya fī al-Mawrūth wa al-Adab al-Shaᶜabī* (Beirut: Bīsān li al-Nashr wa al-Tawzīᶜ wa al-Iᶜlām, 1995).

149. For the most sustained study of wine in Arabic poetic traditions, see Philip F. Kennedy, *The Wine Song in Classical Arabic Poetry: Abū Nuwās and the Literary Tradition* (Oxford: Clarendon Press, 1997).

150. In taverns, coffee was like wine initially drunk from a communal cup that was passed around. Interestingly, this tradition of sharing was also observed in dervish lodges where coffee was drunk to help dervishes stay awake. The move from communal vessel to individual cup occurred quite early in coffee's history in the Middle East, sometime during the middle of the fifteenth century. For more on the history of coffee cups in the Middle East, see Edward J. Keall, 'The evolution of the first coffee cups in Yemen', in Michel Tuchscherer (ed.) *Le Commerce du café avant l'ère des plantations coloniales: espaces, réseaux, sociétés (XVe–XIXe siècle)* (Cairo: Institut français d'Archéologie orientale, 2001) pp. 35–50.

151. Âli, *The Ottoman Gentleman*, p. 52.

152. Walter G. Andrews, *Poetry's Voice, Society's Song: Ottoman Lyrical Poetry* (Seattle: University of Washington Press, 1985) pp. 132, 146–8, 160–3.

153. Walter G. Andrews, Najaat Black and Mehmed Kalpaklı (eds and translators) *Ottoman Lyrical Poetry: An Anthology* (Austin: University of Texas Press, 1997) p. 134.

154. Ibid., p. 60. Coincidentally, in 1532 Figani was flogged and then hung near his home in Tahtakale – the neighbourhood in which Istanbul's

## NOTES FOR CHAPTER 6

first coffee house opened in the middle of the sixteenth century (ibid., pp. 229–31).

155. Khaled El-Rouayheb, 'The love of boys in Arabic poetry of the early Ottoman period, 1500–1800', *Middle Eastern Literatures*, 8 (1) January 2005, p. 10.
156. On the importance of the garden in Ottoman poetry and in Ottoman social life, see Andrews, *Poetry's Voice*, pp. 150–8.
157. Ibid., pp. 161–2. Notice here the use of the female pronoun to refer to the beloved *saki*.
158. Andrews et al., *Ottoman Lyrical Poetry*, p. 150.
159. This is a play on the word *ayak*. See below for explanation.
160. Mustafa İsen (ed.) *Künhü'l-Ahbâr'ın Tezkire Kısmı* (Ankara: Atatürk Kültür Merkezi, 1994) p. 199.
161. ʿÂşik Çelebi, *Meşâʿir Üş-Şuʿarâ*, edited by G. M. Meredith-Owens (London: Luzac, 1971) p. 259a. The immediate provocation that led to this couplet was Sultan Süleyman's burning of Italian wine ships off the coast of Galata in 1562. See Andrews and Kalpaklı, *The Age of Beloveds*, p. 81. My thanks to Walter G. Andrews for alerting me to this couplet and to the previously cited poem and for help with its translation.
162. Andrews and Kalpaklı write that in Ottoman poetry 'a lover's eye always weeps bloody tears'. In this section, they also engage in a very interesting discussion of the shape of the script of the Ottoman word şiʿr (poetry) and its resemblance to a crying eye (Andrews and Kalpaklı, *The Age of Beloveds*, p. 100).
163. Âli, *The Ottoman Gentleman*, p. 112.
164. Coffee's black colour meant that it was often compared with another black stimulant, *berş*, which was a drug concoction of either hemp or opium mixed with syrup (ibid., pp. 53, 53 notes 351–2 and 175). The accompaniment of various drugs with the drinking of coffee no doubt made this connection seem all the more apparent.
165. Andrews et al., *Ottoman Lyrical Poetry*, p. 60.
166. Chelebi, *The Balance of Truth*, pp. 60–2. See also Robert Dankoff, *An Ottoman Mentality: The World of Evliya Çelebi* (Leiden: E. J. Brill, 2004) p. 88.
167. Peçevi, *Tarih-i Peçevi*, vol. 1, pp. 364–5.
168. Âli, *The Ottoman Gentleman*, p. 103 and p. 103 n.618. There was certainly a gendered hierarchy of coffee in the Ottoman world with the 'strongest' coffee – with the fewest additives – at the top and the 'weakest' – with sugar, milk and other spices and additives – at the bottom. Coffee with no sugar was known as *erkek kahvesi* (man coffee) and coffee with sugar was derogatorily termed *kancık kahvesi* (bitch coffee). There was also *sütlü kahve* (milky coffee), which was usually reserved for children (Kayaoğlu, 'Kahve sözlüğü', pp. 162–6).

169. The author of the anonymous Arabic manuscript *Risāla fī Aḥkām al-Qahwa* refers to the presence in coffee houses of 'youths earmarked for the gratification of one's lusts'. The seventeenth-century English poet and traveller George Sandys notes that many café owners in Istanbul 'keep beautiful boyes, who serve as stales [prostitutes] to procure them customers'. For more on these descriptions and for a general discussion of coffee-house boys, see Hattox, *Coffee and Coffeehouses*, pp. 109–10.
170. Andrews and Kalpaklı, *The Age of Beloveds*, pp. 54 and 57.
171. Everett K. Rowson, 'The categorization of gender and sexual irregularity in medieval Arabic vice lists', in Julia Epstein and Kristina Straub (eds) *Body Guards: The Cultural Politics of Gender Ambiguity* (New York: Routledge, 1991) p. 58.
172. Âli, *The Ottoman Gentleman*, p. 97.
173. Ibid., p. 44.
174. Ibid., p. 131.
175. Ibid., p. 17.
176. Ibid., p. 131.
177. Ibid., p. 28.
178. Andrews and Kalpaklı, *The Age of Beloveds*, p. 178.
179. Rowson, 'The categorization of gender, p. 69.
180. Andrews and Kalpaklı, *The Age of Beloveds*, p. 186. Although I am wary of the use of the word 'public' in this context, this quote reiterates both the connections between the spaces of wine and those of coffee and the uniqueness of these places in the spatial geography of Ottoman cities.
181. Âli, *The Ottoman Gentleman*, p. 30.
182. Later, Âli condemns the 'unacceptable behaviour' of male domestic servants, which 'includes entering a room in ranks but then not exiting it, darting about with quick motions and not staying still in one place, and bending the knees when offering pure water or sherbet or coffee, by which I mean bending over and sticking out the behind when serving, so as to make those present at the gathering hope for different joys and pleasures' (ibid., p. 97).
183. On the coffee trade, see Suraiya Faroqhi, 'Coffee and spices: official Ottoman reactions to Egyptian trade in the later sixteenth century', *Wiener Zeitschrift für die Kunde des Morgenlandes*, 76, 1986, pp. 87–93; Mehmed Genç, 'Contrôle et taxation du commerce du café dans l'Empire ottoman fin XVIIe–première moitié du XVIII$^e$ siècle', in Michel Tuchscherer (ed.) *Le Commerce du café avant l'ère des plantations coloniales: espaces, réseaux, sociétés (XVe–XIXe siècle)* (Cairo: Institut français d'Archéologie orientale, 2001) pp. 161–79; Jane Hathaway, *The Politics of Households in Ottoman Egypt: The Rise of the Qazdağlıs* (Cambridge: Cambridge University Press, 1997); Muhammad Husām al-Din Ismāʿil, 'Le café dans la ville de Rosette à l'époque ottomane

XVIe–XVIIe siècle', in Michel Tuchscherer (ed.) *Le Commerce du cafe avant l'ère des plantations coloniales: espaces, réseaux, sociétés (XVe–XIXe siècle)* (Cairo: Institut français d'Archéologie orientale, 2001) pp. 103–9; André Raymond, 'Une famille de grands négociants en café au Caire dans la première moitié du XVIIIe siècle: les Sharāybī', in Michel Tuchscherer (ed.) *Le Commerce du cafe avant l'ère des plantations coloniales: espaces, réseaux, sociétés (XVe–XIXe siècle)* (Cairo: Institut français d'Archéologie orientale, 2001) pp. 111–24; and Michel Tuchscherer, 'Commerce et production du café en Mer Rouge au XVIe siècle', in Michel Tuchscherer (ed.) *Le Commerce du cafe avant l'ère des plantations coloniales: espaces, réseaux, sociétés (XVe–XIXe siècle)* (Cairo: Institut français d'Archéologie orientale, 2001) pp. 69–90.

184. For example, during the numerous instances in which Ottoman officials closed cafés, barber shops often took on the social role of the coffee house as a centre of gathering and discussion (Kafadar, 'Self and others', p. 144).

# References

## Archival documents
Hatt-ı Humayun, Başbakanlık Osmanlı Arşivi, İstanbul

17322 (1241/1825-6)
17351 (1242/1826-7)
17383 (1241/1825-6)
19314/A
19378
19385 (1234/1818-9)
19426 (1243/1827-8)

Mufti Archives of Istanbul, Kısmet-i Askeriye Mahkemesi collection, register 98, Istanbul.

## Published sources
al-ᶜAbd Allah, ᶜAbd al-ᶜAziz ibn Nāṣir ibn Saᶜūd (2000) *Al-Qahwa wa al-Kayf bayna al-Māḍī wa al-Ḥāḍir*, Riyadh: Maṭābiᶜ al-Ḥamīḍī

Abdel-Nour, Antoine (1982) *Introduction à l'histoire urbaine de la Syrie ottomane: XVIe–XVIIIe siècle*, Beirut: Librairie orientale

Abdi Efendi (1943) *1730 Patrona İhtilâli Hakkında Bir Eser: Abdi Tarihi*, edited by Faik Reşit Unat, Ankara: Türk Tarih Kurumu

Abou-El-Haj, Rifaᶜat (1982) 'The social uses for the past: recent Arab historiography of Ottoman rule', *International Journal of Middle East Studies*, 14 (2) pp. 185–201

—— (1988) 'The Ottoman *nasihatname* as a discourse over "morality"', in Abdeljelil Temimi (ed.) *Mélanges Professeur Robert Mantran*, Zeghouan: Centre d'études et de recherches ottomans, morisques de documentation et d'information, pp. 17–30

—— (1991) 'Power and social order: the uses of *kanun*', in Irene A. Bierman, Rifaᶜat Abou-El-Haj and Donald Preziosi (eds) *The Otto-

## REFERENCES

*man City and its Parts: Structures and Social Order*, New Rochelle: A. D. Caratzas, pp. 77-91

(1991) *Formation of the Modern State: The Ottoman Empire, Sixteenth to Eighteenth Centuries*, Albany: State University of New York Press

Abu-Lughod, Janet L. (1987) 'The Islamic city – historic myth, Islamic essence and contemporary relevance', *International Journal of Middle East Studies*, 19 (2) pp. 155-76

Açıkgöz, Nâmık (1999) *Kahvenâme: Klâsik Türk Edebiyatında Kahve*, Ankara: Akçağ Basım Yayım Pazarlama

Afyoncu, Erhan (2004) 'İbrahim Müteferrika'nın Yeni Yayınlanan Terekesi ve Ölüm Tarihi Üzerine', *Türklük Araştırmaları Dergisi*, 15, pp. 349-62

Ahmad, Aijaz (2006) 'Empire comes to Lebanon', *Frontline*. 23 (15) 29 July to 11 August, http://www.hinduonnet.com/fline/fl2315/stories/20060811005800600.htm

Akbar, Jamel (1988) *Crisis in the Built Environment: The Case of the Muslim City*, Singapore: Concept Media

Akgündüz, Ahmed (ed.) (1988) *Şerʿiye Sicilleri: Mahiyeti, Toplu Kataloğu ve Seçme Hükümler*, Istanbul: Türk Dünyası Araştırmaları Vakfı

Aktepe, M. Münir (1958) *Patrona İsyanı, 1730*, Istanbul: İstanbul Edebiyat Fakültesi Basımevi

Alemi, Mahvash (1986) 'Chahar Bagh', *Environmental Design: Journal of the Islamic Environmental Research Centre*, 1, pp. 38-45

Âli, Mustafa (2003) *The Ottoman Gentleman of the Sixteenth Century: Mustafa Âli's Mevāʿidü' n-Nefāʾis fī Kavāʿidi'l-Mecālis* (Tables of delicacies concerning the rules of social gatherings) translated by Douglas Brookes, Cambridge: Harvard University Department of Near Eastern Languages and Civilizations

(1975) *Muṣṭafā ʿĀlī's Description of Cairo of 1599: Text, Transliteration, Translation, Notes*, edited and translated by Andreas Tietze, Vienna: Verlag der Österreichischen Akademie der Wissenschaften

(1979-82) *Muṣṭafā ʿĀlī's Counsel of Sultans of 1581: Edition, Translation, Notes*, edited and translated by Andreas Tietze, 2

# REFERENCES

vols, Vienna: Verlag der Österreichischen Akademie der Wissenschaften

Allouche, Adel (1983) *The Origins and Development of the Ottoman-Safavid Conflict (906–962/1500–1555)*, Berlin: K. Schwarz Verlag

Anastassiadou, Meropi (1993) 'Les inventaires après décès de Salonique à la fin du XIXe siècle: source pour l'étude d'une société au seuil de la modernisation', *Turcica*, 25, pp. 97–135

—— (1999) 'Livres et "bibliothèques" dans les inventaires après décès de Salonique au XIXe siècle', *Revue des mondes musulmans et de la Méditerranée*, 87–88, pp. 111–41

—— (2000) 'Des défunts hors du commun: les possesseurs de livres dans les inventaires après décès musulmans de Salonique', *Turcica*, 32, pp. 197–252

And, Metin (1963–64) *A History of Theatre and Popular Entertainment in Turkey*, Ankara: Forum Yayinlari

—— (1982) *Osmanli Şenliklerinde Türk Sanatlari*, Ankara: Kültüre ve Tuizm Bakanliği

Andrews, Walter G. (1985) *Poetry's Voice, Society's Song: Ottoman Lyrical Poetry*, Seattle: University of Washington Press

—— (1993) 'Singing the alienated "I": Guattari, Deleuze and lyrical decodings of *the subject* in Ottoman *divan* poetry', *Yale Journal of Criticism*, 6 (2) pp. 191–219

Andrews, Walter G. and Mehmed Kalpaklı (2005) *The Age of Beloveds: Love and the Beloved in Early-Modern Ottoman and European Culture and Society*, Durham: Duke University Press

Andrews, Walter G., Najaat Black and Mehmed Kalpaklı (eds and translators) (1997) *Ottoman Lyrical Poetry: An Anthology*, Austin: University of Texas Press

Ankersmit, Frank R. (2001) *Historical Representation*, Stanford: Stanford University Press

Arjomand, Said Amir (1988) 'The Mujtahid of the age and the Mulla-bashi', in Said Amir Arjomand (ed.) *Authority and Political Culture in Shi'ism*, Albany: State University of New York Press, pp. 80–97

Arslan, Mehmed (2002) 'A great Ottoman festivity: circumcision feasts of Prince Mehmed III', in Hasan Celâl Güzel, C. Cem Oğuz and Osman Karatay (eds) *The Turks*, 21 vols, Ankara: Yeni Turkiye, pp. 974–84

Artan, Tülay (1989) 'Architecture as a theatre of life: profile of the eighteenth century Bosphorus', Ph.D. dissertation, Massachusetts Institute of Technology

—— (1998) 'Terekeler Işığında 18. Yüzyıl Ortasında Eyüp'te Yaşam Tarzı ve Standartlarına Bir Bakış. Orta Halliliğin Aynası', in T. Artan (ed.) *18. Yüzyıl Kadı Sicilleri Işığında Eyüp'te Sosyal Yaşam*, Istanbul: Tarih Vakfı, pp. 49–64

Aşgin, Sait (2003) 'Hadikatü'l-Vüzera Üzerine Bir İnceleme', *Ankara Üniversitesi Osmanli Tarihi Arastirma ve Uygulama Merkezi dergisi*, 14, pp. 145–61

Aşıkpâşâzâde, Ahmed (1332/1914) *Âşıkpaşazâde Tarihi*, Istanbul: Matbaa-i Amire

Atâ, Tayyarzâde Ahmed (1876) *Tarih-i Atâ*, 5 vols, Istanbul: n.p.

Atıl, Esin (1969) 'Surname-i Vehbi: an eighteenth century Ottoman book of festivals', Ph.D. dissertation, University of Michigan, Ann Arbor

—— (1986) *Süleymanname: The Illustrated History of Süleyman the Magnificent*, Washington: National Art Gallery and H. N. Abrams

—— (1993) 'The story of an eighteenth-century Ottoman festival', *Muqarnas*, 10, pp. 181–200

—— (1999) *Levni and the Surname: The Story of an Eighteenth-Century Ottoman Festival*, Istanbul: Koçbank

ᶜĀşik Çelebi (1971) *Meşâᶜir Üş-Şuᶜarā*, edited by G. M. Meredith-Owens, London: Luzac

Babaie, Sussan (1994) 'Safavid palaces at Isfahan: continuity and change (1599–1666)', Ph.D. dissertation, New York University

—— (1994) 'Shah ᶜAbbas II, the conquest of Qandahar, the Chihil Sutun, and its wall paintings', *Muqarnas*, 11, pp. 125–42

Babinger, Franz (1927) *Die Geschichtsschreiber der Osmanen und ihre Werke*, Leipzig: Harrassowitz

—— (2004) '18. Yüzyılda İstanbul'da Kitabiyat', in N. Kuran-Burçoğlu (ed.) *Müteferrika ve Osmanlı Matbaası*, Istanbul: Tarih Vakfı Yurt Yayınları

# REFERENCES

al-Bakr, Maḥmūd Mufliḥ (1995) *Al-Qahwa al-ᶜArabiyya fī al-Mawrūth wa al-Adab al-Shaᶜabī*, Beirut: Bīsān li al-Nashr wa al-Tawzīᶜ wa al-Iᶜlām

Barbir, Karl (1999) 'The changing face of the Ottoman Empire in the eighteenth century: past and future scholarship', *Oriente Moderno*, 18 (1) pp. 253–67

Barkan, Ömer Lütfi (1966) 'Edirne Askerî Kassamına ait Tereke Defterleri (1545–1659)', *Belgeler. Türk Tarih Belgeleri Dergisi*, 3 (5–6) pp. 1–479

—— (1975) 'The price revolution of the sixteenth century: a turning point in the economic history of the Near East', *International Journal of Middle East Studies*, 6, pp. 3–28

Barkey, Karen (1994) *Bandits and Bureaucrats: The Ottoman Route to State Centralization*, Ithaca: Cornell University Press

Baysal, Jale (1968) *Müteferrika'dan Birinci Meşrutiyete Kadar Osmanlı Türklerinin Bastıkları Kitaplar*, Istanbul: Edebiyat Fakültesi

—— (1976) 'II. Rákóczi Ferenc'in Çevirmeni Müteferrika İbrahim ve Osmanlı Türklerinin İlk Bastıkları Kitaplar', in *Türk–Macar Kültür Münasebetleri Işığı Altında II. Rákóczi Ferenc ve Macar Mültecileri Sempozyumu/Symposium on Rákóczi Ferenc II and the Hungarian Refugees in the Light of Turco–Hungarian Cultural Relations*, Istanbul: İ. Ü. Edebiyat Fakültesi

—— (1991) *Kitap ve Kütüphane Tarihi'ne Giriş*, Istanbul: Türk Kütüphaneciler Derneği

—— (1992) *Cennetlik İbrahim Efendi (İbrahim Müteferrika Oyunu)* Istanbul: Cem

Beeley, Brian W. (1970) 'The Turkish village coffeehouse as a social institution', *Geographical Review*, 60 (4) October, pp. 475–93

Behar, Cem (2003) *A Neighborhood in Ottoman Istanbul: Fruit Vendors and Civil Servants in the Kasap İlyas Mahalle*, Albany: State University of New York Press

Beinin, Joel (2001) *Workers and Peasants in the Modern Middle East*, Cambridge: Cambridge University Press

Beldiceanu-Steinherr, Irene (1975) 'Le règne de Selim Ier: tournant dans la vie politique et religieuse de l'Empire ottoman', *Turcica*, 6, pp. 34–48

# REFERENCES

Berkes, Niyazi (1962) 'İlk Türk Matbaası Kurucusunun Dinî ve Fikrî Kimliği', *Belleten*, 26 (104) pp. 715–37
— (1964) *The Development of Secularism in Turkey*, Montreal: McGill University Press
— (1985) 'Unitarianizm ve Matbaa', in Niyazi Berkes (ed.) *Felsefe ve Toplumbilim Yazıları*, Istanbul: Adam Yayınları, pp. 85–103 (reprint of Berkes 1962 above)
— (2002) *Türkiye'de Çağdaşlaşma*, edited by A. Kuyaş, Istanbul: Yapı Kredi Yayınları
Berktay, Halil (1992) 'The search for the peasant in Western and Turkish historiography', in Halil Berktay and Suraiya Faroqhi (eds) *New Approaches to State and Peasant in Ottoman History*, London: Frank Cass, pp. 109–84
Beydilli, Kemal (2004) 'Müteferrika ve Osmanlı Matbaası. 18. Yüzyılda İstanbul'da Kitabiyat', *Toplumsal Tarih*, 128 (August) pp. 44–52
Birge, John Kingsley (1937) *The Bektashi Order of Dervishes*, London and Connecticut: Luzac & Co. and Hartford Seminary Press
Blair, S. S. and J. M. Bloom (1995) *The Art and Architecture of Islam 1250–1800*, New Haven: Yale University Press, second edition
Blake, S. P. (1991) *Shahjahanabad: the Sovereign City in Mughal India 1639–1739*, Cambridge: Cambridge University Press
Bozdoğan, S. (1987) 'In search of a national architecture', in H.-U. Khan (ed.) *Sedad Eldem*, Singapore: Concept Media, pp. 61–75
Briggs, Asa and Peter Burke (2003) *A Social History of the Media: From Gutenberg to the Internet*, Cambridge: Polity Press
Brooke-Rose, Christine (1992) 'Histoire palimpseste', in S. Collini (ed.) *Interprétation et surinterprétation*, Paris: Presses Universitaires de France, pp. 115–27
Browne, Edward Granville (1951) *A Literary History of Persia*, Cambridge: Cambridge University Press
Burke, P. (1997) 'Origins of cultural history', in Peter Burke (ed.) *Varieties of Cultural History*, Cambridge: Polity Press, pp. 1–22
Calhoun, Craig (ed.) (1992) *Habermas and the Public Sphere*, Cambridge: Massachussetts Institute of Technology Press
Campo, Juan Eduardo (1991) *The Other Sides of Paradise:*

# REFERENCES

*Explorations into the Religious Meanings of Domestic Space in Islam*, Columbia: University of South Carolina Press

Carleson, Edvard (1979) *İbrahim Müteferrika Basimevi ve Bastiği ilk Eserler/İbrahim Müteferrika's Printing House and its First Printed Books*, edited by M. Akbulut, Ankara: Türk Kütüphaneciler Derneği

Cerasi, Maurice (1998) 'The formation of Ottoman house types: a comparative study in interaction with neighboring cultures', *Muqarnas*, 15, pp. 116–56

Cevdet, Ahmed (1854–84) *Vekayi-i Devlet-i Aliyye-i Osmaniyye* (or *Tarih-i Cevdet*) 12 volumes, Istanbul: Matbaa-i Âmire

Chakrabarty, Dipesh (2000) *Provincializing Europe: Postcolonial Thought and Historical Difference*, Princeton: Princeton University Press

Chardin, J. (1711) *Voyages de Monsieur Chevalier Chardin en Perse et autres lieux d'Orient*, 4 vols, Amsterdam: Chez Jean Louis de Lorme

Chelkowski, Peter J. (1979) 'Ta'ziyeh: indigenous avant-garde theatre of Iran', in Peter J. Chelkowski (ed.) *Ta'ziyeh: Ritual and Drama in Iran*, New York: New York University Press, pp. 1–11

Clery, E. J. (1991) 'Women, publicity and the coffee-house myth', *Women: A Cultural Review*, 2 (2) Summer, pp. 168–77

Coşkun, Menderes (1999) 'Osmanlı Hac Seyahatnamelerinde Hac Yolculuğu', in G. Eren (ed.) *Osmanlı*, 12 vols, Ankara: Yeni Türkiye

(2000) 'The most literary Ottoman pilgrimage narrative: Nabi's Tuhfetü'l-Haremeyn', *Turcica*, 32, pp. 363–88.

Crecelius, Daniel (1980) 'Review of *Islamic Roots of Capitalism: Egypt, 1760–1840* by Peter Gran', *American Historical Review*, 85 (1)

Çamuroğlu, Reha (1991) *Yeniçerilerin Bektaşiliği ve Vaka-i Şerriye*, Istanbul: Ant Yayınları

al-Dabbāgh, 'Abd al-Khāliq (n.d.) *Mu'ajam al-Amthāl al-'Āmiyya fī al-Mūṣul*, Baghdad: al-Hadaf Press

Dallal, Ahmad (1993) 'The origins and objectives of Islamic revivalist thought, 1750–1850', *Journal of the American Oriental Society*, 113 (3) pp. 341–59

## REFERENCES

Dâniş Bey, Mehmed (1994) *Netîcetü'l-Vekayi^c: Yeniçeri Ocağının Kaldırılışı ve II. Mahmud'un Edirne Seyahati: Mehmet Dâniş Bey ve Eserleri*, edited by Şamil Mutlu, Istanbul: Edebiyat Fakültesi Basımevi

Dankoff, Robert (2004) *An Ottoman Mentality: The World of Evliya Çelebi*, Leiden: E. J. Brill

Darling, Linda (1996) *Revenue Raising and Legitimacy: Tax Collection and Finance Administration in the Ottoman Empire, 1560–1660*, Leiden: E. J. Brill

David, Jean-Claude (1982) *Le Waqf d'Ipšīr Pāšā à Alep (1063/1653): Étude d'urbanisme historique*, Damascus: Institut français de Damas

Deguilhem, Randi (1993) 'Le café à Damas et le traité du Šayh^c Ǧamāl al-Dīn al-Qāsamī al-Dimašqī', *Bulletin d'études orientales*, 45, pp. 21–32

De Jong, F. and Peter Gran (1982), 'On Peter Gran, *Islamic Roots of Capitalism: Egypt, 1760–1840*: a review article with author's reply', *International Journal of Middle East Studies*, 14, pp. 381–99

Deleuze, Gilles and Félix Guattari (1987) *A Thousand Plateaus: Capitalism and Schizophrenia*, translated by Brian Massumi, Minneapolis: University of Minnesota Press

Demeerseman, André (1955) 'Un mémoire célèbre qui préfigure l'évolution moderne en Islam', *Institut des belles lettres arabes*, 18, pp. 5–32

Desmet-Grégoire, Hélène and François Georgeon (eds) (1997) *Cafés d'Orient revisités*, Paris: Centre National de la Recherche Scientifique Editions

Dols, Michael W. (1992) *Majnūn: The Madman in Medieval Islamic Society*, edited by Diana E. Immisch, Oxford: Clarendon Press

Douglas, Mary (1966) *Purity and Danger: An Analysis of Concepts of Pollution and Taboo*, London: Routledge & Kegan Paul

Doumani, Beshara (1995) *Rediscovering Palestine: Merchants and Peasants in Jabal Nablus, 1700–1900*, Berkeley: University of California Press

Dürrî, Ahmed Efendi (1810) *Relation de Dourry Effendy, ambassadeur de la Porte Othomane auprès du Roi de Perse, en 1720, présentée au Sultan Ahmed III*, edited by Louis-Mathieu Langlès, Paris: Ferra

# REFERENCES

Eisenstein, Elizabeth L. (1979) *The Printing Press as an Agent of Change: Communications and Cultural Transformations in Early-Modern Europe*, Cambridge: Cambridge University Press

(1982) 'The fifteenth century book revolution, some causes and consequences of the advent of printing in Western Europe', *Le Livre dans les sociétés pré-industrielles*, Athens: Kentron Neoelleon Ereunon, pp. 57–76

(1983) 'From scriptoria to printing shops: evolution and revolution in the early printing book trade', in Kenneth E. Carpenter (ed.) *Books and Society in History, Papers of the Association of College and Research Libraries Rare Books and Manuscripts Preconference, 24–28 June, 1980, Boston, Massachusetts*, New York and London: Bowker, pp. 29–42

Eldem, Edhem, Daniel Goffman and Bruce Masters (1999) *The Ottoman City between East and West: Aleppo, Izmir and Istanbul*, Cambridge: Cambridge University Press

Eldem, Sedad Hakkı (1968–74) *Köşkler ve Kasırlar: A Survey of Turkish Kiosks and Pavilions*, 2 vols, Istanbul: Kutulmuş Matbaasi

(1977) *Sa'dabad*, Istanbul: Devlet Kitapları Müdürlüğü

Ellis, Markman (2001) 'Coffee-women, "The Spectator" and the public sphere in the early eighteenth century', in Elizabeth Eger, Charlotte Grant, Clíona Ó Gallchoir and Penny Warburton (eds) *Women, Writing and the Public Sphere, 1700–1830*, Cambridge: Cambridge University Press, pp. 27–52

El-Rouayheb, Khaled (2004) 'Sunni Muslim scholars on the status of logic, 1500–1800', *Islamic Law and Society*, 11 (2) pp. 213–32

(2005) 'Was there a revival of logical studies in eighteenth-century Egypt?' *Die Welts des Islams*, 45 (1) pp. 1–19

(2005) 'The love of boys in Arabic poetry of the early Ottoman period, 1500–1800', *Middle Eastern Literatures*, 8 (1) January, pp. 3–22

(2005) *Before Homosexuality in the Arab–Islamic World, 1500–1800*, Chicago: Chicago University Press

(2006) 'Opening the gate of verification: the forgotten Arab-Islamic florescence of the 17th century', *International Journal of Middle Eastern Studies*, 38 (2) pp. 263–81

REFERENCES

Erdem, Yahya (1999) 'Sahaflar ve Seyyahlar: Osmanlı'da Kitapçılık', in Güler Eren (ed.) *Osmanlı*, 12 vols, Ankara: Yeni Türkiye, pp. 720–31
Erdoğan, Muzaffer (1958) 'Osmanlı Devrinde İstanbul Bahçeleri', *Vakıflar Dergisi*, 4, pp. 149–82
Ergin, Osman Nuri (1995) *Mecelle-i Umûr-ı Belediyye*, Istanbul: İstanbul Büyükşehir Belediyesi
Ergürbüz, Şefik (1947) *Matbaacılık Tarihi*, Izmit: Işıl Kitabevi
Erimtan, Can (2006) 'The sources of Ahmed Refik's *Lâle Devri* and the paradigm of the 'Tulip Age': a teleological agenda', in M. Kagar and Zeynep Durukal (eds) *Festschrift in Honour of Professor Ekmeleddin İhsanoğlu*, Istanbul: IRCICA, pp. 259–78
(1999) 'The case of Saadabad: Westernization or revivalism?' *Art turc/Turkish Art, 10e Congrès international d'art turc, Proceedings of the 10th International Congress of Turkish Art, Geneva, Fondation Max van Berchem, September 1995*, Geneva: Fondation Max van Berchem
Ersoy, Osman (1980) 'İlk Türk Basımevi'nde Basılan Kitapların Fiyatları', in *Basım ve Yayıncılığımızın 250. Yılı Bilimsel Toplantısı, 10–11 Aralık 1979, Ankara. Bildiriler*, Ankara: Türk Kütüphaneciler Derneği, pp. 69–77
Ertuğ, Hasan Refik (1970) *Basın ve Yayın Hareketleri Tarihi*, Istanbul: Yenilik Basımevi
Esʿad Efendi, Mehmed (1293/1876–77) *Üss-i Zafer*, Matbaa-i Süleyman Efendi
(2000) *Vakʿanüvis Esʿad Efendi Tarihi*, edited by Ziya Yılmazer, Istanbul: Osmanlı Araştırmaları Vakfi
(2005) *Üss-i Zafer: Yeniçeriliğin Kaldırılmasına Dair*, edited by Mehmed Arslan, Istanbul: Kitabevi
Establet, Colette and Jean-Paul Pascual (1992) 'Damascene probate inventories of the 17th and 18th centuries: some preliminary approaches and results', *International Journal of Middle East Studies*, 24 (3) pp. 373–93
(1998) *Ultime voyage pour la Mecque: les inventaires apres deces de pelerins morts à Damas vers 1700*, Damas: Institut français d'études arabes de Damas

# REFERENCES

(1999) 'Les livres des gens à Damas vers 1700', *Revue des mondes musulman et de la Méditerranée*, 87–8, pp. 143–75.

Ettinghausen, R. (1976) 'Introduction', in E. B. Macdougal and R. Ettinghausen (eds) *The Islamic Garden*, Washington: Dumbarton Oaks, pp. 3–10

Evliya Çelebi (1896) *Narrative of Travels in Europe, Asia and Africa in the Seventeenth Century*, translated by Joseph von Hammer-Purgstall, 2 vols, New York: Johnson Reprint Corp

(1896–1938) *Anadolu, Suriye, Hicaz (1671–1672)* vol. 9 of *Evliya Çelebi Seyahatnamesi*, 10 vols, Istanbul: Devlet Matbaası

(1896–1938) *Mısır, Sudan, Habeş (1672–1680)*, vol. 10 of *Evliya Çelebi Seyahatnamesi*, 10 vols, Istanbul: Devlet Matbaası

Evren, Burçak (1996) *Eski İstanbul'da Kahvehaneler*, Istanbul: Milliyet Yayınları

Faroqhi, Suraiya (1984) *Towns and Townsmen of Ottoman Anatolia: Trade, Craft and Food Production in an Urban Setting, 1520–1650*, Cambridge: Cambridge University Press

(1986) 'Coffee and spices: official Ottoman reactions to Egyptian trade in the later sixteenth century', *Wiener Zeitschrift für die Kunde des Morgenlandes*, 76, pp. 87–93

(1987) *Men of Modest Substance: House Owners and House Property in Seventeenth-Century Ankara and Kayseri*, Cambridge: Cambridge University Press

(1994) 'Crisis and change 1590–1699', in Halil İnalcık and Donald Quataert (eds) *An Economic and Social History of the Ottoman Empire: 1300–1914*, 2 vols, Cambridge: Cambridge University, pp. 411–636

(1995) *Coping with the State: Political Conflict and Crime in the Ottoman Empire, 1550–1720*, Istanbul: Isis Press

(1995) *Kultur und Alltag im osmanischen Reich*, Munich: C. H. Beck'sche

(1995) *Making a Living in the Ottoman Lands, 1480–1820*, Istanbul: Isis Press

(1995) 'Wealth and power in the land of olives: the economic and political activities of Müridoğlu Hacı Mehmed Ağa, notable of Edremit (died in or before 1823)', in *Making a Living in the Ottoman Lands 1480–1820*, Istanbul: Isis Press, pp. 291–311

(1999) *Approaching Ottoman History: An Introduction to the Sources*, Cambridge: Cambridge University Press

(2000) *Subjects of the Sultan: Culture and Daily Life in the Ottoman Empire*, London: I.B.Tauris

Fay, Mary Ann (1996) 'The ties that bound: women and households in eighteenth-century Egypt', in Amira El Azhary Sonbol (ed.) *Women, the Family and Divorce Laws in Islamic History*, Syracuse, NY: Syracuse University Press, pp. 155–72

(1997) 'Women and *waqf*: property, power and the domain of gender in eighteenth-century Egypt', in Madeline C. Zilfi (ed.) *Women in the Ottoman Empire: Middle Eastern Women in the Early Modern Era*, Leiden: E. J. Brill, pp. 28–47

Febvre, Lucien and Henri-Jean Martin (1958) *L'Apparition du livre*, Paris: A. Michel

Fekete, Lajos (1965) 'XVI. Yüzyılda Taşralı Bir Türk Efendisinin Evi', *Belleten*, 29 (116) pp. 615–38

Fleischer, Cornell (1986) *Bureaucrat and Intellectual in the Ottoman Empire: The Historian Mustafa Âli (1541–1600)*, Princeton: Princeton University Press

Foran, John (1992) 'The long fall of the Safavid dynasty: moving beyond the standard views', *International Journal of Middle East Studies*, 24 (2) May, pp. 281–304

Foucault, Michel (1980) 'The eye of power', in Colin Gordon (ed.) *Power/Knowledge: Selected Interviews and Other Writings, 1972–1977*, New York: Pantheon Books, pp. 226–40

(1986) 'Of other spaces', translated by Jay Miskowiec, *Diacritics*, 16 (1) Spring, pp. 22–7

Friedl, Erika (1991) 'The dynamics of women's spheres of action in rural Iran', in Nikki R. Keddie and Beth Baron (eds) *Women in Middle Eastern History: Shifting Boundaries in Sex and Gender*, New Haven: Yale University Press, pp. 195–214

Fryer, John (1698) *A New Account of East India and Persia in Eight Letters*, London: R. Chiswell

Gdoura, Wahid (1985) *Le Début de l'imprimerie arabe à Istanbul et en Syrie: évolution de l'environnement culturel (1706–1787)*, Tunis: Institut superieur de documentation

# REFERENCES

Geertz, Clifford (1980) *Negara: The Theater State in Nineteenth-Century Bali*, Princeton: Princeton University Press

Genç, Mehmed (1975) 'Osmanlı Maliyesinde Malikane Sistemi', in Osman Okyar (ed.) *Türkiye İktisat Tarihi Semineri Metinler/Tartışmalar*, Ankara: Hacttepe Üniversitesi Yayınları, pp. 231–96

(2001) 'Contrôle et taxation du commerce du café dans l'Empire ottoman fin XVIIe–première moitié du XVIIIe siècle', in Michel Tuchscherer (ed.) *Le Commerce du cafe avant l'ère des plantations coloniales: espaces, réseaux, sociétés (XVe–XIXe siècle)*, Cairo: Institut français d'archéologie orientale, pp. 161–79

Gerelyes, Ibolya (1985) 'Inventories of Turkish estates in Hungary in the second half of the 16th century', *Acta Orientalia Academiae Scientiarum Hungaricae*, 39 (2–3) pp. 275–338

Gibb, H. A. R. and H. Bowen (1950–57) *Islamic Society and the West: A Study of the Impact of Western Civilization on Muslim Culture in the Near East*, vol 1, parts 1 and 2, *Islamic Society in the Eighteenth Century*, London: Oxford University Press

Goodwin, Godfrey (1971) *A History of Ottoman Architecture*, London: Thames & Hudson

(1997) *The Janissaries*, London: Saqi Books

Göçek, Fatma Müge (1987) *East Encounters West: France and the Ottoman Empire in the Eighteenth Century*, New York: Oxford University Press

(1996) *Rise of the Bourgeoisie, Demise of Empire: Ottoman Westernization and Social Change*, Oxford: Oxford University Press

Gökman, M. (1978) *Tarihi Sevdiren Adam: Ahmet Refik Altınay – Hayatı ve Eserleri*, Istanbul: İş Bankası Yayınları

Gran, Peter (1979) *Islamic Roots of Capitalism: Egypt, 1760–1840*, Austin: University of Texas Press

(1980) 'Political economy as a paradigm for the study of Islamic history', *International Journal of Middle East Studies*, 11 (4) pp. 511–26

(1996) *Beyond Eurocentricism: A New View of Modern World History*, Syracuse: State University of New York Press

Grehan, James Paul (1999) 'Culture and consumption in eighteenth-century Damascus', Ph.D. dissertation, University of Texas at Austin

# REFERENCES

(2003) 'Street violence and social imagination in late-Mamluk and Ottoman Damascus (c.1500–1800)', *International Journal of Middle East Studies*, 35 (2) pp. 214–36

Gündüz, Mahmud (1978) 'Matbaanın Tarihçesi ve İlk Kur'anı Kerim Basmaları', *Vakıflar Dergisi*, 12, pp. 335–50

Habermas, Jürgen (1989) *The Structural Transformation of the Public Sphere: An Inquiry into a Category of Bourgeois Society*, translated by Thomas Burger, Cambridge: Massachussetts Institute of Technology Press

Hakim, Besim Selim (1986) *Arabic–Islamic Cities: Building and Planning Principles*, London: KPI

Halaçoğlu, Y. (1995) *XIV–XVII: Yüzyıllarda Osmanlılarda Devlet Teşkilâtı ve Sosyal Yapı*, Ankara: Türk Tarih Kurumu Basımevi

Hamadeh, Shirine (2004) 'Ottoman expressions of early modernity and the "inevitable" question of Westernization', *Journal of the Society of Architectural Historians*, 61 (1) March, pp. 32–51

(forthcoming) 'Public spaces and the garden culture of Istanbul in the eighteenth century', in Virginia Aksan and Dan Goffman (eds) *The Early Modern Ottomans: Remapping the Empire*, Cambridge: Cambridge University Press

Hanebutt-Benz, Eva, Dagmar Glass and Geoffrey Roper (eds) (2002) *Sprachen des Nahen Ostens und die Druckrevolution: eine interculturelle Begegnung*, Mainz: Johann Gutenberg Museum

Hanna, Nelly (1991) *Habiter au Caire: la maison moyenne et ses habitants aux XVIIe et XVIIIe siècles*, Cairo: Institut français d'archéologie orientale

(2003) *In Praise of Books: A Cultural History of Cairo's Middle Class, Sixteenth to the Eighteenth Century*, Syracuse: Syracuse University Press

Hathaway, Jane (1997) *The Politics of Households in Ottoman Egypt: The Rise of the Qazdağlıs*, Cambridge: Cambridge University Press

(2004) 'Rewriting eighteenth-century Ottoman history', *Mediterranean Historical Review*, 19 (1) pp. 29–53

Hattox, Ralph S. (1985) *Coffee and Coffeehouses: The Origins of a Social Beverage in the Medieval Near East*, Seattle: University of Washington Press

REFERENCES

Haykel, Bernard (2003) *Revival and Reform: The Legacy of Muḥammad al-Shawkānī*, Cambridge: Cambridge University Press
Heinz, Wilhelm (1962) 'Die Kultur der Tulpenzeit des Osmanischen Reiches', *Wiener Zeitschrift für die Kunde des Morgenlandes*, 61, pp. 62–116
Hershatter, Gail (1997) *Dangerous Pleasures: Prostitution and Modernity in Twentieth-Century Shanghai*, Berkeley: University of California Press
Heyd, Uriel (1960) *Ottoman Documents on Palestine, 1552–1615: A Study of the Firman According to the Mühimme Defteri*, Oxford: Clarendon Press
Hillenbrand, R. (1986) 'Safavid architecture', in P. Jackson and L. Lockhart (eds) *The Cambridge History of Iran*, 7 vols, Cambridge: Cambridge University Press, vol. 6, *The Timurid and Safavid Periods*, pp. 759–842
Hofheinz, Albrecht (n.d.) 'Illumination and enlightenment revisited, or: pietism and the roots of Islamic modernity', available at http://195.37.93.199/hofheinz/HOFHEINZ.htm
Holdermann, Jean Baptiste Daniel (1734) *Grammaire turque ou Méthode courte et facile pour Apprendre la Langue turque*, Constantinople: İbrahim Müteferrika
Hopp, L. (1975) 'İbrahim Müteferrika (1674/75?–1746): fondateur de l'imprimerie turque', *Acta Orientalia Academiae Scientiarum Hungaricae*, 29 (1) pp. 107–13
Horniker, Arthur Leon (1944) 'The corps of the Janizaries', *Military Affairs*, 8 (3) Autumn, pp. 177–204
Hourani, Albert (1957) 'The changing face of the Fertile Crescent in the XVIIIth century', *Studia Islamica*, 8, pp. 89–122
—— (1968) 'Ottoman reform and the politics of notables', in W. R. Polk and R. L. Chambers (eds) *The Beginnings of Modernization in the Middle East: The Nineteenth Century*, Chicago: University of Chicago Press, pp. 41–68
—— (1991) *A History of the Arab Peoples*, New York: Warner Books
Houston, Robert A. (1988) *Literacy in Early Modern Europe: Culture and Education 1500–1800*, London: Longman
Hudson, Nicholas (2002) 'Challenging Eisenstein: recent studies in print culture', *Eighteenth-Century Life*, 26 (2) pp. 83–95

# REFERENCES

Imber, C. (1992) 'Süleyman as Caliph of the Muslims: Ebu's-Su'ûd's formulation of Ottoman dynastic ideology', in G. Veinstein (ed.) *Soliman le Magnifique et son temps*, Paris: Documentation française, pp. 179–84

Ismāʿil, Muhammad Husām al-Din (2001) 'Le café dans la ville de Rosette à l'époque ottomane XVIe–XVIIe siècle', in Michel Tuchscherer (ed.) *Le Commerce du cafe avant l'ère des plantations coloniales: espaces, réseaux, sociétés (XVe–XIXe siècle)* Cairo: Institut français d'Archéologie orientale, pp. 103–9

Issawi, Charles (1979) 'Review of *Islamic Roots of Capitalism: Egypt, 1760–1840* by Peter Gran', *Journal of Economic History*, 39 (3) pp. 800–1

Işın, Ekrem (2001) 'Bir içecekten daha fazla: kahve ve kahvehanelerin toplumsal tarihi' ('More than a beverage: a social history of coffee and coffeehouses'), in Selahattin Özpalabıyıklar (ed.) *Tanede Sakli Keyif, Kahve (Coffee, Pleasures Hidden in a Bean)* Istanbul: Yapı Kredi Kültür Sanat Yayıncılık, pp. 10–43

Itzkowitz, Norman (1959) 'Mehmed Raghib Pasha: the making of an Ottoman vezir', Ph.D. dissertation, Princeton University

—— (1962) 'Eighteenth-century Ottoman realities', *Studia Islamica*, 16, pp. 73–94

İhsanoğlu, Ekmeleddin (2000) 'Osmanlı Medrese Tarihçiliğinin İlk Safhası (1916–1965) – Keşif ve Tasarlama Dönemi', *Belleten*, 164, August, pp. 541–82

İnalcık, Halil (1954) '15. Asır Türkiye İktisadî ve İçtimaî Tarihi Kaynakları', *İstanbul Üniversitesi İktisat Fakültesi Mecmuası*, 15 (1–4) pp. 51–73

—— (1975) 'The socio-political effects of the diffusion of fire-arms in the Middle East', in V. J. Parry and M. E. Yapp (eds) *War, Technology and Society in the Middle East*, London: Oxford University Press, pp. 195–217

—— (1977) 'Centralization and decentralization in Ottoman administration', in Thomas Naff and Roger Owen (eds) *Studies in Eighteenth Century Islamic History*, Carbondale: Southern Illinois University Press, 27–52

# REFERENCES

(1978) 'The impact of the *Annales School* on Ottoman studies, and new findings', *Review*, 1 (3–4) pp. 69–96

(1980) 'Military and fiscal transformations in the Ottoman Empire, 1600–1700', *Archivum Ottomanicum*, 6, pp. 283–337

İnalcik, Halil and Donald Quataert (eds) (1994) *An Economic and Social History of the Ottoman Empire*, 2 vols, Cambridge: Cambridge University Press

İsen, Mustafa (ed.) (1994) *Künhü'l-Ahbâr'ın Tezkire Kısmı*, Ankara: Atatürk Kültür Merkezi

İskit, Server (1939) *Türkiye'de Neşriyat Hareketleri Tarihine Bir Bakış*, Istanbul: Maarif Vekaleti

İslamoğlu-İnan, Huri (1987) 'Introduction: "Oriental despotism" in world-system perspective', in Huri İslamoğlu-İnan (ed.) *The Ottoman Empire and the World Economy*, Cambridge: Cambridge University Press, pp. 42–7

—— (ed.) (1987) *The Ottoman Empire and the World Economy*, Cambridge: Cambridge University Press

İslamoğlu-İnan, Huri and Çağlar Keyder (1977) 'Agenda for Ottoman history', *Review*, 1 (1) pp. 31–56

al-Jabartī, ʿAbd al-Raḥmān (1998) *ʿAjāʾib al-Āthār fī al-Tarājim wa al-Akhbār*, 4 vols, Cairo: Maṭbʿat Dār al-Kutub al-Miṣriyya

Jeltyakov, A. D. (1979) *Türkiye'nin Sosyo-Politik ve Kültürel Hayatında Basın (1729–1908 Yılları)*, Ankara: Basın Yayın Genel Müdürlüğü

Johns, Adrian (1998) *The Nature of the Book: Print and Knowledge in the Making*, Chicago: University of Chicago Press

Kafadar, Cemal (1981) 'Yeniçeri–esnaf relations: solidarity and conflict', MA thesis, McGill University

—— (1989) 'Self and others: the diary of a dervish in seventeenth century Istanbul and first-person narratives in Ottoman literature', *Studia Islamica*, 69, pp. 121–50

—— (1991) 'On the purity and corruption of the Janissaries', *Turkish Studies Association Bulletin*, 15, pp. 273–9

—— (1993) 'The myth of the golden age: historical consciousness in the post-Suleymanic era', in Halil İnalcık and Cemal Kafadar (eds) *Suleyman the Second and his Time*, Istanbul: Isis Press, pp. 37–48

# REFERENCES

(1997–98) 'The question of Ottoman decline', *Harvard Middle Eastern and Islamic Review*, 4 (1–2) pp. 30–75

(2002) 'A history of coffee', paper presented at the thirteenth Economic History Congress, Buenos Aires, Argentina, July

(2003) 'Coffee and the conquest of the night in the early modern era', the eleventh annual Eugene Lunn Memorial Lecture, Davis, California, 15 May

Karácson, Imre (1910) 'İbrahim Müteferrika', *Tarih-i Osmanî Encümeni Mecmuası*, 3, pp. 178–85

(1994) 'Müteferrika İbrâhîm', *Müteferrika*, 4, pp. 145–55

Karakışla, Yavuz Selim (1998) 'Osmanlı Kitap Tarihinde Bir Katkı: Osmanlı Devlet Arşivi'nde Bulunan, Kitap ile İlgili Bazı Belgeler (1844–1854)', *Müteferrika*, 14, pp. 41–59

Karataş, Ali İhsan (1999) 'Tereke Kayıtlarına Göre XVI. Yüzyılda Bursa'da İnsan–Kitap İlişkisi', *Uludağ Üniversitesi İlâhiyat Fakültesi Dergisi*, 8 (8) pp. 317–28

(2002) 'Osmanlı Toplumunda Kitap (XIV–XVI. Yüzyıllar)', in H. C. Güzel, K. Çiçek and S. Koca (eds) *Türkler*, 21 vols, Ankara: Yeni Türkiye

Katip Chelebi (1957) *The Balance of Truth*, translated by G. L. Lewis, London: George Allen & Unwin

Kayaoğlu, İ. Gündağ (2001) 'Kahve sözlüğü' (The coffee glossary), in Selahattin Özpalabıyıklar Yayıncı (ed.) *Tanede Saklı Keyif Kahve (Coffee, Pleasures Hidden in a Bean)* Istanbul: Yapı Kredi Kültür Sanat Yayıncılık

Kaye, Alan (1986) 'The etymology of "coffee": the dark brew', *Journal of the American Oriental Society*, 106 (3) July–September, pp. 557–8

Keall, Edward J. (2001) 'The evolution of the first coffee cups in Yemen', in Michel Tuchscherer (ed.) *Le Commerce du café avant l'ère des plantations coloniales: espaces, réseaux, sociétés (XVe–XIXe siècle)*, Cairo: Institut français d'Archéologie orientale

Kemal, Namık (1868) 'Usûl-u Meşveret Hakkında Mektuplar', *Hürriyet*, 14 September

Kennedy, Philip F. (1997) *The Wine Song in Classical Arabic Poetry: Abū Nuwās and the Literary Tradition*, Oxford: Clarendon Press

Keskioğlu, Osman (1967) 'Türkiye'de Matbaa Te'sisi ve Mushaf

Basımı', *Ankara Üniversitesi İlâhiyat Fakültesi Dergisi*, 15, pp. 121–39

Keyder, Çağlar and Faruk Tabak (eds) (1991) *Landholding and Commercial Agriculture in the Middle East*, Albany, NY: State University of New York Press

Khouri, Dina Rizk (1996) 'Drawing boundaries and defining spaces: women and space in Ottoman Iraq', in Amira El Azhary Sonbol (ed.) *Women, the Family and Divorce Laws in Islamic History*, Syracuse: Syracuse University Press, pp. 173–87

Khoury, Dina Rizk (1997) 'Slippers at the entrance or behind closed doors: domestic and public spaces for Mosuli women', in Madeline C. Zilfi (ed.) *Women in the Ottoman Empire: Middle Eastern Women in the Early Modern Era*, Leiden: E. J. Brill, pp. 105–27

Kırlı, Cengiz (2000) 'The struggle over space: coffeehouses of Ottoman Istanbul, 1780–1845', Ph.D. dissertation, State University of New York, Binghamton

—— (2000) 'Kahvehaneler ve Hafiyeler: 19. Yüzyıl Ortalarında Osmanlı'da Sosyal Kontrol', *Toplum ve Bilim*, 83, pp. 58–79

—— (2003) 'İstanbul: Bir Büyük Kahvehane', *İstanbul Dergisi*, 47, pp. 75–8

—— (2004) 'Coffeehouses: public opinion in the nineteenth-century Ottoman Empire', in Armando Salvatore and Dale F. Eickelman (eds) *Public Islam and the Common Good*, Leiden: E. J. Brill, pp. 75–97

Koch, E. (1994) 'Diwan-i Amm and Chihil Sutun: the audience halls of Shah Jahan', *Muqarnas*, 11, pp. 143–65

Koçu, Reşad Ekrem (1964) *Yeniçeriler*, Istanbul: Koçu Yayınları

Koloğlu, Orhan (1987) *Basımevi ve Basının Gecikme Sebepleri ve Sonuçları*, Istanbul: İstanbul Gazeteciler Cemiyeti

Kömeçoğlu, Uğur (2001) 'Historical and sociological approach to public space: the case of Islamic coffeehouses in Turkey', Ph.D. dissertation, Boğaziçi University

Korom, Frank J. (2003) *Hosay Trinidad: Muharram Performances in an Indo-Caribbean Diaspora*, Philadelphia: Pennsylvania University Press

Krautheimer, Richard (1939) *Studies in Iconology*, New York: Oxford University Press

(1942) 'Introduction to an iconography of mediaeval architecture', *Journal of the Warburg and Courtauld Institutes*, 5, pp. 1–33

Krüger, H. (1978) *Fetwa und Siyar. Zur internationalrechtlichen Gutachterpraxis der osmanischen Scheich ül-Islam vom 17. bis 19 Jh. unter besonderen Berücksichtigung des 'Behcet ül-Fetwa'*, Wiesbaden: Harrassowitz

Krusinski, T. J. (1728) *The History of the Revolution of Persia*, translated by Father J. A. du Cerceau, 2 vols, London: J. Pemberton

Kuran-Burcuoğlu, Nedret (2002) 'Matbaacı Osman Bey: Saray'dan İlk Defa Kur'an-ı Kerim Basma İznini Alan Osmanlı Hattatı', *Türklük Bilgisi Araştırmaları/Journal of Turkish Studies*, 26, pp. 97–112

Kut, A. Turgut (1994) 'Terekelerde Çıkan Kitapların Matbu Satış Defterleri', *Müteferrika*, 2, pp. 3–24

Kut, Turgut and Fatma Türe (eds) (1996) *Yazmadan Basmaya: Müteferrrika, Mühendishane Üsküdar*, Istanbul: Yapı Kredi Yayınları

Lane, Edward William (2000) *Description of Egypt*, edited by Jason Thompson, Cairo: The American University in Cairo Press

Lebelski, George (1963–64) 'A true description of the magnificall tryumphes and pastimes', in M. And, *A History of Popular Entertainment and Theatre in Turkey*, Ankara: Forum, pp. 118–30

Le Goff, Jacques (1985) *Les Intellectuels au Moyen Âge*, Paris: Éditions du Seuil

Lewis, Bernard (1958) 'Some reflections on the decline of the Ottoman Empire', *Studia Islamica*, 9, pp. 111–27

—— (1962) *The Emergence of Modern Turkey*, London: Oxford University Press

Lewis, Thomas V. (1972) *A Study of Naima*, edited by Norman Itzowitz, New York: New York University Press

Liman von Sanders, Otto (1977) *Five Years in Turkey*, Annapolis, MD: United States Naval Institute

Lybyer, Albert Howe (1913) *The Government of the Ottoman Empire in the Time of Suleiman the Magnificent*, Cambridge, MA: Harvard University Press

McGowan, Bruce (1994) 'The age of the Ayans, 1699–1812', in Halil İnalcık and D. Quataert (eds) *An Economic and Social History of the*

*Ottoman Empire, 1300–1914*, 2 vols, Cambridge: Cambridge University Press, pp. 639–757

McKitterick, David John (2003) *Print, Manuscript and the Search for Order, 1450–1830*, Cambridge: Cambridge University Press

Marcus, Abraham (1983) 'Men, women and property: dealers in real estate in 18th century Aleppo', *Journal of the Economic and Social History of the Orient*, 26, pp. 137–63.

—— (1986) 'Privacy in eighteenth-century Aleppo: the limits of cultural ideals', *International Journal of Middle East Studies*, 18 (2) pp. 165–83

—— (1989) *The Middle East on the Eve of Modernity: Aleppo in the Eighteenth Century*, New York: Columbia University Press

Mardin, Şerif (1973) 'Center–periphery relations: a key to Turkish politics', *Daedalus*, 102 (1) Winter, pp. 169–91

—— (1988) 'Freedom in an Ottoman perspective', in Metin Heper and Ahmed Evin (eds) *State, Democracy and the Military: Turkey in the 1980s*, Berlin: Walter de Gruyter, pp. 23–35

Marsot, Afaf Lutfi al-Sayyid (1995) *Women and Men in Late Eighteenth-Century Egypt*, Austin: University of Texas Press

Meier, Astrid (2004) 'Perceptions of a new era? Historical writing in early modern Ottoman Damascus', *Arabica*, 4, pp. 419–34

Meriwether, Margaret Lee (1997) 'Women and *waqf* revisited: the case of Aleppo, 1770–1840', in Madeline C. Zilfi (ed.) *Women in the Ottoman Empire: Middle Eastern Women in the Early Modern Era*, Leiden: E. J. Brill, pp. 128–52.

—— (1999) *The Kin Who Count: Family and Society in Ottoman Aleppo, 1770–1840*, Austin: University of Texas Press

Mortada, Hisham (2003) *Traditional Islamic Principles of Built Environment*, London: RoutledgeCurzon

Muir, Edward (1997) *Ritual in Early Modern Europe*, Cambridge: Cambridge University Press

[al-Nīsābūrī] Muslim Ibn al-Ḥajjāj al-Qushayrī (1995) *Ṣaḥīḥ Muslim*, 5 vols, Beirut: Dār Ibn Ḥazm

Müteferrika, İbrahim Efendi (1732) *Usûl ül-Hikem fi Nizâm ül-Ümem*, Istanbul: Matbaa-ı Âmire

—— (2004) 'Osmanlı Matbaasının Kuruluşu ve Başlangıcı', in N. Kuran-

Burçoğlu and M. Kiel (eds) *Müteferrika ve Osmanlı Matbaası*, Istanbul: Tarih Vakfı Yurt Yayınları

Naff, Thomas and Roger Owen (eds) (1977) *Studies in Eighteenth Century Islamic History*, Carbondale: Southern Illinois University Press

Nafi, Bashir (2002) 'Taṣawwuf and reform in pre-modern Islamic culture: in search of Ibrāhīm al-Kūrānī', *Die Welts des Islams*, 42 (3) pp. 307–55

Nagata, Yuzo (1979) *Materials on the Bosnian Notables*, Tokyo: Institute for the Study of Languages and Cultures of Asia and Africa

Naʿīmā, Mustafa Efendi (1281–3) *Târîh-i Naʿîmâ: Ravdat-ül Hüseyn fî Hülâsat-i Ahbâr-il Hâfikeyn*, 6 vols, Istanbul: Matbaa-i Âmire, third edition

Necipoğlu, Gülru (1986) 'Plans and models in 15th- and 16th-century Ottoman architectural practice', *Journal of the Society of Architectural Historians*, 45 (3) September, pp. 224–43

—— (1990) 'From international Timurid to Ottoman: a change of taste in sixteenth-century ceramic tiles', *Muqarnas*, 7, pp. 136–70

—— (1991) *Architecture, Ceremonial, and Power: The Topkapi Palace in the Fifteenth and Sixteenth Centuries*, Cambridge: Massachussetts Institute of Technology Press

—— (1993) 'Framing the gaze in Ottoman, Safavid and Mughal palaces', *Ars Orientalis*, 23, pp. 303–42

—— (1997) 'The suburban landscape of sixteenth-century Istanbul as a mirror of classical Ottoman garden culture', in Attilio Petruccioli (ed.) *Gardens in the Time of the Great Muslim Empires: Theory and Design*, Leiden: E. J. Brill, pp. 32–71

Nedim, Ahmed (n.d.) *Nedim Divanı*, edited by A. Gölpınarlı, Istanbul: İnkılâp ve Aka Kitapevleri, second edition

Neubauer, Hans-Joachim (1999) *The Rumour: A Cultural History*, translated by Christian Braun, London: Free Association Books

Neumann, Christoph K. (1996) 'Arm and reich in Qaraferye', *Der Islam*, 73, pp. 259–312

Nuhoğlu, Hidayet (1999) 'Müteferrika Matbaası ve Bazı Mulâhazalar', in G. Eren (ed.) *Osmanlı*, 12 vols, Ankara: Yeni Türkiye, vol. 7, pp. 221–9

(2000) 'Müteferrika Matbaası ve Bazı Mulâhazalar', in M. Armağan (ed.) *İstanbul Armağanı*. 4 vols, Istanbul: İstanbul Büyükşehir Belediyesi Kültür İşleri Daire Başkanlığı Yayınları, vol. 4, *Lâle Devri*, pp. 211–25

Ocak, A. Y. (2002) 'Osmanlı Kaynaklarında ve Modern Türk Tarihçiliğinde Osmanlı-Safevî Münasebetleri (XVI–XVII Yuzyıllar)', *Belleten*, 66 (246) pp. 503–16

(2003) 'Islam in the Ottoman Empire: a sociological framework for a new interpretation', *International Journal of Turkish Studies*, 9 (1 and 2) Summer, pp. 183–97

O'Fahey, R. S. and Bernd Radtke (1993) 'Neo-Sufism reconsidered', *Der Islam*, 70, pp. 52–87

Olson, Robert W. (1974) 'The esnaf and the Patrona Halil rebellion of 1730: a realignment in Ottoman politics?' *Journal of the Economic and Social History of the Orient*, 17, pp. 329–44

(1975) *The Siege of Mosul and Ottoman–Persian Relations 1718–1743*, Bloomington: Indiana University Press

(1977) 'Jews, Janissaries, esnaf and the revolt of 1740 in Istanbul: social upheaval and political realignment in the Ottoman Empire', *Journal of the Economic and Social History of the Orient*, 20, pp. 185–207

(Câbî) Ömer Efendi (2003) *Câbî Târihi (Târîh-i Sultân Selîm-i Sâlis ve Mahmûd-ı Sânî)* edited by Mehmed Ali Beyhan, 2 vols with consecutive pagination, Ankara: Türk Tarih Kurumu

Omont, H. (1926) 'Nouveaux documents sur l'imprimerie à Constantinople au XVIIIe siècle', *Revue des bibliothèques*, 33, pp. 1–10

Owen, Roger (1976) 'The Middle East in the eighteenth century: an "Islamic" society in decline? A critique of Gibb and Bowen's *Islamic Society and the West*', *Bulletin of the British Society of Middle Eastern Studies*, 3 (2) pp. 110–17

'Review of *Islamic Roots of Capitalism: Egypt, 1760–1840* by Peter Gran', *Economic History Review*, 33 (1) pp. 150–1

Özdeğer, Hüseyin (1988) *1463–1640 Yılları Bursa Şehri Tereke Defterleri*, Istanbul: İ. Ü. İktisat Fakültesi

Öztürk, Said (1995) *Askerî Kassama ait Onyedinci Asır İstanbul Tereke*

*Defterleri (Sosyo-Ekonomik Tahlil)*, Istanbul: Osmanlı Araştırmaları Vakfı

Pardoe, Julia (1839) *The Beauties of the Bosphorus*, London: George Virtue

Peçevi, İbrahim (1864–1867) *Tarih-i Peçevi*, 2 vols, Istanbul: Matbaa-i Âmire

Peirce, Leslie P. (1993) *The Imperial Harem: Women and Sovereignty in the Ottoman Empire*, Oxford: Oxford University Press

—— (1997) 'Seniority, sexuality and social order: the vocabulary of gender in early modern Ottoman society', in Madeline C. Zilfi (ed.) *Women in the Ottoman Empire: Middle Eastern Women in the Early Modern Era*, Leiden: E. J. Brill, pp. 169–96.

—— (2003) *Morality Tales: Law and Gender in the Ottoman Court of Aintab*, Berkeley: University of California Press

Pera, Le Vigne de (1863) 'Letter from Constantinople ... to the English court', *Calendar of State Papers, Foreign Series of the Reign of Elizabeth*, edited by Joseph Stevenson, vol. 16, May–December 1582, London: HM Stationery Office

Perry, Charles (1743) *A View of the Levant: Particularly of Constantinople, Syria, Egypt and Greece: In which their Antiquities, Government, Politics, Maxims, Manners, and Customs, (with Many Other Circumstances and Contingencies) are Attempted to be Described and Treated on. In Four Parts*, London: T. Woodward & J. Shuckburgh

Perry, John. R. (1999) 'Toward a theory of Iranian urban moieties: the Haydariyyah and Niʿmatiyyah revisited', *Iranian Studies*, 32, pp. 51–70

Petruccioli, Attilio (ed.) (1997) *Gardens in the Time of the Great Muslim Empires: Theory and Design*, Leiden: E. J. Brill

Philipp, Thomas (1984) 'Jews and Arab Christians: their changing positions in politics and economy in eighteenth century Syria and Egypt', in Amnon Cohen and Gabriel Baer (eds) *Egypt and Palestine: A Millennium of Associations (868–1948)*, New York: St Martin's Press

—— (1985) *The Syrians in Egypt*, Stuttgart: Franz Steiner Verlag

Pietilä, Tuulikki (1999) *Gossip, Markets and Gender: The Dialogical*

Construction of Morality in Kilimanjaro, Department of Sociology Research Report no. 233, Helsinki: University of Helsinki

Piterberg, Gabriel (2001) 'The variety of territorial sites in the poetic and historical imagination of the Ottomans', paper presented at 'The Meanings of Land: Law, Ideology and Identity in the Ottoman Period', Berkeley, California, 20 October

(2003) *An Ottoman Tragedy: History and Historiography at Play*, Berkeley: University of California Press

al-Qaradawi, Yusuf (1985) *The Lawful and the Prohibited in Islam*, translated by Kamal El-Helbawy, M. Moinuddin Siddiqui and Syed Shukry, London: Shorouk International

Quataert, Donald G. (1981) 'Review of *Islamic Roots of Capitalism: Egypt, 1760–1840* by Peter Gran', *Business History Review*, 55 (3) pp. 464–5

(ed.) (2000) *Consumption Studies and the History of the Ottoman Empire, 1550–1922: An Introduction*, Albany: State University of New York

Radtke, Bernd (2000) *Autochthone islamische Aufklärung im 18. Jahrhundert, Theoretische und filolgische Überlegungen: Fortsetzung einer Debatte*, Utrecht: M. Th. Houtsma Stichting

Rafeq, Abdul-Karim (1970) *The Province of Damascus*, Beirut: Khayyats

(1994) 'The Syrian ʿulamāʾ, Ottoman law, and Islamic sharīʿa', *Turkica*, 26, pp. 9–32.

(1994) 'Registers of succession and their importance for socioeconomic history: two samples from Damascus and Aleppo, 1277/1861', in J.-L. Bacqué Grammont, İ. Ortaylı and E. van Donzel (eds) *CIÉPO. Osmanlı Öncesi ve Osmanlı Araştırmaları Uluslararası Komitesi. VII. Sempozyumu Bildirileri: Peç: 7–11 Eylül 1986*, Ankara: TTK, pp. 479–91

(1999) 'Relations between Syrian ʿulamāʾ and the Ottoman state in the 18th century', *Oriente Moderno*, 18, pp. 67–95

Rahimi, Babak (2004) 'The Safavid camel sacrifice rituals', *Iranian Studies*, 37 (3) pp. 451–78

Rahman, Fazlur (1979) *Islam*, Chicago: Chicago University Press, second edition

Râşid, Mehmed Efendi (1865) *Tarih-i Râşid*, 6 vols, Istanbul: Matbaa-ı Âmire, second edition

# REFERENCES

Raven, Diederick (1999) 'Elizabeth Eisenstein and the impact of printing', *European Review of History/Revue européene d'histoire*, 6 (2) pp. 223–34

Raymond, André (1973–74) *Artisans et commerçants au Caire au XVIIIe siècle*, 2 vols, Damascus: Institut français de Damas

(1995) *Le Caire des Janissaires: l'apogée de la ville ottomane sous Abd al-Rahman Kathuda*, Paris: Centre National de la Recherche Scientifique Editions

(2001) 'Une famille de grands négociants en café au Caire dans la première moitié du XVIIIe siècle: les Sharāybī', in Michel Tuchscherer (ed.) *Le Commerce du cafe avant l'ère des plantations coloniales: espaces, réseaux, sociétés (XVe–XIXe siècle)*, Cairo: Institut français d'archéologie orientale, pp. 111–24

(2002) *Arab Cities in the Ottoman Period: Cairo, Syria and the Maghreb*, Aldershot: Ashgate

Refik, Ahmed [Altınay] (n.d.) *Fatma Sultan: Garyrî Matbû Vesikalara Nazaran Yazılmışdır*, Istanbul: Diken Matbaası

(1913) 'Lâle Devri', *İkdam*, no. 5763, 9 March 1913

(1331/1915) *Lâle Devri (1130–1143)* Istanbul: Kitabhâne-i İslam ve Askeriyye, first edition

Reichmuth, Stefan (2002) 'Arabic literature and Islamic scholarship in the 17th/18th century: topics and biographies', *Die Welt des Islams*, 42 (3) pp. 281–8

Richardson, Brian (1999) *Printing, Writers and Readers in Renaissance Italy*, Cambridge: Cambridge University Press

Rigney, A. (1991) 'Narrativity and historical representation', *Poetics Today*, 12 (3) Fall, pp. 591–605

Rosenow-von Schlegell, Barbara (1997) 'Sufism in the Ottoman Arab world: Shaykh ᶜAbd al-Ghanī al-Nābulusī', Ph.D. dissertation, University of California, Berkeley

Rowson, Everett K. (1991) 'The categorization of gender and sexual irregularity in Medieval Arabic vice lists', in Julia Epstein and Kristina Straub (eds) *Body Guards: The Cultural Politics of Gender Ambiguity*, New York: Routledge, pp. 50–79

Russell, Alexander (1794) *The Natural History of Aleppo*, 2 vols, London: G. G. and J. Robinson

# REFERENCES

Sabev, Orlin (2003) 'Private book collections in Ottoman Sofia, 1671–1833 (preliminary notes)', *Études balkaniques*, 1, pp. 34–82

Sahillioğlu, Halil (1999) 'Ottoman book legacies', in Halil Sahillioğlu (ed.) *Studies on Ottoman Economic and Social History*, Istanbul: Research Centre for Islamic History, Art and Culture, pp. 189–91

Said, Edward (1978) *Orientalism*, New York: Pantheon Books

Sajdi, Dana (2004) 'A room of his own: the "history" of the barber of Damascus (fl. 1762)', *The MIT Electronic Journal of Middle East Studies*, 4, pp. 19–35

Sakal, Fahri (1999) 'Osmanlı Ailesinde Kitap', in G. Eren (ed.) *Osmanlı*, 12 vols, Ankara: Yeni Türkiye, vol. 11, pp. 732–8

Saleh, Nabil (1996) *The Qadi and the Fortune Teller: Diary of a Judge in Ottoman Beirut (1843)* London: Quartet Books

Salibi, Kamal Suleiman (1958) 'The Banu Jamaᶜa: a dynasty of Shafiᶜite jurists in the Mamluk period', *Studia Islamica*, 9, pp. 97–109

Salzmann, Ariel (1993) 'An ancien regime revisited: "privatization" and political economy in the eighteenth-century Ottoman Empire', *Politics and Society*, 21 (4) pp. 393–423

—— (2000) 'The Age of Tulips: confluence and conflict in early modern consumer culture (1550–1730)', in Donald Quataert (ed.) *Consumption Studies and the History of the Ottoman Empire, 1550–1922: An Introduction*, Albany: State University of New York, pp. 83–106

—— (2004) *Tocqueville in the Ottoman Empire: Rival Paths to the Modern State*, Leiden: E. J. Brill

Sâmî, Mustafa, Hüseyin Şâkir and Mehmed Subhî (1198/1789) *Tarih-i Sâmî ü Şâkir ü Subhî*, Istanbul: Darüttiboat-ı Âmire

Scalenghe, Sara (2004–5) 'The deaf in Ottoman Syria, 16th–18th centuries', *Arab Studies Journal*, 12–13, pp. 10–25

Schulze, Reinhard (1990) 'Das islamische achtzehnte Jahrhundert: Versuch einer historiographischen Kritik', *Die Welt des Islams*, 30, pp. 140–59

—— (1996) 'Was ist die islamische Aufklärung?' *Die Welt des Islams*, 36 (3) pp. 276–325

Schwartz, Gerhard (1990) *Die Janitscharen: geheime Macht des Türkenreichs*, Vienna: Amelthea, second edition

Seng, Yvonne J. (1991) 'The Üsküdar estates (tereke) as records of daily life in an Ottoman town 1521-24', Ph.D. dissertation, University of Chicago
(1991) 'The Şerʿiye Sicilleri of the Istanbul Müftülüğü as a source for the study of everyday life', *Turkish Studies Association Bulletin*, 15 (2) pp. 307-25
Sennet, Richard (1977) *The Fall of Public Man*, New York: Alfred A. Knopf
Shaw, Ezel Kural (1972) 'The double veil: travellers' views of the Ottoman Empire', in Ezel Kural Shaw and C. J. Heywood (eds) *English and Continental Views of the Ottoman Empire, 1500-1800*, Los Angeles: William Andrews Clark Memorial Library, pp. 1-29
Shaw, S. J. and E. K. Shaw (1977) *History of the Ottoman Empire and Modern Turkey*, 2 vols, Cambridge: Cambridge University Press
Shaw, Stanford S. (1965) 'The origins of Ottoman military reform: the Nizam-ı Cedid army of Sultan Selim III', *The Journal of Modern History*, 37 (3) pp. 291-306
Silay, Kemal (1994) *Nedim and the Poetics of the Ottoman Court: Medieval Inheritance and the Need for Change*, Bloomington: Indiana University Press
Singer, Amy (1999) 'Review of *State and Provincial Society in the Ottoman Empire: Mosul, 1540-1834* by Dina Rizk Khoury', *International Journal of Middle East Studies*, 31 (2) pp. 300-3
Spacks, Patricia Ann Meyer (1985) *Gossip*, New York: Knopf
Spivak, Gayatri Chakravorty (1988) 'Can the subaltern speak?' in Cary Nelson and Lawrence Grossberg (eds) *Marxism and the Interpretation of Culture*, Urbana: University of Illinois Press
Stajnova, Mihaila (1979) 'Ottoman libraries in Vidin', *Études balkaniques*, 2, pp. 54-69
Steinberg, Sigfrid H. (1977) *Five Hundred Years of Printing*, Harmondsworth: Penguin Books
Stout, Robert Elliott (1966) 'The Sūr-i Humāyun of Murad III: a study of Ottoman pageantry and entertainment', Ph.D. dissertation, Ohio State University
Strauss, Johann (1992) 'Les livres et l'imprimerie à Istanbul (1800-1908)', in P. Dumont (ed.) *Turquie: Livres d'hier, livres d'aujourd'hui*, Strasbourg-Istanbul: Centre de recherche sur la

# REFERENCES

civilisation ottomane et le domaine turc contemporain, Université des Sciences Humaines–Éditions ISIS (1993) 'İstanbul'da Kitap Yayını ve Basımevleri', *Müteferrika*, 1, pp. 5–17

Subrahmanyam, Sanjay (2005) 'Beyond incommensurability: understanding inter-imperial dynamics'. http://repositories.cdlib.org/uclasoc/trcsa/32

Szyliowicz, J. S. (1988) 'Functional perspectives on technology: the case of the printing press in the Ottoman Empire', *Archivum Ottomanicum*, 11, pp. 249–59

Şânîzâde, Atâullah (1284–91/1867–75) *Târîh-i Şânîzâde*, 4 vols, Istanbul: various publishers

Şemdânizâde, Süleyman Efendi (1976) *Şem'dâni-zâde Fındıklı Süleyman Efendi Târihi Mûr'it-Tevârih*, edited by M. M. Aktepe, 3 vols, Istanbul: Edebiyat Fakültesi Matbası

al-Tabarī, Muḥammad İbn Jarīr (1998) *The History of al-Tabari: Biographies of the Prophet's Companions and their Successors*, translated by Ella Landau-Tasseron, New York: State University of New York Press

Taib, Osmanzade et al. (1969) *Hadikat ül-Vüzerâ*, Istanbul: Ceride-i Havadis Matbaası, 1271/1854–5, Freiburg, facsimile edition

Tanpınar, A. H. (1942) *Ondokuzuncu Asır Türk Edebiyatı Tarihi*, Istanbul: İstanbul Üniversitesi Edebiyat Fakültesi Yayınları

Terzioğlu, Derin (1995) 'The imperial circumcision festival of 1582: an interpretation', *Muqarnas*, 12, pp. 84–100

—— (2002) 'Man in the image of God in the image of the times: Sufi self-narrative and the diary of Nıyāzı-i Mışrī (1618–94)', *Studia Islamica*, 94, pp. 139–65

Thály, Coloman de (ed.) (1909) *Lettres de Turquie (1730–1739) et Notices (1740) de César de Saussure*, Budapest: Academie Hongroise des Sciences

Tilly, C. (1985) 'War making and state making as organized crime', in P. Evans, D. Rueschemeyer and T. Skocpol (eds) *Bringing the State Back In*, Cambridge: Cambridge University Press, pp. 295–315

Timur, Taner (2004) 'Matbaa, Aydınlanma ve diplomasi: Said Mehmed Efendi', *Toplumsal Tarih*, 128, August, pp. 54–61

# REFERENCES

Toledano, Ehud R. (1990) *State and Society in Mid-Nineteenth-Century Egypt*, Cambridge: Cambridge University Press

Topdemir, Hüseyin Gazi (2002) *İbrahim Müteferrika ve Türk Matbaacılığı*, Ankara: T. C. Kültür Bakanlığı

Tuchscherer, Michel (ed.) (2001) *Le Commerce du café avant l'ère des plantations coloniales: espaces, réseaux, sociétés (XVe–XIXe siècle)*, Cairo: Institut français d'archéologie orientale

―― (2001) 'Commerce et production du café en Mer Rouge au XVI$^e$ siècle', in Michel Tuchscherer (ed.) *Le Commerce du cafe avant l'ère des plantations coloniales: espaces, réseaux, sociétés (XVe–XIXe siècle)*, Cairo: Institut français d'Archéologie orientale, pp. 69–90

Turner, Victor (1995) *The Ritual Process: Structure and Anti-Structure*, New York: Aldine

Ubicini, A. (1853) *Lettres sur la Turquie, ou tableau statistique, religieux, politique, administratif, militaire, commercial, etc. de l'Empire ottoman, depuis le Khatti-Cherif de Gulhanè (1839): Première Partie, Les Ottomans*, Paris: Librairie militaire de J. Dumaine

Uluç, Lale (1999) 'Ottoman book collectors and illustrated sixteenth century Shiraz manuscripts', *Revue des mondes musulmans et de la Méditerranée*, pp. 85–107

Unan, Fahri (1997) 'Taşköprülü-zâde'nin Kaleminden XVI. Yüzyılın "İlim" ve "Âlim" Anlayışı', *Osmanlı Araştırmaları/Journal of Ottoman Studies*, 17, pp. 149–264

―― (2002) 'Osmanlı Medrese Ulemâsı: İlim Anlayışı ve İmî Verim', in H. C. Güzel, K. Çiçek and S. Koca (eds) *Türkler*, 21 vols, Ankara: Yeni Türkiye, vol. 11, pp. 436–45

Unat, F. R. (1968) *Osmanlı Sefirleri ve Sefâretnâmeleri*, edited by B. S. Baykal, Ankara: Türk Tarih Kurumu

Ünver, A. Süheyl (1967) *Ressam Ali Rıza Beye göre Yarım Asır Önce Kahvehanelerimiz ve Eşyası*, Ankara: Ankara Sanat Yayınları

Ursinus, Michael (1994) *Quellen zur Geschichte des Osmanischen Reiches und ihre Interpretation*, Istanbul: Isis

Uzunçarşılı, İsmail Hakkı (1988) *Osmanlı Tarihi*, 4 vols, Ankara: Türk Tarih Kurumu

Vandal, A. (1887) *Une Ambassade française en Orient sous Louis XV:*

*La Mission du Marquis de Villeneuve 1728–1741*, Paris: E. Plon, Nourrit & Cie

Veinstein, Gilles (1978) 'Note sur les inventaires après décès ottomans', in Rémy Dor and Michel Nicolas (eds) *Quand le crible était dans la paille: hommage à Pertev Naili Boratav*, Paris: Maisonneuve & Larose, pp. 383–95

—— (1981) 'Les pèlerins de la Mecque à travers quelques inventaires après décès ottomans (XVIIe–XVIIIe siècles)', *Revue de l'occident musulman et de la Méditerranée*, 31, pp. 63–71

—— (1992) 'Les inventaires après décès des campagnes militaires: le cas de la conquête de Chypre', *Bulletin of the Turkish Studies Association*, pp. 293–305

Veinstein, Gilles and Yolande Triantafyllidou-Baladic (1980) 'Les inventaires après décès ottomans de Crète', in Ad van der Woude and Anton Schuurman (eds) *Probate Inventories: A New Source for Historical Study of Wealth, Material Culture and Agricultural Development, Papers Presented at the Leemwenborch Conference, Wageningen, 5–7 May*, Utrecht: HES Publishers, pp. 191–204

Vigenère, Blaise de (1660) 'Les illustrations de Blaise de Vigenère Bourbonnois', in Laonicus Chalcondyle, *Histoire de la decadence de l'Empire grec et establissement de celuy des Turcs*, Paris: C. Sonnius

Voll, John O. (1975) 'Muḥammad Yaḥyā al-Sirhindī and Muḥammad ibn ᶜAbd al-Wahhāb: an analysis of an intellectual community in eighteenth century Madina', *Bulletin of the School of Oriental and African Studies*, 38 (1) pp. 32–9

—— (1987) 'Linking groups in the networks of eighteenth century revivalist scholars: the Mijzāzī family of Yemen', in Nehemia Levtzion and John O. Voll (eds) *Eighteenth Century Renewal and Reform in Islam*, Syracuse: Syracuse University Press, pp. 69–92

—— (2002) 'ᶜAbdallah Ibn Salīm al-Baṣrī and 18th century Ḥadīth Studies', *Die Welts des Islams*, 42 (3) pp. 356–72

von Hammer-Purgstall, Joseph (1831) *Geschichte des Osmanischen Reiches*, 10 vols, Pest: C. A. Hartleben

—— (1835–37) *Histoire de l'Empire ottoman depuis son origine jusqu'à nos jours*, 18 vols, Paris: Bellizard, Barthès, Dufour & Lowell

# REFERENCES

Walcher, Heidi A. (1998) 'Between paradise and political capital: the semiotics of Safavid Isfahan', in Jeff Albert, Magnus Bernhardsson and Roger Kenna (eds) *Transformations of the Middle Eastern Environments: Legacies and Lessons*, New Haven: Yale University Press, pp. 330–48

Watenpaugh, Heghnar Zeitlian (2004) *The Image of an Ottoman City: Imperial Architecture and Urban Experience in Aleppo in the 16th and 17th Centuries*, Leiden: E. J. Brill

Waters, Clara Erskine Clement (1895) *Constantinople: The City of the Sultans*, Boston: Estes & Lauriat

Watson, William J. (1968) 'İbrāhīm Müteferrika and Turkish Incunabula', *Journal of the American Oriental Society*, 88, pp. 435–51

Weber, M. (1991) *From Max Weber: Essays in Sociology*, edited and translated by H. H. Gerth and C. W. Mills, London: Routledge

Weinberg, Bennett Alan and Bonnie K. Bealer (2002) *The World of Caffeine: The Science and Culture of the World's Most Popular Drug*, New York: Routledge

Wheatcroft, Andrew (1993) *The Ottomans*, London: Viking

White, Charles (1845) *Three Years in Constantinople; or, Domestic Manners of the Turks in 1844*, 3 vols, London: Henry Colburn

White, Hayden V. (1974) 'The historical text as a literary artefact', *Clio*, 3 (3), pp. 81–100

—— (1985) *Tropics of Discourse: Essays in Cultural Criticism*, Baltimore and London: Johns Hopkins University Press

Williams, Raymond (1992) *The Long Revolution*, London: Hogarth

Yaşar, Ahmed (2003) 'The coffeehouses in early modern Istanbul: public space, sociability and surveillance', MA thesis, Boğaziçi University

Yücel, H.-Â. (1937) 'Ahmed Refik', *Akşam*, 18 October 1937

Ze'evi, Dror (1996) *An Ottoman Century: The District of Jerusalem in the 1600s*, Albany: State University of New York Press

—— (2004) 'Back to Napoleon? Thoughts on the beginning of the modern era in the Middle East', *Mediterranean Historical Review*, 19 (1) 2004, pp. 73–94

Zilfi, Madeline C. (1988) *The Politics of Piety: The Ottoman Ulema in*

# REFERENCES

the Post-Classical Age (1600–1800), Minneapolis: Bibliotheca Islamica

(1997) Women in the Ottoman Empire: Middle Eastern Women in the Early Modern Era, Leiden: E. J. Brill

Мейер, М. С. (1980)) 'К характеристике правящего класса в Османской империи XVI–XVII вв. (По данным 'тереке дефтерлери')', *Средневековый Восток. История, культура, источниковедение*, Москва: Наука, pp. 180–9

(1991) *Османская империя в XVIII веке. Черты структурного кризиса*, Москва: Наука

Събев, Орлин (2002) 'Книгата в ежедневието на мюсюлманите в Русе (1695–1786)', *Алманах за историята на Русе*, 4, pp. 380–94

(2004) *Първото османско пътешествие в света на печатната книга (1726–1746): Нов поглед*, София: Авангард Прима

# Index

Abbas I, Shah, 43, 58, 180 n.9
Abbas II, Shah, 53
Abdel-Nour, Antoine, 141
Abdullah Efendi, Yenişehirli, 56, 60
Abou-El-Haj, Rifaᶜat ᶜAli, 1, 8, 11, 16–17, 25, 36, 90–1, 113
Ağakapısı, 127
Ahmed III, Sultan, 6, 34–5, 43–4, 46–50, 53, 55–62, 92, 99, 180 n.2, 187 n.84
Aksan, 1
Aktepe, Münir, 47
Alemi, Mahvash, 54
Aleppo, 22, 37, 133, 138, 141, 146, 150–1, 165
ᶜAlī, Muḥammad, 156, 159
Âli, Mustafa, 10, 25, 138, 143–4, 146–7, 155, 157–8, 161, 163, 166–9, 217 n.121
Ali Ağa, Kahveci, 124
ᶜAlī Bey, 139
Anatolia, 15, 156
Andrews, Walter, 134, 167, 169
Ankersmit, Frank, 51
*Annales School*, 15
Armenians, 159
Asiatic mode of production, 4, 13
Atâ, Tayyarzâde Ahmed, 45
Atıl, Esin, 183 n.44
Atlantic, 13, 15
Atpazarı, 124
al-ᶜAṭṭār, Ḥasan, 12
Austria, 72
axe-hanging, 129, 131

Babaie, Sussan n.54, 184
*Bagçe-i Karabâli*, 54 185 n.65
Balyan family, 120
Barbir, Karl, 8
Barkan, Ömer Lütfi, 15
Barkey, Karen, 1, 18
Başçavuşu Mustafa Ağa, Segban, 124, 132
Bayezid, Prince, 197 n.49
Baysal, Jale, 63, 64, 65, 81, 82
Beeley, Brian, 212 n.75
Behar, Cem, 134, 146
Bektashi/Bektashism, 125–7, 131, 204 n.51
Beligi, 164, 165, 166, 167
Berkes, Niyazi, 65
Beşiktaş, 139
Beyazid II, 185 n.67
Birgivi Mehmed, 25, 77, 81
Blake, Stephen, 52
Bosnavi, Ömer, 69, 70
Bosporus, 96, 125, 139
Bowen, Harold, 9–11, 52
Brook-Rose, Christine, 63
Būlāq, 139

Cairo, 31, 37, 133, 138–40, 142–3, 146
camel sacrifice, 114
Canbaz Kürd Yusuf, 125
Canbuladoğlu Ali Pasha, 15
capitalism, 11–12, 135
Carleson, Edvard, 73
*Cedvel-i Sim*, 41, 55
Celali rebellions, 15, 19

# INDEX

Cevdet, Ahmed, 44, 45
Chahar Bagh, 52–3, 55, 58
Chihil Sutun, 35, 53, 55, 57, 59, 184 n.54, 185 n.57
Christianity, 46
Cihangir, Prince, 197 n.49
circumcision, 34, 36, 92, 95–111, 113–16
coffee-house boys, 168, 169
Cohen, 1
Constantinople, 42; *see also* Istanbul
Cuno, 1
Çaksu, Ali, 36, 178 n.74
Çardak İskelesi, 120, 124, 127, 132
(Küçük) Çelebizâde Efendi, 58, 59, 69
Çızakça, 1

Damad (Nevşehirli) İbrahim Paşa, 34, 43–51, 55, 57–62, 183 n.44, 187 n.84
Damascus, 3, 30, 138, 165
Dâniş Bey, Mehmed, 122, 125
Darling, 1
David, Jean-Claude, 150
de Laria, M., 81
decline thesis, 2–3, 6–7, 9, 11, 19, 21, 27–9, 38–40
dervishes, 96
*devlet sohbeti*, 122, 157, 161
*divan*, 55, 149, 160
Douglas, Mary, 36, 103, 104, 107
Doumani, Beshara, 1, 14, 17
Dûrrî, Ahmed Efendi, 55

Ebussuud Efendi, 60
Edirne, 96, 99
Egypt, 3, 5, 12, 14, 24, 31, 70, 96, 128, 143, 165; French occupation of, 140
Eisenstein, Elizabeth, 79
Eldem, Sedad Hakki, 42, 57
Ellialtı Kahvesi, 127
El-Rouayheb, Khaled, 24, 164
Engels, Frederick, 10

England, 17, 94
Erdoğan, Muzaffer, 185 n.65
Erimtan, Can, 35
Ersoy, Osman, 66, 73
Eski Saray, 102, 104
Ettinghausen, Richard, 52
Eurasia, 33
Europe, 4, 12–13, 15, 17, 30, 39–40, 48, 62, 66, 72, 74, 79, 92, 94
Evliya Çelebi, 99, 143, 150

Fahmy, 1
Faroqhi, Suraiya, 1, 15, 28, 97, 103, 174 n39, 195 n.3
Fatma Sultan, 46
Figani, Baba, 164, 166
First World War, 6, 38
Fleischer, Cornell, 8, 10, 25
Fontainebleau, 42
Foucault, Michel, 37, 137, 160, 218 n.122
Foundation of the Turkish State Theatre and Ballet, 63
France, 43, 46, 49, 55, 72, 94, 183 n.44
Fryer, John, 141
Fust, Johann, 78

Galata, 130
Galib, Sheyh, 164
gardens, 28, 33, 41, 52, 54, 58, 102–4, 146, 149, 164, 169
Geertz, Clifford, 93
Genç, Mehmed n.42, 175
gender, 4, 19, 77, 133, 136–7, 161–5, 167–70, 207
Germany, 23
al-Ghammāz, Ibn, 153
Gibb, H. A. R., 9, 10, 11
Göçek, Fatma Müge, 42, 47, 180 n.6
Goff, Jacque le, 79
Golden Horn, 96, 120
Goodwin, Godfrey, 48 183 n.40
gossip, 117, 145, 148, 155, 157–9, 161

# INDEX

Gran, Peter, 12
guild associations, 92, 112
Gutenberg, Johann, 78

Habermas, Jürgen, 37, 135–7, 160
Hacı Bektaş Veli, 125
Hacı Hâfız, 128
Hacı Ömer Ağa, 82
Halil, Patrona, 34, 124; see also Patrona Halil rebellion
Halil, Sur Emin, 102
Hamadeh, Shirine, 53
Hanna, Nelly, 31, 140
Haravi, Qasim Ibn Yusuf Abu Nasri, 54
haremlik, 146–7, 160, 163
Hasan, Fasihi, 60
Hathaway, Jane, 1, 23
Hattox, Ralph, 148
Hershatter, Gail, 155, 156
heterotopia, 37, 137, 160, 169, 218 n.122
Hickok, 1
Hillenbrand, Robert, 57
Hippodrome, 96, 99
Hoexter, 1
Holdermann, Jean Baptiste Daniel, 69, 72–3, 76
Hopp, Jajos, 65
Hourani, Albert, 7–11, 17, 25
House of Osman, 21
Houston, Robert A., 79
Husain, Shah Sultan, 55–8
Husayn (the Prophet's grandson), 101, 113
Ḥadīth, 12, 23
Ḥibbān, Ibn, 133

Iran, 24, 39, 43, 55–6, 58–60, 62, 113, 180 n.2
Iraq, 38
Isfahan, 43, 52–3, 55, 57–9, 114–15, 184 n.54, 186 n.68, 187 n.84, 180 n.9
Islam, 22, 24, 46, 49, 52, 56, 60–2, 81, 152, 159; Islamic Enlightenment, 23
Ismaʿil I, Shah, 54, 60, 113, 185 n.67
Ismāʿīl Bey, 139
Ismihan Sultan, 107
Istanbul, 3, 6, 20, 25, 36–7, 41, 44–8, 50–1, 53–6, 59, 61, 67, 75–6, 81, 96–8, 100, 117–18, 120, 125, 127, 130, 133–4, 137, 139, 146, 156, 159; see also Constantinople
Itzkowitz, Norman, 9–10, 11
Ivan the Terrible, 95
Iznik, 59
İnalcık, Halil, 7, 15
İpshîr Pasha, 150, 151
İslamoğlu-İnan, Huri, 13, 16, 29, 174 n.35

al-Jabartī, ʿAbd al-Raḥmān, 12, 139–41, 143, 157
Janissary/Janissaries, 5, 36, 97, 99, 117–31, 133
Jeltyakov, A. D., 65
Jerusalem, 141, 143

Kabakçı Mustafa revolt, 124
Kabataş, 54
Kadızadeli movement, 25
Kafadar, Cemal, 8, 11, 26–7, 30–1, 123
Kağıthane, 55, 58
Kağıthane river, 41, 46, 48, 57
Kahvecioğlu, (Kalyunu Burunsuz) Mustafa Ağa, 128, 132, 206 n.78
Kalpaklı, Mehmed, 167, 169
Karabali, 54
Karácson, Imre, 64, 65
Karbala, 101, 113
Karlowitz, Treaty of, 43
Kasap İlyas, 146
Kātip Çelebi, 70, 78, 138–9, 162, 166
Kaye, Alan, 162

# INDEX

Kefri Cedid, 143
Kefri Nahe, 143
Keyder, Çağlar, 13
Khan, Murteza Kuli, 55
al-Khaṭṭāb, Caliph ʿUmar Ibn, 153
Khoja Bey, 8
Khoury/Khouri, Dina Rizk, 1, 146, 161
Khwandamir, Ghiyath ad-Din Muhammad, 59
Kipling, Rudyard, 10
Kırlı, Cengiz, 125, 139, 156, 159–60
Koch, Eba, 52
Koçu Bey, 8, 11, 17
Köprülü Mehmed Pasha, 19
Korkut, Dede, 197 n.45
Krautheimer, Richard, 53
Kremlin, 95
Krusiński, Juda Tedeusz, 70
Krusinski, Tadeusz Jan, 57
Küçük Kaynarca, Treaty of, 44
Kunt, 1

Lebanon, 38
Levant, 5, 24
Levni, 102
Lewis, Bernard, 10, 11, 26
Lewis, Thomas V., 10
Liman von Sanders, Otto, 45, 182
Lokman, 97
Louis XIV, King, 95
Lubenau, Reinhold n.66, 185
Lybyer, Albert Howe, 9

McGowan, Bruce, 43
*mahalle*, 133, 143, 146, 148–9, 154, 161, 170
Mahmud I, Sultan, 46, 61
Mahmud II, Sultan, 52
Mansurizâde, 60
Marcus, Abraham, 1, 21, 141
Mardin, Şerif, 49
Marx, Karl, 10
Mecca, 23, 77

Medina, 23
Mediterranean, 7, 31
Mehmed II 'the Conqueror', Sultan, 90, 199 n.4
Mehmed IV, Sultan, 57, 99, 180 n.2
Mehmed, Sultan, 97, 107, 110
Meier, Astrid, 31
Meninski, Franciszek, 158
Middle East, 10, 12, 17, 21, 24, 30, 38–9, 137
Mikhail, Alan, 37
Mir Mahmud, 56
modernity, 2, 5–6, 12, 14, 22, 27, 30–1, 136
Mosul, 146, 161
Mughal, 52
Muhammad, Prophet, 77, 113, 133, 152
Muharram rituals, 36, 93, 101, 113–15
Münif Pasha, 82
Murad III, Sultan, 98, 107, 151
Murad IV, Sultan, 56, 122
Musa Dede, Sheikh, 60
Mustafa Pasha, Alemdar, 124
Müteferrika, Ibrahim, 34–5, 46, 63–74, 76–82

Nablus, 14
Nahifi Mustafa, 60
*nahil*, 36, 92–3, 100–10, 112, 114–15
Naima/Naʿima/Naʿīmâ, Mustafa Efendi, 10, 17, 69–72, 122, 161
*nasihatname*, 8, 17, 25–6, 30
Nazmizade Efendi, 70
Necipoğlu, Gülru, 53–4, 59
Nedim, Ahmed Efendi, 58, 164
Nevres-i Kadim, 63, 82
Nile, River, 139
Nıyazı Mısri, 30
Nizâm-ı Cedîd, 123
North Africa, 24
Nuhoğlu, Hidayet, 65

# INDEX

Nuri, Celal, 82

Ocak, Ahmed Yaşar, 52
Old Palace, 102, 104, 106–8; see also Topkapi Palace
Olson, Robert, 47, 48
Oriental despotism, 4, 10, 12
Owen, Roger, 10
Ömer Efendi, Dilaverzâde, 46

Palestine, 5, 14
Panofsky, Erwin, 185 n.58
Paris, 42, 47–8, 50–1
Passarowitz, Treaty of, 43, 47–8, 51–2
Patrona Halil rebellion, 34–5, 47, 61, 124, 183 n.41
Peçevi, İbrahim, 138–9, 142, 151, 166
Peirce, Leslie, 19–20, 134, 144
Perry, Charles, 41
Perry, John R., 113
Persia, 78, 96
Philipp, Thomas, 7
Piterberg, Gabriel, 134
Porte, 97

al-Qaraḍāwī, Yūsuf, 152
al-Qāsim, Ibn, 153
Qāsim Bey Abū Sayf, Amīr, 140
Qizilbash, 56
Quataert, Donald, 28

Radtke, Bernd, 23
Rafeq, Abdul-Karim, 7
Raghip Pasha, 10
Rahimi, Babak, 36
Rahman, Fazlur, 23
Rákoczi, Ferenc, 64
al-Rāmī, Ibn, 153, 154
Raşid Efendi, 69–71, 73, 186 n.71
Raymond, André, 21
Redhouse, Sir James, 158
Refik, Ahmed, 35, 44–7, 49–50
Reichmuth, Stefan, 24

Richardson, Brian, 80
Rigney, Ann, 48
Rowson, Everett, 167
rumour, 136, 155, 157–61
Russell, Alexander, 138
Russia, 72

Saadabad, 34–5, 41–3, 46–53, 55–61, 179 n.2, 187 n.84
Sabev, Orlin, 35
Sadi Efendi, 60
Safavid, 35–6, 43, 52–60, 62, 93, 97, 113–15
Said, Edward, 7, 10
Salonica, 82
Salzmann, Ariel, 1, 17, 33–6, 48, 91
Sami, Şemseddin, 158
Sâmî, Mustafa (vakanüvis), 61
Sandıkçılar, 130
Sani, 165
Saussure, Czezarnak (César) de, 64, 65, 73, 76, 79
Schulze, Reinhard, 23
selamlık, 146, 147, 161
Selim I 'the Grim', Sultan, 54, 185 n.66, 186 n.15
Selim III, 1, 46
Şemdânizâde Süleyman Efendi, 45
Sennett, Richard, 161
Sepetçiler, 125
Seydi Ali Paşa, 128
Shahjahanabad, 52
Shanghai, 155
Shiʿi, 56
Silay, Kemal, 49
Singer, Amy, 1, 27
Spain, 94
Spivak, Gayatri, 155
Steinberg, Sigfrid, 78, 79
Subrahmanyam, Sanjay n.52, 184
Sufi, 30, 36, 96, 125, 127, 131;
Sufism, 23, 117, 126
Süleyman I 'the Magnificent', Sultan, 1, 5, 8–9, 26, 164, 199 n.4
Süleymaniye, 127

# INDEX

Süleymaniye mosque, 98
Sunni, 24, 56, 59, 60
Sweden, 72
Syria, 15, 39, 128, 156, 165
Szyliowicz, J. S., 66

Tahmasb, Shah, 114
Tahtakale, 138
al-Ṭahṭāwī, 12
Tanzimat, 5–6, 14, 17–18, 27, 45, 50
*Tarih-i Osmanî Encümeni* (TOE), 43–5
Tehran, 55
Tekfur Sarayı, 59
Tersane Başağası, 128
Tersane Corps, 102
Terzioğlu, Derin, 30, 98
theatre state, 36, 92–3, 95, 98–100, 103, 112–16
Timur, 59
Timurid, 59
Todorova, 1
Toledano, Ehud R., 1, 148
Topdemir, Hüseyin Gazi, 66
Topkapi Palace, 96, 159; *see also* Old Palace
Topkapi Palace Museum, 97
Tower of Skulls, 114
Tulip Age/Period, 2, 34–5, 42, 44, 47–50, 56, 60–1, 92
Turan, Şerafettin, 67
Turhan Sultan, 19
Turkey, 11, 26, 48, 64, 165
Turner, Victor, 108

Ubucini, A., 78
Unkapanı, 128

Uzbeks, 59, 115

Vakᶜa-i Hayriyye, 120, 125
van Gennep, Arnold, 109
Vandal, Albert, 47
Vankulu dictionary, 70–1, 73, 77
Vehbi, 97
Versailles, 35, 42, 46–9, 51, 61
Villeneuve, Marquis de, 47
Voll, John, 23
von Hammer-Purgstall, Joseph, 101, 107

Walcher, Heidi, 180 n.9
Watenpaugh, Heghnar Zeitlian, 151
Watson, William, 78
Weber, Max, 195 n.8
Wheatcroft, Andrew, 47
White, Charles, 82, 139, 142, 161
White, Hayden V., 50
Williams, Raymond, 79
wine, 162–5, 167, 169
world-systems theory, 12

Yali Köşk, 96
Yaşar, Ahmed, 123
Yazıcıoğlu Mehmed, 77
Yemiş İskelesi, 127
Yetimoğlu, 130
Yirmisekiz Çelebi Mehmed Efendi, 42, 47–8, 51, 62
Yücel, Hasan Ali, 45

Zeʾevi, Dror, 1, 141
Zilfi, Madeline, 25
*zorba*, 129, 130

www.ingramcontent.com/pod-product-compliance
Ingram Content Group UK Ltd.
Pitfield, Milton Keynes, MK11 3LW, UK
UKHW022105120525
458442UK00003B/81